Choose Adventure

Choose Adventure

Safe Travel in Dangerous Places

GREG ELLIFRITZ

Dedication

To Lauren- You have read this book more times than anyone should. You diligently edited the drafts, acted as my photographer, and supported this entire project. I couldn't have done it without you. Te quiero, siempre.

To my fellow travelers- Thank you for sharing your adventures, inspiring stories, and long days of travel with me. I hope hard-won knowledge from this book keeps you safe in all your future adventures.

Contents

WARNING

The information in this book is for educational and entertainment purposes and is the result of the author's experiences and research. It should not be considered either legal or medical advice. While the information within can be very valuable, it does not replace hands-on combative training, qualified medical care, or legal advice. The author is not a doctor or lawyer.

Laws vary from country to country. Please research local laws and customs before utilizing any advice from this book. Consult a local medical practitioner or attorney if you have any doubts. I encourage you to respect local laws and customs. The author does not in any way endorse illegal activities of any kind and disclaims any liability from any injury or financial loss that may result from the use or misuse of information provided in this book.

Furthermore, exercise some common sense. If you think that a strategy I advocate in this book might get you hurt or killed, don't listen to me. Trust your gut and do your best to avoid being incarcerated in the developing world.

Introduction

"So what else is there to worry about beside disease and sanitation, running out of gas or unavailability of medical care? Well, maybe rockslides and landslides, storms and floods, frozen roads and crazy drivers, marauding bandits and slippery thieves, insurrections and civil wars, spewing volcanoes and other such precarious hazards one might stumble upon... Frankly, I do not have any good advice for the reader about such things. Just try to avoid them if you can." – Stan Diamond

"How the hell are you still alive?" is probably the most common question I am asked whenever I share my travel adventures with friends or co-workers.

In the last 20 years I've traveled through all seven continents and through more than 50 countries and territories, most which would be considered the so-called "third world."

I've ridden donkeys in Egypt, dirt bikes in Vietnam, ATVs in the jungles of Costa Rica, and in overnight buses throughout South America. I've trekked the Inca Trail, climbed Mt. Kilimanjaro, and lived with an Amazonian tribe in Ecuador. I've eaten guinea pig, llama, alpaca, kangaroo, ostrich, horse, snake, scorpions, caterpillars, and tarantulas. I've lived through a surprise volcanic eruption, a couple of hurricanes, and a few riots over the years. It's truly been an amazing journey.

People who haven't been outside of the USA have some serious misconceptions about travel to foreign countries, especially if those countries happen to be in the developing or the third world. Certainly, dangers exist in third world countries, but the risks are not quite as serious as the media makes them out to be. Even if not completely eliminated, many travel risks can be mitigated to the point where you are less likely to be hurt or killed in a third world country than you are here at home. You may also be surprised at how comfortable you can be in the developing world. This book is all about enhancing your travel experience, reducing dangers, and making your travels through the third world as comfortable and easy as possible.

While discussing this book with a friend and veteran world traveler, he made an astute statement:

*"If I was going to write this book, it would only have one page. In fact, it would only have one sentence...***'Don't do stuff'.***"*

It's great advice. I wholeheartedly concur. The problem, as both my friend and I agreed, is that people lack the cultural literacy, life experience, or traveling knowledge to truly be able to differentiate between what is "stupid" and what is "not stupid." A lot of this book is simply identifying the "stupid stuff" that you may not yet understand and showing you how to make better traveling decisions.

There are hundreds of travel books that talk about important topics like finding great deals on flights and rental cars. Other books and websites talk about "travel hacking" and how to use credit cards perks or bonus points to pay for their trips. I feel no need to rehash these tired topics. I want to give you a unique perspective, information gleaned through travel to several dozen third world countries and tempered by nearly a quarter century of experience as a street cop. I will teach you how to make your travels safe and enjoyable. All of these tips come from my own personal experiences and those of some trusted friends who have traveled as much (or more) than I have.

I like to be prepared. If you are reading this book, then you likely feel the same way. You will definitely enjoy your travel in developing countries far more after you've done a little pre-planning. But don't go overboard. You can't plan for or be prepared for all of the situations you are going to face. That's the appeal of third world travel. It has an edge.

That edge can be dulled, but never eliminated. Don't go insane trying to take all of my advice or come up with a contingency plan for every possible eventuality. If you do, you'll never leave home. You'll turn into one of those arm chair travelers who is always "planning a trip" to someplace incredible, but who never actually leaves home. Be smart. Take some sensible precautions. But in the end, you have to make the leap into the deep end of the pool.

It's time to jump.

A note on terminology...

Some readers will (probably correctly) have issue with my use of the term "third world." The original definition came shortly after World War II when academics wanted to describe the distinction between the "first world" non-theocratic democracies with market-based economies, the "second world" communist Soviet Bloc along with its allies, and the "third world" leftovers.

Many will argue that the previous "second world" countries are fading away. Some have embraced capitalism and have become much more developed while some have fallen off the economic cliff and are commonly considered the equivalents of the economically depressed "third world."

Although not true to the original definition, during the 1960's, the term "third world" became more popularly descriptive not of political alliances, but of social and economic conditions. The "third world" came to define those countries that share the characteristics of having both a colonial heritage and a high rate of poverty among the majority of the country's population. When I speak of "third world" countries in this book, I am referring to the more commonly used modern connotation rather than the original meaning based on political ideology.

I also use the term "developing world" interchangeably. The term "developing world" is even more controversial than the term "third world." In 2016, the World Bank declared that it would no longer use the term "developing world." The International Monetary Fund has labeled 159 different countries with "developing world" status, but has failed to actually define the term. In this work, I use the term "developing world" to mean the same thing as "third world," an economically depressed country with a colonial heritage.

My Story

Unlike many travel experts, my traveling experiences began later in life. When I was growing up, my parents had no interest in travel. Consequently, I rarely left my home state, let alone the country.

I graduated college with a science degree and plans to work for the National Park Service. In a change of fate, I got hired as a police officer three months later. My police career became an obsession. I didn't take many trips in my early policing days because I was too entranced with the job of catching criminals. I was afraid I would miss out on a big arrest if I took time off to travel. Within a few years, I was assigned to be the full-time training officer for my police department. That job came with the requirement of thousands of hours of additional training in the field of firearms, self-defense tactics, legal issues, and crime prevention.

In total, I ended up with over 75 different police instructor certifications, mostly in the subject matter of police use of force. In short, I became a court recognized expert in the fighting arts. I taught police officers how to psychologically manipulate contacts with violent criminals to avoid violence. If those tactics failed, I taught officers how to win physical fights with pepper spray, impact weapons, their firearms, and their bare hands. My teaching skills became increasingly in demand and I started a side business teaching the same techniques to the general public. My demanding teaching schedule further delayed my opportunities to travel.

I booked my first international trip at the age of 28, more for familial support than a desire to see the world. My sister was getting married. She chose to have a destination wedding at a resort in Jamaica. As I was a groomsman, I had to go. I was worried about crime and the dangers of traveling to a third world country. I obsessively researched the destination, local crime trends, and tactics to avoid kidnapping. When I arrived on the island, I was pleasantly surprised. Everyone was friendly and nice. Things seemed a bit chaotic compared to home, but the environment was nothing like I had suspected. There were no gunfights or riots in the streets.

Everyone employed by the resort cautioned the guests to never leave the hotel grounds. They said things were "too dangerous" to venture into town. After a few days of all-inclusive resort fare, I found myself getting bored. I craved some adventure so I decided to take a walk to the nearest town and see what was going on there. I walked a couple miles and stopped in a local store to get a drink. As I was coming out of the store, I was approached by a Jamaican taxi driver. He introduced himself and offered his services as a tour guide. He had recently gotten out of the military and seemed like a friendly and knowledgeable guide. I took a chance and allowed him to show me the town where he lived.

The taxi driver took me to local markets, bars, and scenic beach vistas. I wasn't attacked, robbed, or murdered. In fact, I had so much fun that I got the taxi driver's phone number and booked a second island tour for the rest of my family with him on the following day.

Surprisingly, I really enjoyed learning about different people and cultures. That first trip sparked a curiosity that led to several more "safe" trips to tourist areas in

Mexico, the Bahamas, and Costa Rica. After a couple of these fun experiences, I was seriously consumed by the travel bug. Travel became one of my few hobbies. I quickly started booking solo trips to the most primitive third world countries, craving the challenge and adventure that only travel in the developing world could provide.

I went from seldom taking a day off work to working overtime so I could accumulate more comp-time vacation hours. For more than a decade, I combined my busy police training job with spending at least six weeks a year traveling in the developing world. I picked the most remote destinations, the most physically difficult challenges, and refused to travel in any country with potable water flowing from the tap. In the last 15 years, I've traveled through more than 50 countries and territories on all seven continents.

I've made lots of mistakes and learned many lessons. My remote travel experiences combined with my passion for education and my skills dealing with criminals as a police officer consolidated in the advice I share in this book. Reading it will give you the equivalent of a graduate level education in the field of third world travel. You'll learn the relatively mundane (but important) travel skills of safely choosing lodging and transportation, dealing with airplane flights, long haul buses, taxi drivers, handling money, and language issues.

You will learn the social skills necessary to navigate an unfamiliar environment. This book will also prepare you for the relatively rare occasions where you might have to face greater danger. I will show you how to survive natural disasters, riots, and crowd violence. I will teach you how to use improvised weapons, how to avoid criminals and scam artists, and how to escape a kidnapping attempt or terrorist attack.

The book is organized by chapters. Each chapter contains information on a specific topic. The book is designed to flow chronologically from the first stages of planning your trip, through to your arrival in country and then on to the challenges you will face as a traveler in the developing world. Feel free to read the book cover to cover or to only read the chapters that interest you.

Planning Your Trip: What To Do Before You Leave

> "A real adventure vacation will make you the proud owner of a backpack full of sweat-soaked clothes, a T-shirt tan and unfashionable facial growth, will generate outspoken opinions and rekindle a deep love for life. Upon your return you will find yourself pursued by women who want to trace the outlines of your fresh pink scars, cheat on their boyfriends and ride too fast on your noisy motorcycle."
> – Robert Young Pelton

Passports– Before you leave, check your passport. If you don't have at least six months remaining before it expires, some countries will not allow you to enter. Renew your passport before the six month limit if possible. I've also seen people hassled by immigration officials if their passport looked overly worn or had torn pages. If you are rough on your possessions, consider a case or cover for your passport. Such covers can also prevent others from identifying your nationality, thereby protecting you from scams targeting individuals from particular countries.

Also, avoid putting your passport through a washing machine. It will survive, but may not actually be acceptable as an entry document in the country you are visiting. I actually saw a fellow passenger denied entry into El Salvador because his passport had been laundered.

Visas– It is also important to determine if you need a visa for entry. If you need a visa, it will be handled in one of three ways. The first is that you may be required to send your passport to an embassy or consulate in your home country. That process can take up to several weeks before the embassy grants the visa and returns your passport.

Alternatively, some countries allow you to buy a visa upon entry. Others simply require that you fill out a form online prior to arrival. The most important part of this process is to realize you may need a visa well before you actually have to obtain it to allow for enough processing time. It will be disastrous to realize the night before your departure that you need a visa you don't currently have.

Often, visas involving work, business, or a change in residence require different pre-requisites and a longer lead time. If you are traveling for any reason other than pleasure, budget additional time to get your visa approved. Research the costs, necessary supporting documentation, and other requirements to ensure a smooth visa application process.

If you are a United States Citizen, take a look at the Visa quick check page at http://cibtvisas.com/visa-quick-check to determine the visa requirements for the country you are planning to visit. The Sky Team Visa and Health Portal http:/www.skyteam.com/en/flights-and-destinations/visa-and-health/ is another good reference to check before your trip. You simply enter your nationality, residence, and the countries you will be visiting. The site will then give you a customized report telling you what visa are needed and how to apply for them. The site lists current health concerns in the area where you will be traveling as well as a list of recommended vaccines.

When checking visa requirements, also check to see if you need a "transit visa" for the countries where you might be making flight connections. Most countries allow passengers to enter without a visa as long as they have a connecting flight and don't leave the airport. Some require a special visa that must be arranged in advance. Be sure to look at your layover times as well. Some countries require full tourist visas if your layover is longer than a set time (somewhere between four and twelve hours), even if you have no plans to leave the airport.

Location Research– Research the areas you want to visit well in advance. There are narrower safety margins in third world countries. You can very easily get yourself in trouble by visiting the "wrong" city or country. Do your homework and you will save yourself endless amounts of hassle and improve your safety profile as well.

There is no single best source to do research. All sources have their own biases and inaccuracies. You should be looking at guidebooks, government sites, public rating websites (like Yelp or Trip Advisor), personal references, and travel forums. Make sure you consult a wide variety of sources to get an accurate picture of what your chosen vacation site is truly like. Be cautious about relying on any single reference. Make sure any guidebook you select is the most up to date one available. Beware of fake reviews (both good and bad) on the travel websites. It's best to research your destination broadly.

One good source of information is countryreports.org. After going there, I generally consult some governmental websites. While I often start with U.S. government sites, I find many other countries' travel information websites to be much more useful and less paranoid than the US Consular Affairs site. I prefer to do most of my research using The UK, Canada, and Australia's sites instead.

In addition to general governmental and private information sites, you should also check to see if there are any disease epidemics where you will be traveling and what medical precautions you should take. I use the Health Map website at http://www.healthmap.org/en/. You can search its database by either country or disease type and get up to date information on recent epidemics and medical concerns.

The ProMedMail site (http://www.promedmail.org) is also useful for tracking disease epidemics. It is important that you are aware of this information because most U.S. doctors will be unfamiliar with the risks of third world travel. If you can provide a list of what you need, or participate actively in the discussion with your health care provider, your health and safety will be better assured.

Embassies- Determine where your local embassies are located in the country using goabroad.com (http://embassy.goabroad.com) and add their addresses and phone numbers to your cell phone. In some emergencies, assistance from your home country's embassy can be invaluable.

Check Dates- Triple check the dates of your trip with a list of national, local, and bank holidays (days where most businesses and government offices are closed) in the countries you will visit. Activities in some areas completely shut down during certain holidays. Museums and public recreation areas may be closed and it might be tough to find an open restaurant. It's best to avoid visiting during most holidays; unless of course, the holiday (like Carnival in Brazil) is the entire purpose of your trip.

You should also check guidebooks for closures particular to individual cities as well. This is very important if your plan on visiting lots of museums or exhibits. You will find that such places are regularly closed citywide on at least one weekday every week. If it's important for you to see something, make sure it will be open on the day of your visit.

Decide if you want to travel with a group or on your own. Group travel doesn't always take the form of the stereotypical senior citizen bus tour. There are many companies that provide small group tours with local guides and using local transportation (often public buses). There is a significant amount of time scheduled to use freely for individual exploration. You don't have to constantly accompany the group.

I enjoy small group adventure travel. Local guides enhance your experience and group members tend to be friendly, fun, and open-minded. These groups are especially good for female travelers who have concerns about travel safety in foreign countries. Take a look at the following tour companies and what types of tours they offer. There are likely many great travel guiding services, but I have personally traveled with each of these companies and can vouch for the quality of their guides and itineraries:

Exodus Travels

Explore

G Adventures

Intrepid

Additionally, my older readers might want to check out some of the programs through Road Scholar. They conduct small group tours focused more on education than adventure. Although I've never done any of their trips, several of my friends have recommended them to me.

Solo travel in the third world, while especially rewarding to introverts, presents more danger than traveling with a group. In a group, the pooled resources of the numerous group members are extremely useful in any critical incident. Just having someone else available to bring you some food when you are sick or take you to the hospital when injured is a tremendously valuable asset. Even more important is having someone to call your family when you are hospitalized or bail you out of jail when you get in trouble. Those activities are harder to accomplish when you are traveling by yourself.

If you decide to travel solo, it's generally a good practice to find a local resident that you can trust. Keep him around however possible, whether it is by paying him as a guide, or by buying dinner or a few beers. Having a local you can trust on your side in an emergency or as someone who can keep you away from the most dangerous parts of town is an indispensable resource.

A local guide also helps give you a more balanced perspective, highlighting an area's true character. He or she can also show you the best places to go, and create a more authentic experience with cultural exposure that you won't find in your favorite guidebook. Check out the Tours by Locals website at https://www.toursbylocals.com/ to find a local guide in the city you will be visiting.

Booking Flights- When looking for airfare I first check Skyscanner.com to get an idea of what the general price range of my flight might be. I tend to avoid buying my fares from some of the lesser known companies on Skyscanner. I prefer to use better known sites for safety purposes.

Skyscanner will often provide local flight options and additional routes that the common American flight search engines might not catalog. If I find a good flight, I generally book it on the individual airline's own site to get the cheapest fare.

Besides Skyscanner, I've also had good luck using the following lesser-known flight search sites:

Dohop

Momondo

Vayama (also very good for hotels)

Triple Check Booking Arrangements– One of the most common mistakes made by even the most veteran travelers is hurriedly making booking arrangements. Take the extra time necessary to verify that your flight and hotel reservations have your name spelled correctly. This is critically important with regard to plane tickets. If your name is misspelled, you may not be flying. If you are a recently married woman, ensure that your travel documents match the name on your passport, regardless of the fact that you may have legally changed your name. If your tickets don't match the name on your passport, you won't be leaving the United States.

Triple check all of your travel dates as well. Taking these two simple steps during the booking process will save you the hassle of massive inconvenience should you make a mistake typing a name or picking a date from a pull-down menu. Be extra cautious when crossing the International Date Line as well. I once had a layover in Hawaii that ended up being 24 hours longer than I had intended after I screwed up my flight bookings when crossing the International Date Line. An additional day in Hawaii wasn't a terrible burden, but it did add some significant unexpected costs to my trip.

When conducting price comparison research for your trip, be sure to clear your internet browser cache and erase your cookies before you return to a particular site at a later date. Travel companies occasionally use data obtained on your previous visits to artificially raise prices on your subsequent searches. If you see a dramatic price change in your flight or hotel in a short time frame, this is likely what has happened. Delete your cookies and try again.

When buying international airfare, most research shows the best time to buy your tickets is sometime between six and eight weeks prior to your departure. Prices will go up about 40% when you get closer than four weeks before scheduled departure. Don't waste your money by waiting too long to book your flights.

Check your Airlines' Luggage Policies– You don't want to get hit with expensive fees for overweight luggage or too many bags. It's best if you consider baggage costs when booking the flight, but if you forget, make sure to check before you leave for the airport. That overweight suitcase may end up costing you several hundreds of dollars to check.

When flying internationally and then taking domestic airlines within your destination country, take extra care. The baggage regulations may not be the same if you are flying different airlines. What is acceptable weight and size on your international flight may not work on the small plane you have to take to reach a more remote location. It's also important to note that many foreign airlines (especially budget airlines) have very tight restrictions on both carry-on and checked luggage. It's not uncommon to see five kilogram (11 pounds) limits on carry-on bags and 15 kilogram (33 pounds) limits on checked luggage. Do your research BEFORE you show up at the airport.

Estimate your travel costs so that you can plan to bring enough money. If you are having problems estimating costs for your trip, you can try out the travel budget calculator at the Practical Money Skills website.

(http://www.practicalmoneyskills.com/calculators/
calculate/travelBudgeting.php?calcCategory=family)

For a longer stay, look at Numbeo's cost of living
calculator (https://www.numbeo.com/cost-of-living/)
sorted by country. Rough flight estimates to every country
in the world are available at Kayak.com's Explore site
(https://www.kayak.com/explore/).

One more useful cost of living estimator is the Expatistan
Cost of Living Index (https://www.expatistan.com/cost-
of-living). That one compares actual costs in your home
town with costs for food, housing, transportation, and
other commodities in the city you want to visit.

Call your bank- Notify your bank and credit card
companies that you are going to be using the card outside
your home country. Otherwise, if the company sees some
unusual charges from another country, they might block
the card out of fear of fraud. In most places outside the
United States, the toll-free customer service number on
the back of your card isn't "toll free." Look for the
International Collect number and store it in your phone in
case you need to unblock a card or report one stolen from
outside the USA.

While you are looking at credit card info, check to see
if your credit card provides free accidental death, lost
baggage, or travel delay insurance coverage. Many people
fail to realize that some companies offer free insurance if
any part of the trip was booked using the company's credit
card. It makes no sense to purchase extra coverage if your
credit card provides it free of charge.

Also, check and see if your credit card company offers
"traveler emergency assistance." Some companies provide
a phone number that their customers can call if they have
a travel emergency. The card company will put you in

contact with translators, doctors, pharmacies and people who can expedite the return of lost or stolen travel documents. Usually, the call and the arrangements are free. You only pay for the particular service you need. Put the emergency assistance number into your phone. It may be useful if you have a problem and have exhausted all of your other options.

Make sure that you have at least one credit card that has a four-digit numeric PIN for cash advances. Even if you don't normally make cash advances on your credit card, it's useful to have the capability to do so if you bank or debit card is lost, stolen, or doesn't function in the country you are visiting.

Have backup copies of all documents-Take screen shots of your hotel reservation confirmation, airline tickets, and directions from the airport to the hotel and save them on your phone. You may not have an internet connection at the airport when you arrive. It wouldn't be a bad idea to stash hard copies of these documents in your carry-on bag as well.

Photocopy all of your credit cards, identity documents, and passport. Scan or photograph them as well. Put the scanned document on an online cloud storage site so that you can access it from any computer in the world. It will make replacing lost or stolen documents much easier. Also send an electronic copy of all important documents to a family member or someone you can trust as a backup plan.

Clean out your wallet/purse- Get rid of all of the extraneous cards, receipts, and identifying paperwork from your wallet or purse. If these items will not be used on your trip, there's no reason to take them. They are likely to be lost or stolen and it's always difficult to replace identity documents in a foreign country. Even worse, the information could be used by a criminal to commit identity theft.

Take your identification, passport, airline mileage cards, health insurance card (if valid in the country where you are traveling), and whatever other credit/ATM cards you are actually planning to use. Remove all other cards and/or identifying documents and leave them at home.

Clean out your carry-on bag and luggage– I have lots of friends who use their carry-ons for backpacking trips while not engaged in international travel. Even worse, some friends load their bags up with ammunition and supplies for their excursions to the shooting range. Both of these activities make it far more likely that you will accidentally leave some prohibited item in your luggage. Empty your carry-on bag completely before you repack it to ensure that you don't get arrested for smuggling a prohibited item through airport security.

Check your bags – Check for pills (even non-prescription), aerosol cans, water bottles, stray bullets, pocket knives, batteries, lighters, matches, fireworks, fuel tabs, fruit, or anything else that could be considered "contraband" by the airlines, the TSA, or the government of the country you are visiting.

I don't use any of my international travel bags for any other purpose. Because of this precaution, I'm unlikely to have any "prohibited" items in my bags. Even so, whenever I'm packing, I completely clean out all of my bags and make sure they are totally empty before I start filling them up. Yes, this precaution is a pain, but it isn't nearly as bad as spending a couple years in prison after foreign customs officials find a stray bullet left over from your last shooting session.

Look out for eating utensils as well. A girlfriend has been pulled aside for additional screening on several instances when she packed a butter knife or metal fork with her food in a carry-on bag. Although these items are not specifically forbidden by the TSA, some agents go a little overboard and won't let them onto the plane. If you need eating utensils for a packed meal, make sure they are plastic.

Learn a little about the culture you will be visiting. If you are unsure about local customs, check out the following reference books before your trip. It's much better to spend some time doing some basic research than to ignorantly offend a gracious host.

Kiss, Bow, Shake Hands by Terri Morrison

Bodytalk by Desmond Morris

When Cultures Collide by Richard D. Lewis.

Download city maps of the areas you are visiting to your phone, laptop, and e-reader. Being lost in a new city could spoil your travels or potentially place you in danger of being criminally victimized.

Check out the currency exchange rate between your home country and the one(s) you will be visiting. You'll need to know the rate because all local purchases will be listed in the host country's currency instead of the U.S. Dollar. The best website I've found for researching foreign currency values is XE (xe.com.)

There is a handy checklist summarizing these steps located in the Appendix at the end of the book.

What to Pack

> "A foreign country is not designed to make you comfortable. It's designed to make its own people comfortable."
> – Clifton Fadiman

Despite the title of this chapter, I really can't tell you what to pack. Where you are going, the length of your stay and your personal preferences will dictate that everyone's packing list will be different. Besides, there are countless websites and mobile apps that will give you detailed packing lists for any conceivable destination. Most guidebooks include packing lists as well.

The basics of packing are up to you. You know what you need far better than I do. The list of items below is designed to be a supplement to your own packing list. All of my recommendations are items that I've found indispensable (or at least pretty handy) in my travels, but are not usually included in the "normal" packing lists.

My best advice is to pack light. You never know when you'll have to carry your luggage. You may encounter political unrest. In unstable third world countries, it's always a possibility. When there are political demonstrations in the streets, public transportation often stops working and roadblocks are everywhere. Your quick taxi to the airport won't be coming. You may have to walk (with your bags) for a significant distance in order to facilitate your escape from the city. Keep that in mind when packing.

Quality Luggage – I'm not a minimalist traveler. I always tend to carry bigger bags and more luggage than I truly need. Despite my lack of ability to do so, I recognize the benefits of packing light. You should be able to carry your bag for an hour and lift it over your head. Wheels are nice, but they can't always be used (think about cobblestone streets). Don't rely on the wheels. Make sure you can actually carry your bag, in addition to rolling it.

I prefer baggage that has the ability to convert to a backpack if necessary. In an emergency, I can place my larger checked bag on my back and hand-carry my smaller bag. When purchasing luggage, make sure it is light weight. Some suitcases weigh up to 15 pounds empty. The amount of gear you can pack is dramatically reduced when you suitcase itself takes up half of your allowable packed weight.

Ensure that your luggage is well-labeled. I don't like the paper luggage tags provided by the airlines. I prefer something more durable. Any army surplus store should have the ability to stamp out military-style metal dog tags for a reasonable price. Stamp a dog tag with your name, address, cell phone, and email. Rivet it or otherwise permanently attach it to the outside of your bag. Place a business card or some other identification inside the bag as well. If you use a commercial luggage tag, reinforce the strap with a zip tie so it doesn't break as easily.

Here are some items that I always pack when I'm traveling in the developing world:

A Laundry Bag– If you are visiting third world countries, your clothes will get dirtier and smellier than you've ever experienced. There's nothing worse than taking "clean" clothes out of your bag only to find that they smell of stale sweat and week-old campfire smoke. Have something to separate clean and dirty clothes in your luggage.

I use a "dry bag" to hold my dirty laundry. It's a waterproof bag commonly used for keeping things dry on diving or white water rafting trips. They are waterproof and contain odors extremely well. I carry the Sea to Summit brand bags because they are lighter and more flexible than most other dry bags, but there are a lot of other options as well.

Throw a few scented fabric softener sheets in the bottom of the bag. Disperse them throughout your dirty clothes to further reduce the pungent smell as you fill your bag with laundry.

Bandanna-A bandanna is a critically essential travel accessory. It can be used as a sweat towel (important for us big guys), a head cover, sleep mask, a dust mask, a water pre-filter, as well as a bandage or emergency tourniquet. Get a couple of cotton bandannas for your trip and carry at least one everywhere you go.

Drain Plug-A flat rubber drain plug is a useful item to carry as well. It allows the use of hotel or hostel sinks for washing clothing or dishes. They don't take up much space and will undoubtedly prove useful if your hotel sink doesn't have a stopper. It will also be useful in the event of an impending natural disaster like a hurricane or tsunami. Such events occasionally knock out city water supplies. Being able to plug the bathtub in your hotel room and fill it with water in advance of the storm may help you survive the water shortage.

Paracord and Duct Tape- These two items can be used to repair almost everything that you could possibly need to fix. In addition, the duct tape can be used to prevent blisters, as a band aid, or to patch a sucking chest wound. Wrap some around your water bottle to save space. You can also buy duct tape in flat packs.

Paracord (also called 550 cord) is cordage that is about the diameter of shoelaces but contains seven inner strands surrounded by an outer covering. It gets its name because it is capable of holding up to 550 lbs. of weight. It can be used in addition to a poncho or tarp to make a sleeping or rain shelter, to tie down luggage on the top of a bus or car, as replacement shoe laces, or even as an emergency clothes line. The inner strands can be removed and used for sewing, fishing, or lashing small items together. Twenty feet of paracord actually gives you more than 150 feet of total cordage. You can also buy paracord woven into bracelets that may provide a convenient albeit not very stylish way to carry some emergency cordage.

To make a clothes line for easily drying clothes without having to pack clothes pins, use a piece of paracord that is about twice as long as the length of line you want. Tie both ends together to form a loop. Tie one end of the loop to a doorknob, window latch, or any other object. Insert a pen or toothbrush through the other end of the loop and pull it taut. Twist the pen until the two sides of the "loop" become entwined. Tie or tape the pen to another object or wall. Push a corner of each clothing item you want to dry in between the two tightly wound pieces of cord and it will hang without using clips or clothes pins.

Trust me. Bring some paracord. If you pack it, you'll use it.

A couple of binder clips– Pack a couple small binder clips and a couple of larger binder clips in your luggage. You will find all kinds of uses for them once you arrive in country. Combined with a little paracord (mentioned above) they can be used for hanging just about anything anywhere you need to in your hotel room. I use the small ones to clip my visa or immigration paperwork inside my passport so I don't lose it. Most commonly I use the larger binder clips to hold curtains closed in my hotel room to create a darker sleeping environment. Any gaps in the curtains can be quickly closed with a couple of clips. They are also useful for keeping curtains from blowing open when using a fan or air conditioning in your room.

Binder clips holding hotel room curtains closed.

A pen (or two) – Pack a pen in your carry-on bag for your flight. On the plane you will be given your destination country's customs and immigrations forms to fill out. It will save you lots of time on the ground if you arrive at the immigration desk with these forms already completed. You will need a pen to do that. I think every trip I've taken has involved someone in my row on the plane asking to borrow a pen. Don't be that guy. Carry your own pen. Better yet, carry two so that you can help the clueless traveler in the seat next to you on the plane. Having an extra pen will also help when your loaned pen fails to be returned. Everyone is a pen thief.

A Door Stop– These are great for providing an extra layer of security in your hotel room. Shove a doorstop under the closed and locked door to make it even harder for someone to get in to your room. Pack two. On doors with large gaps between the bottom of the door and the floor, you can place two door stops on top of each other to better secure the door. If you want the ultimate door stop that will work under the broadest range of conditions, get the "Wedge-It." Whichever type you choose, it will be cheap insurance and will provide much better peace of mind when staying in shady hotels or hostels.

A Book (or E-Reader)- I read a lot, so I'm seldom without my Kindle reader. When I travel, I supplement my Kindle with at least one paperback book in the event my e-reader can't be charged or gets stolen. Even if you don't regularly read at home, you'll want to pack a book. Inevitably during your travels, you will be stranded someplace and waiting for something. A book is a great way to kill time as you wait. If you are thinking "*I don't need a book, I have my phone*," you might want to skip ahead to the telephone chapter. The super expensive foreign data plans make Facebooking from your phone a far less desirable option. Bring a book.

Other uses for books are as a source of paper for writing, kindling for emergency fire starting, or emergency toilet paper (crumple the pages thoroughly first.) I know it is sacrilegious to suggest burning books. I am no Ray Bradbury; but I would certainly use pages from my book to start a fire or as toilet paper if I were in trouble. You can also trade physical books for new reading material in some hostels or hotels.

An Inflatable Pillow– Most people think about inflatable pillows as things that are used on long airplane flights. They certainly are often used in that role, but you will find far more uses when traveling in a third world country. When you arrive late in a new city only to find that your hotel lost your reservations and the only place you can find to sleep is a nasty hostel that doesn't provide pillows or bed linen, you'll be glad you packed your own pillow. They are also useful on the beach, on long bus rides, and if you get stranded and have to sleep in an airport.

I use the Aeros inflatable pillow by Sea-to-Summit. It packs down into a tiny size and is amazingly comfortable. I don't travel anywhere without it.

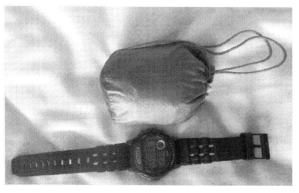

The Aeros inflatable pillow shown in size
comparison with a men's wristwatch

Sleep Mask– Sleep masks are also very useful for both bus/
plane travel and hotel rooms with inadequate curtains.
They will make all the difference if you are trying to sleep
late after a long night of travel or partying. Most of your
hotels/hostels will get VERY bright as soon as the sun
comes up. You can also use a thin stocking cap as a sleep
mask. If it isn't too warm, just pull it down over your eyes.
If the thought of packing such a specialty item like a sleep
mask offends your travel sensibilities, just pack the
stocking cap. It will do double duty keeping you warm and
asleep at the same time. In the worst case scenario, simply
pull a brimmed baseball cap down over your face and eyes.
You won't be able to sleep on your side, but it will block a
lot of the light that may interfere with your slumber.

Zip Lock Bags– You can never have too many quart-size
Ziploc bags. In addition for them being necessary to get
your liquids through TSA security in the airport, they are
also handy for organizing and separating small items. If you
have any liquids that may leak, the Ziploc may be critical to
preventing spills or contamination.

I tend to use Ziploc bags of all sizes to organize and
protect my clothing inside my luggage. I separate socks,
underwear, shorts, and pants by using individual large
Ziploc bags inside my suitcase. It makes finding things easy
and protects everything in your bag from the unexpected
rain storm, spill, or bedbug contamination.

They are also useful if you have to pack used toilet paper
or feminine hygiene products out of the back country when
hiking or when stuck on a bus without trash cans. Speaking
of bus rides, larger (gallon-sized) Ziploc bags can also hold

vomit, urine, or feces when your bus driver won't make a stop in the event you are sick or need to use the toilet.

Sun protection– Many third world countries are in tropical conditions. You will be spending time outside and the equatorial sun will fry your lily-white skin. Your trip will suck if you have to visit a third world hospital for severe sunburn.

I know what you are thinking: "*Sunscreen is sold everywhere.*" Not true. In many rural areas in developing countries, the locals can't afford sunscreen. They rely on long sleeves and hats to keep from getting burned instead. There's a good chance you won't be able to find sunscreen for sale in any of the local stores.

If you do find it for sale (generally only in beach areas) it will be two to three times more expensive than it is at home. I don't know why sunscreen costs so much in other countries, but it does. It's better that you bring some from home (packed in a Ziploc bag in your checked luggage). If you get caught without sunscreen and don't want to pay exorbitant prices, check the local flea markets. Vendors there regularly sell the partial bottles of sunscreen left in hotel rooms or thrown away by other tourists. You can probably find a mostly-full bottle of sunscreen for a relatively inexpensive price.

Don't forget to pack high quality sunglasses and sunscreen-containing lip balm as well. Both of these items are also significantly more expensive in other countries. You can buy a four dollar pair of fake Oakley sunglasses on the street in most developing countries, but the lenses will be distorted and they will break within a couple days. Again, it's better to bring some from home.

Headlamp– A headlamp is very useful. In case of a power outage, a headlamp can be worn, leaving your hands free to carry luggage, cook a meal, or care for an injured person. It can also provide a handy reading lamp if the overhead light in your room or on your bus is broken or if you are staying in a location that doesn't have 24 hour electrical service.

Condoms- If you think there is a possibility of engaging in sexual intercourse with a local or a fellow traveler, bring your own condoms from home. Condoms are notoriously difficult to find in developing countries. The locally-made rubbers that you can find will have a much higher breakage rate than condoms manufactured in the USA, Europe, and Japan.

Condom sizes are also different from what you might find in the USA. Condoms in Asia and South America are sized several millimeters smaller in both length and diameter than their counterparts in the United States. Asian "large" size condoms are sized smaller than the "regular" sized condoms found in the USA. Additionally, if you are latex sensitive, you are unlikely to find any non-latex alternative condoms in the developing world. You will stay much safer from sexually transmitted infections if you bring condoms from your home country.

Condoms (the unlubricated ones) also work well as emergency water carriers in a survival situation. It's useful to carry a few on your travels, even if you don't plan on using them for their intended purpose. You can fill a condom with a tremendous amount of water. If you use this water transportation method in a survival situation, place the condom full of water inside a sock for protection during transport. Don't tie the neck like a balloon. It will be difficult to untie when you need to get to the water. Use a piece of string or cloth to tie off your emergency water carrier instead.

Multi-tool or Swiss Army Knife– Items you need will unexpectedly break at the most inopportune moment when you are traveling in the developing world. Having a means to make small repairs will prove to be invaluable. Whenever I travel, I carry a multi-tool that contains pliers, screwdrivers, bottle openers, and a knife blade. I end up using it all the time. Multi-tools are small, easily carried and can perform many different functions. They can even be pressed into service as an improvised weapon if necessary.

The problem with carrying most multi-tools is that they have a knife blade. That will prevent you from bringing it onto a plane in carryon luggage. Some folks travel light and don't like to check bags. If that describes your style of travel, you'll have to avoid packing a multi-tool. Depending on the country you are visiting, you may be able to pick one up locally and use it for the duration of your trip. A final option is to choose one of the Swiss army knives that doesn't contain a knife blade, only tools. Whichever option you choose will prove to be useful in your travels.

Airports

"It can hardly be a coincidence that no language on earth has ever produced the expression "As pretty as an airport." Airports are ugly. Some are very ugly. Some attain a degree of ugliness that can only be the result of a special effort. This ugliness arises because airports are full of people who are tired, cross, and have just discovered that their luggage has landed in Murmansk (Murmansk airport is the only exception of this otherwise infallible rule), and architects have on the whole tried to reflect this in their designs."

– Douglas Adams

Airport Safety– Since 9/11, when people think of terrorism, they usually think about airline hijackings. While hijackings can occur, more often it is the airport itself that is targeted by terrorists rather than any specific plane. The Moscow airport was bombed in 2011. The Las Angeles airport was attacked in 2013. Most recently, an active killer targeted people in the baggage claim area of the Ft. Lauderdale Florida airport. One of the largest airport attacks happened in Istanbul in 2016. In that attack, ISIS terrorists killed 42 people and wounded 238 more. All of these attacks occurred outside of the secured area of the airport.

Think about it. A terrorist could cause exactly the same result (mass casualties and a crippling strike to the economy) as bringing down a plane without ever having to board. If terrorist groups bombed or shot up the unsecured ticketing areas of several airports sequentially, they would kill thousands and force everyone to stop flying. And the terrorists could do it without having to remove their shoes at the security check or try to smuggle a bomb past the body scanner. It would be easy. That's why terrorists worldwide choose airports as their targets.

Here are some quick safety rules to keep you from getting killed at the airport, either foreign or domestic:

1. **Don't rush**. Get to the airport with plenty of extra time to spare. When you are hurried and worrying about catching your flight, you aren't paying proper attention to what's going on around you. Not rushing to catch your plane will give you more time to keep an eye on your surroundings and avoid anything that makes you uncomfortable. Download the TSA app to get real time updates on American airport delays and specific security wait times at the airport of your choosing. Check the data and plan ahead so that you don't have to hurry

2. **Avoid standing at the ticketing counter.** Fly with carryon luggage only or check your luggage at the curb (this is not allowed if you are checking firearms) to avoid standing in the ticketing line. Print your boarding pass in advance or use the airline's app on your phone. The less time spent where people gather (especially lots of clueless people) the better.

3. **Get through security as quickly as you can**. Even though most airport security is a farce, you are still safer inside the checkpoint than outside. Don't eat or have coffee in restaurants outside the security checkpoint. Clear security quickly and then find a place to eat inside the secured area. The best advice for clearing security quickly is in this Wired Magazine article (http://howto.wired.com/wiki/

Fly_Through_Airport_Security)

4. **Once you clear security, find your gate,** any emergency exits, and any place where you might be able to acquire weapons for a more serious hostage situation or terrorist bombing. Food preparation areas will generally have knives. Maintenance areas will generally have tools. Look for cleaning carts or closets to find long-handled mops or brooms that can be used as impact weapons. You might need any of those items if things go really bad.

5. **Get away from as many people as possible.** Terrorists target large groups of people. I'm a big fan of avoiding such groups and thus, I'm also a huge proponent of using airport lounges. You will most likely have access to a lounge if you are traveling in Business or First Class or have preferred status with a certain airline. If not, look at the "Lounges" subheading later in the chapter to find out how you can get in to one. The more walls you put between you and the crowd of "targets" the terrorist wants to bomb, the safer you will be.

6. **If your airport has multiple levels, wait on an upper floor until your plane begins to board**. In every recent airport terrorist bomb/active killer attack, the terrorists began their attack on the ground floor. None of the worldwide attacks have reached victims located in the upper levels of any airport. The higher up you go, the safer you will be.

Getting through security- When trying to make it through security quickly in the airport, watch for a couple of seconds before choosing your security line. Many airports will have some lines that are routed through the metal detectors and some lines that are routed through the x-ray body scanner. The body scanner lines ALWAYS take longer. If there is an option, choose the line that doesn't go through the scanner and you will make it through the security procedures more quickly.

You can also save time if you organize your carryon items more efficiently as they go through the x-ray machine. First, remove your belt, watch, and anything in your pockets. Put all of that stuff in the outside pocket of your carryon bag while waiting in line before you approach the scanners. You can put all of those items back on when you arrive at your gate rather than holding up the security line.

Next, place your shoes and wallet on the conveyor belt first. You can then put your shoes back on and secure your money as you wait for your other items to be scanned. Place your carryon bag on the belt after your shoes. Finally place your computer and Ziploc bag of liquids on the belt. As soon as you get your shoes on, your bag should be coming out. Open the pockets where you plan to store your computer and liquids. When they finally clear the scanner, place them in your bag and move on to your gate.

As soon as you make it through the security checkpoint, quickly stash your passport and boarding passes. I see lots of travelers dropping these items or misplacing them as they try to gather their carryon luggage. If you leave your passport and boarding passes in your hand or hanging out of a pocket, they are far more likely to be lost or stolen. Stash them some place safe as soon as you can. Having a designated pocket in your clothing or in your carryon bag where you consistently store your travel documents will help you find them easily and ensure that you don't lose anything important.

Keep good control of both your travel documents and any luggage you may be carrying. There are numerous scam artists working in third world airports. Thieves, pickpockets, and scammers will often congregate in the luggage pickup area. Keep an eye on your belongings and watch your wallet and passports to ensure they aren't stolen.

In smaller local airports there may not be any security procedures, jet bridges, or luggage handling. You will likely have to carry your own bags out to the plane and load them yourself before climbing up a small ladder to get inside. These planes won't have large overhead storage for your luggage and often have very strict baggage weight limits. Pack light!

Expect to carry your own bags if you are flying a local airline. This one is in Placencia, Belize.

To prevent theft from baggage (by transportation personnel), make valuable items harder to steal. Duct tape, cable lock, or zip-tie all valuables together inside your suitcase. The large bundle will be harder for an airport baggage handler to stick in his pocket.

Third World Airports may look a little different. Here is my departure gate on a flight from Belize to Guatemala

Food and Drink at the Airport– The cell phone app Gate Guru provides detailed maps of all major airports and lists of amenities and restaurants. Pull up your airport terminal and check out the terminal layout before you arrive in the airport. I generally do this as I am waiting to disembark my plane during layovers.

Bring plenty of food and water with you in foreign airports. They probably will not have the same type of services you are used to. Many airports require that passengers flying internationally be at their gates at least an hour before departure. After checking in at the gate, they move all the passengers into a small room without chairs, water fountains, or restrooms for up to an hour before boarding. Have everything you need when you arrive at the gate because you may not be able to leave. Plan for some emergencies. If your plane is delayed, you may get hungry. A couple of protein bars are a great addition to your carry-on supplies.

You probably shouldn't drink airline coffee, tea, or water that doesn't come out of a bottle. Water from the plane tap (either in the galley or in the restroom) comes from a large water tank in the plane. That tank is often filled by the same person who empties the plane's waste. On some planes the waste water and drinking water ports are located in very close proximity. Several government studies have found that water from an airplane tap can contain more than 10 times the amount of bacteria that is present in municipal water supplies.

Don't assume that there will be food at the airport.
Here is the one-room arrivals, departures, and
baggage claim area in a Nicaraguan airport.

Staying Healthy on the Plane– There's nothing like being
trapped in the stale, virus-filled exhalations of 200 fellow
passengers for a long international flight on an airplane.
There's a reason that many people get sick after flying.

Although most people are fearful of germs floating
around in the cabin of the plane, statistically you are more
likely to catch a virus on a plane from something you touch,
not the air you breathe. Studies have shown that the
highest concentrations of viral and bacterial particles in an
airplane are on the surfaces of arm rests, tray tables, and

the restroom door handle. If you are exceptionally germ phobic, avoid touching these items with you bare hands and stay away from the aisle seats. Aisle seats are touched by many people boarding and leaving the plane. They have much higher pathogen concentrations.

Besides avoiding contact with germs, there are a few other strategies you can employ to keep healthy:

- **Stay Hydrated**. Your immune system works better when you are fully hydrated. That's hard to do on a plane unless you bring extra water. The combination of the low humidity and the low air pressure (which makes you breathe faster) tends to dehydrate people at a faster rate than they would experience at home. I fill up several water bottles (where allowed) and take them on to the flight with me. Even where TSA or airport policy doesn't allow liquid-containing bottles, they rarely have any limitations on bringing through an empty bottle. I have the flight attendants refill my bottles as often as possible. I personally try to drink at least eight ounces of water for every two hours I'm flying.
- **Keep your hands clean**. It's likely that every surface of the plane is completely contaminated with viruses and bacteria. I regularly see people changing babies' diapers on the tray tables where people eat. It's disgusting. Use an anti-bacterial wipe to clean the surfaces of your tray table and arm rests. You can't avoid touching things, but you can keep your hands and anything you touch as clean as possible. Don't touch the airline magazines. They cannot be disinfected and are likely contaminated with the viruses shed when the last passenger stuffed his/her

dirty tissues in the seat back pocket next to it. Don't wash your hands with dirty plane water unless no other options exist. I prefer to use alcohol hand sanitizers or anti-bacterial wipes to clean my hands. Look for an alcohol hand sanitizer that has at least 60% alcohol. Less concentrated gels give you the false impression of cleanliness but don't do the job very well. It's especially important to clean your hands before eating to reduce the chance that microbes will enter your body.

- **Adjust the overhead vent to blow air away from your face**. You should adjust the vent so that it is blowing straight down in front of your face. If your hands are in your lap, they should feel the air. This creates a "screen" of air in front of your face. If any passenger sneezes or otherwise contaminates the air with viral particles, this 'wind screen" should blow the particles down toward the floor and away from your face where they could contaminate you.

Other Health Issues – besides being concerned about viral exposures, all travelers should also work to prevent deep vein thrombosis (DVT). These are blood clots that form in the leg, usually caused by a combination of the high altitude and lack of motion for an extended period of time. Get up and move every hour or so. That"s one of the reasons I like aisle seats.

Compression socks, like the ones worn by diabetics, will help prevent DVT, as will taking an aspirin before your flight. Research this condition thoroughly. It's no joke and can have fatal consequences. If you notice numbness, discoloration, excessive swelling or pain in an extremity after a long flight, seek medical attention without delay.

Insecticides- More than 30 countries around the world require that airline staff spray aerosol insecticide (called "disinsection") throughout the plane's cabin on take-off or arrival. Flight attendants walk up and down the aisles spraying the insecticide (usually a chemical called permethrin) in the air and inside the overhead luggage compartments. The chemical is supposed to kill alien insects that might harm crops or any mosquitoes which might be carrying dangerous viruses.

The insecticide is generally considered safe and rarely causes problems. If you have a respiratory ailment, it's probably a good idea to avoid inhaling the aerosol mist. Cover your mouth and look away from the aisle until you can no longer smell or feel the chemicals in the air.

A plane I was supposed to take in Honduras. It was out of service because it hit a cow on the runway a couple days earlier.

Crash Safety– Certain parts of a plane have greater crash survival rates than others. In general, sitting in the rear of the plane is best in the event of a crash. One study noted that passengers in the front of the plane (first and business class) had a 49% survival rate after a plane crash. Passengers sitting at the extreme rear of the plane had a 69% crash survival rate.

Passengers nearest emergency exits also fare better in crashes. Passengers seated more than five rows away from an emergency exit have a significantly decreased chance of surviving a crash as compared to those who sit closer to an emergency exit.

Lounges- If you aren't flying first or business class, it may be worth your effort to get a temporary airport lounge pass. Many third world airports are hot, crowded, unsanitary, and dangerous. Spending your wait time in a first class lounge is much more comfortable than waiting at the gate, especially if you have a long layover. Lounges regularly have amenities like more comfortable seating, free food and drinks, internet access, air conditioning, showers, and private toilets.

I use Priority Pass (https://www.prioritypass.com/en) whenever I'm not flying business class. For less than $100 a year (or free with some credit cards), I can get one-time lounge passes for almost any airport in the world. Lounge Buddy is an App that will tell you each airport's available lounges and what the requirements are for entry.

If you really want (or need) to get into a first class lounge and don't have a membership or ticket, there are a couple of sneaky ways to do it.

Many lounges have policies that allow a legitimate lounge customer to bring a guest for free or for a very small fee. Find a lounge you want to visit and hang out near the entrance. When you see a customer who appears friendly and isn't in a hurry, ask if you can join him as a guest. Smile, act friendly and have a good reason. Say something like: "Hi! I'm flying coach today and have a really long layover. I'd like to get a little work done in the lounge, but don't have access. Do you mind taking me in as your guest?"

You may have to ask several people, but if you are persistent enough, you should find someone who will take you in with them.

Another (less ethical) way of getting lounge access is to buy a FULLY REFUNDABLE first class ticket on the day of your flight. Print out your ticket and use it to get in the lounge. Once inside, cancel the ticket by phone or internet. These tickets are expensive. Make sure you read all the small print and conditions if you purchase one of these tickets! Be absolutely certain that you will be able to cancel the ticket with a FULL refund and no penalties before you try this trick.

Airport toilet in Hurghada, Egypt. At least the cockroach was dead. The toilets are cleaner in the lounges.

Arriving at Your Destination

"Once you reach the Immigration officer, don't try to impress him with the three new words of native language you learned on the plane. He may think you know the language and try to ask more questions than necessary. Most of the time playing dumb with a friendly face gets you a lot farther than trying to be intelligent. Appearing unimportant is the best route to take during 90% of your travel."
– Randall and Perrin in *Adventure Travel in the Third World.*

It had been a long, rough flight. Being crammed into the back of a plane that was shaken by turbulence for more than 12 hours had weakened my resolve to live. That's what I get for trying to find the cheapest airfare on the internet.

The plane touched down in Lima, Peru just after midnight. It was my first solo trip to the third world. Like many Americans, I had been on holidays to Mexico and Jamaica. I had even taken a guided tour in Costa Rica with my family a few years earlier. But this time it was different. I was alone and exhausted.

Sitting in the back of the plane ensured that I was one of the final people to disembark. As I walked off the plane, the single file line to get through immigration was several hundred yards long. There were only two immigrations officers working and three international flights had arrived at roughly the same time. I was in for a wait.

It took almost two hours to get through the immigration queue. By the time I made it to my designated luggage carousel, it had stopped running. The baggage claim area was virtually empty except for a few straggling passengers who looked worse than I did and a couple bored security guards. None of the baggage carousels were running. Where was my bag?

I walked to each of the carousels and waited a few minutes. None of the carousels had any bags. What the hell? I was sure someone had taken my bag.

I walked to the "lost baggage" office nearby to file a claim. In my pitiful Spanish, I attempted to explain to the clerk that my bag was missing. She didn't understand me, but pointed to a corner of the baggage claim area. There was a six-foot high mountain of luggage. Apparently, once a bag has made a couple passes around the carousel, the porters remove it from the conveyor belt and throw it in a big pile in the corner of the room. I dug through all the bags, found mine and was on my way, but I wish someone had told me about this strange custom before I found myself stranded in a third world airport at 2 a.m. My Lonely Planet Guidebook didn't cover half of the things I needed to know on that first solo trip.

Customs and Immigration

When your plane lands, move quickly through the airport to the immigration line. You will save a tremendous amount of time if you jog past the other passengers disembarking from your flight. Many immigration posts are staffed by only one or two officers. When an entire plane-load of passengers arrives, it can take hours to process everyone. You want to be as close to the front of the line as possible.

Some third world airports do not have computers. Immigration officers must manually write travelers' information in large ledger books. I once flew into an airport in Nicaragua that did not contain either a computer or telephone. The immigration officials locked all of the flight's passengers into a small room without air conditioning and wouldn't allow anyone to leave until all passenger names had been manually entered into the log book. It was unpleasant even though I was at the front of the line. It would have been even worse if I had dawdled getting off the plane.

You will likely have to fill out a few forms (given to you on the plane) and hand them to the customs and immigration officers. Immigration is always first. They'll check your passport and your immigrations form. Then you get your bags and report to customs, handing them your customs form.

Some of the customs and immigration forms are not printed in English, some are in broken English and some are completely indecipherable. Don't worry too much about "getting it right." These forms are just a part of the country's revenue collection scheme. As long as you brought the right amount of cash for your visa, you'll get in. Customs officials in third world countries rarely even look at any of your forms. If you've screwed up something critical, they will allow you to fix it.

As highlighted in the opening quote of this chapter, I endorse Randall and Perrin's "play dumb" technique when dealing with foreign customs and immigration officials. I have all of my paperwork in order and present that to the officer with my passport. I greet the officer in English even if I speak the language of the country I'm visiting. I smile and pretend not to understand most of the questions he or she asks unless they are in fluent English. I just smile and say *"I'm sorry. I don't understand."* The officer usually just shakes his head, stamps my paperwork and allows me to enter. I've crossed international borders more than 150 times in my travels and I've never been searched or been detained by any foreign customs officials, even though my appearance is far from innocuous. The local officials are generally happy to have the economic boost from foreign travelers and will let you in as long as their dogs don't smell drugs or fruit.

In addition to the "play dumb" advice, if you want to speed through customs, be prepared to answer two questions. The most common questions that customs and immigrations officials ask are "*Why are you here?*" and "*Where are you staying?*" No matter how groggy or jet-lagged you may be, you should have simple, coherent, and plausible answers for those two questions. If you do, you'll most likely get a quick stamp in your passport and a welcome from the immigration official.

Some of you are saying: "*This advice doesn't apply to me. I'm not a drug smuggler. I have nothing to hide.*" Unfortunately, being innocent doesn't save you from the inconveniences of an interrogation conducted by third world customs officials. You really don't want to be chosen for "secondary screening," even if you have nothing to hide. In addition to a potential time delay, some immigrations/customs officers will use secondary screening as an opportunity to solicit a bribe. This is especially true in many African countries. The officers know that they have you over a barrel. They will honestly tell you: "*Give me $50 or we will question you for the next three hours.*" They have the power to make your life hell and they know it. It's best to have honest answers about the common immigration questions and avoid the "secondary screening" area of the airport.

A lot of countries use the "traffic light" system for determining whose luggage to search. As you go through customs, you push a button. The button triggers either a red or a green light to flash. If you get a green light, you can pass. If the light is red, your luggage is thoroughly searched by the customs officers. In some countries known for valuable natural resources or wildlife, you will also undergo the traffic light process to search your luggage when you leave the country just like you did for entry.

If they don't employ the traffic light system, many countries just run everyone's luggage through an X-ray machine. They seem to be looking mostly for fruit or agricultural items. I've never had any problems with any of the items I carry. Most countries (outside the USA) really don't care what you bring in. The one exception is high dollar electronic items like computers. If you have a lot of electronic gadgets in your luggage, you may be scrutinized closely and required to pay import duties. Check the customs requirements for each country you visit and determine what is legal to bring in and what is not.

Take a look around as you are walking through the airport on your arrival into the country. If you are leaving through the same airport, it will be useful to get an idea of the basic layout for your return. Take note of where the ticketing counters and security checkpoints are located. Also, check to see if there are any available restaurants and restrooms. I've been in quite a few third world airports that didn't have so much as a snack bar. You'll want to know if you have to eat before arriving for your flight or if you can actually eat in the airport itself.

When crossing international borders, you may be given some paperwork or a "tourist card." Keep these documents in your passport and do not lose them! Depending on the country visited, you may be fined or have your departure delayed if you can't produce this paperwork when you are leaving. It may be prudent to attach a paperclip or small binder clip to your passport to keep your travel documents secure.

Passport with binder clip for tourist registration card.

When returning home (for Americans) you will endure a similar process. You will go through immigration controls first, and then you will pick up your checked bag to pass through a customs inspection. After passing through customs, you will re-check your bag (make sure you place any duty-free liquid purchases inside your checked bags at this time) and then go through security again.

Lots of travelers unfamiliar with returning home from foreign travel become frustrated and confused because they don't understand the process. You must get your checked bags so that customs can inspect them if they so desire. That's relatively rare, but it does occasionally happen. You must then go through security again because you had access to your checked bags, where you could have accessed a weapon or something unsafe to carry in the passenger compartment of the plane.

Be patient and budget lots of time for this process. Don't pick a connecting flight with a layover less than two hours. Having Global Entry will dramatically speed up the process as will downloading the government's "Mobile Passport" app on your phone. I find the mobile passport lines move about twice as fast as the standard immigration queues.

Be aware of a recent Customs and Border Protection innovation in some locations that is called "preclearance." In locations that have preclearance, American travelers will go through customs and immigration screenings at the airport in the departing country before they board their flight instead of upon landing in the USA.

Preclearance speeds up the process when you land in the USA, but it adds a tremendous amount of time to your airport check in. In preclearance locations, you will have to arrive at the airport three to four hours before your plane takes off.

Most of the current preclearance locations are in Canada, the Caribbean, and the Middle-East. If you are traveling to those locations, check the customs and border protection website to see if your trip will be affected.

Money

There are usually ATMs available in most airports. Making cash withdrawals in local currency is far cheaper than changing money at an exchange window. In most third world countries, you will need local currency to pay taxi drivers. Hit the ATM and withdraw some emergency cash as soon as you land. The exchange rates at the ATM will be better and the lines will be much shorter than at the money changing window.

Transportation

If you haven't pre-arranged airport transportation, read up in advance about how to get a taxi in the safest manner possible. Every city and country is different. You don't want to get ripped off or kidnapped, both of which can happen easily when dealing with gypsy cabs and criminals posing as taxi drivers. Most travel guidebooks have sections covering these issues. Read them BEFORE you land. Nothing screams "victim" like reading a Lonely Planet Guidebook in the baggage claim area.

Third world taxi queue. This is what you will see when you step out of the Cairo airport after midnight. You better have things figured out before you arrive.

Occasionally, you will walk outside the airport and see that the taxi queue is astronomically long with a line of people that is virtually unmoving. If you don't want to wait, go to the airport DEPARTURES door rather than the ARRIVALS door. Catch a taxi that is dropping off a passenger instead of waiting in the long line with all the other tourists. Often times these taxis will be cheaper as well. The driver will be willing to drop the price a bit if it means he gets a fare without wasting time in a long queue.

The single most common way I see tourists scammed is by cab drivers is at the airport. I've been the victim of airport taxi scams myself. I once pre-booked transportation to my hotel from the airport in Rio de Janeiro, Brazil. I arrived at the designated meeting point and waited an hour but my transportation didn't arrive. I wasn't prepared, didn't know the local customs, and didn't have a functioning cell phone or phone numbers for the transportation company.

As I was waiting with a clueless look on my face, I was approached by a very well dressed man who asked me if I needed a taxi. Being unprepared and frustrated, I said "yes." The man escorted me past the cab queue outside and up to the airport parking garage where his car was waiting. He took me to my hotel and then charged me $70 for the "private limousine transfer." I later learned that a regular cab outside would have cost me around $20. I paid the "gringo tax" because I was stupid and unprepared. An entire economy is built around travelers who act like I did.

A naïve tourist will walk outside and see the chaotic taxi queue. He will be approached by a well-spoken local "taxi agent" offering to take the tourist directly to a private cab to bypass the line and the chaos. The "private" taxi will charge the tourist three to four times the going rate for the fare. Follow the locals and watch what they do. If anyone approaches you in the taxi queue, ignore them.

Another common scam among airport taxi drivers is to tell their passengers that their hotel is either closed or full. They then offer to take the passenger to another hotel (where they get a kickback from the owner). Don't fall for this scam. If a cab driver refuses to take you to your desired location, get out of the cab and find another one.

If you have pre-booked transportation in an especially dangerous country, make sure that the driver meeting you doesn't use your real name on the sign he is holding. Use a fake name or a company name instead. You may also want to set up a security question as verification with your driver. This prevents being picked up by a kidnapper instead of your designated driver.

If kidnappers know you will be arriving, it is very easy for them to wait in the passenger pickup area of the airport and look for a driver bearing a sign with your name on it. Depending on the kidnapper's motivations, he will then either bribe your driver to "disappear" or will abduct the driver. The kidnapper will then take the sign with your name on it and wait for you himself. Having a designated security question or pass phrase to be given by the driver might alert you to the fact that something isn't right.

If the country you are visiting is a known kidnapping hotspot, you may want to institute an additional security protocol. Before leaving with the driver, take a photograph of both him and his vehicle's license plates and send it to a friend at home. Most kidnappers won't stick around to pose for a picture if you insist on taking one before you leave the airport parking lot.

Luggage Issues

> *"I'm a guy who tends to fall in love with hot, messy, barely functional places–where fiery arguments are common–and one is pleasantly surprised if one's luggage arrives in good order– if at all."*
> – Anthony Bourdain

Third world airports have very short baggage carousels. There isn't enough room for the whole plane's luggage. Baggage handlers will remove all bags that have made more than one pass on the carousel without pickup. They will place the bags in a pile somewhere in the baggage claim area. If you are delayed from getting your bag for any reason, look for the luggage pile. It is more likely your bag has been placed there and won't be on the designated carousel.

Keep your baggage claim ticket if you checked a bag. Unlike what happens in the United States, in some third world countries you will have to show a security guard a claim ticket and identification in order to leave the baggage claim area with a piece of luggage. Don't lose your claim ticket.

As soon as you clear the secure baggage claim area, rip the airline baggage tags off your luggage. No one needs to know your name or where you came from. Quick-witted scam artists can use this information to target you as you leave the airport or arrive at your hotel.

In addition to the scam artists, kidnappers can also use baggage tag information to target travelers. Criminal groups will employ people who hang around the baggage carousels at international airports looking at luggage tags. These criminals read the name on your bag tag and then conduct a quick internet search to see if you are a valuable target.

If the internet search shows that you might be wealthy or that you are a business executive, the criminals will look outside for the driver holding a sign bearing your name. The kidnapper will then either bribe the driver or threaten him with force, ordering him to leave. The kidnapper or his associate will then take the sign with your name and pose as your driver. When you walk out to meet him, you won't be going to your hotel as expected. Instead, you will need the information I provide in the upcoming "Kidnapping" chapter.

Lost Luggage– If your baggage is ever lost or delayed, file a report with the airline immediately. Do it before you leave the airport. Most airports have a "lost baggage" office somewhere near the baggage carousel. Having a photo of your luggage will be useful when you are asked to provide a description of your lost bag and the baggage claim worker doesn't speak English.

After you file your report, ask the agent for a stipend to purchase replacement clothing and equipment. It's often easier to get the payment in advance rather than submitting receipts at a later date. You might be surprised how easy it is to get payment up front. My bag was once lost in China. I filed the lost bag report with some difficulty and then asked the agent for a stipend. He opened a desk drawer and handed me the equivalent of $200 US in Chinese Yuan. Cash. No questions asked. No forms to sign. I was grateful I didn't have to get receipts from the

Chinese street merchants where I had to buy some replacement clothing.

There is one good outcome when your luggage is lost; the airline is required by federal regulations to refund any checked baggage fees if they lose your luggage. Don't forget to get your money back from the airline if they lose your bags.

If you are exceptionally worried about your bags being lost by the airlines, there are a couple of technological solutions that may help you locate your lost bags. The service Trakdot (https://trakdot.com/en) places a small tracking device in your bags that sends you a text message when your baggage arrives at your destination. Another option is I-Trak (https://www.i-trak.com/home.aspx). This company will call or email you with the exact location of your luggage if requested. I haven't personally used either option, but they seem like great ideas if one is worried about losing precious cargo.

When your flight is delayed or the airline loses your luggage, you may be entitled to a reimbursement. Each country's regulations are different, but if your European flight is delayed for more than three hours, you may be eligible for up to $800 in cash. U.S. passengers who are bumped from a flight may be entitled to up to $1300. Unfortunately, the airlines don't make it easy to collect the money. Only 2% of eligible claims are paid out annually.

If you don't want to go through the "customer service" hassle to get your refund, check out Airhelp (https://www.airhelp.com/en/). They will submit your claim for you and only require some basic details about your cancelled or delayed flight. If your claim is rejected, you won't owe any money. If you get a refund, Airhelp will take 25% as a fee for their service.

Hotels

"Basically, there are a few primary forewarnings about staying at a specific hotel: Never stop at a hotel where every car in the parking lot is painted primer grey. Never stop at a hotel where the cashier's office consists of a steel cage and bulletproof glass. Never stop at a hotel where the occupants have Mongoloid facial features and are seated on the porch strumming banjo duets. You have to use a piece of mind to have peace of mind."
– Louis Awerbuck

It was pouring rain when my plane landed at midnight in Bogota, Colombia. The jet bridge wasn't working, so we all had to use the stairs to exit the plane onto the runway. The half mile walk to customs outside in monsoon-like conditions and 45 degree weather made the trip unforgettable. I cleared customs and immigration and got a taxi to my pre-booked hotel. I arrived at the hotel a little before 2 a.m. They had no record of my reservation. Despite showing them printed copies of my reservation, the hotel manager insisted that the reservation *"wasn't in the system"* and that they had no spare rooms. They suggested a hostel down the street.

Being stuck walking with all of my luggage on the streets of a dodgy neighborhood in Bogota at 2 a.m. isn't recommended in most guidebooks. Luckily, the pouring rain kept even the criminals inside. I found the recommended hostel and took their last available single room. I quickly took a hot shower and jumped into bed, exhausted after a full day of travel. Soon after crawling under the covers, I felt some kind of insect biting my legs. Bedbugs. I was too tired to even complain. Fortunately, my trip involved some camping, so I had my sleeping bag in my luggage. I rolled the sleeping bag on the bare floor and went to sleep. Luckily, I was able to find a better hotel in the morning.

That was one of the worst hotel experiences I've had in all my years of travel. With hope, your luck will be better than mine and you won't have to endure the problems associated with lost reservations and parasitic bed infestations. Pay attention to the tips below and you'll have a much better chance of having a great experience.

Hotels vs. Apartments vs. Hostels- If you are staying in a single city more than a few consecutive days, you will likely get a better place to stay by looking at short term apartment rentals in lieu of hotels. AirBnB (https://www.airbnb.com/) is probably the best known site advertising such rentals, but there are others as well. Tripping.com searches 18 of the largest apartment rental sites on the net with just a couple keystrokes. It does not however, search AirBnB. If you are looking for a short term apartment rental, I would try tripping.com first and then comparison shop on AirBnB if you can't find anything you like.

If you book your hotel accommodations in advance, be cautious of hotel scammers. There are a lot of criminals who list phony hotels or apartments on rental sites. These scammers will ask for full prepayment or a large deposit. After you pay and arrive in country, you'll find that the hotel room you reserved doesn't exist. To avoid being taken by a scam like this, don't pre-pay your accommodations. You should also avoid paying deposits in cash or by wire transfers. Insist on using a credit card for payment. Most scammers won't be able to process the card and will insist on a wire transfer. That should be a clear indication that something is amiss. Paying with a credit card avoids those issues and also gives you recourse in getting your money back if the hotel room doesn't meet your standards.

On any of the apartment rental sites, you should take photos of the apartment or room as soon as you arrive. Document any obvious damage. Occasionally unscrupulous owners will allege you damaged their property and demand additional payment. It's good to have proof that any damage was pre-existing. The photos will also help you put furniture back in its original position should you move it during your stay.

If you are looking for a hostel, check out the Hostelworld app (https://www.hostelworld.com/mobile-app) for your phone. You can book more than 30,000 different hostel properties in more than 180 different countries from your smart phone. This app allows you to sort by price, rating, property type, or name. It may be the easiest way to find and book a hostel when your travel plans unexpectedly change and you find yourself without lodging.

When you are new to traveling, it may make sense to ease yourself into a new cultural experience rather than jumping in with both feet. It's easy to be overwhelmed when dealing with a completely different culture, language, and food. If you're worried about being overwhelmed, start your stay in a Western style hotel and eat Western food for a couple days. Gradually introduce yourself to new foods and find more local accommodations once you get your feet on the ground. Traveling is supposed to be fun. Don't stress yourself unnecessarily.

Smaller and slightly run down hotels just outside the main tourist areas are usually the safest places to stay. There will be fewer drunken tourists causing problems in the hotel itself if it is slightly out of the way or a bit dingy. Most of the thieves will also be concentrating their efforts on the wealthier and more clueless travelers in the tourist trap hotels.

A final advantage is that being on the outskirts of the downtown or tourist areas buys you a little more time to escape. I like staying on the side of town closest to the airport as most third world airports tend to be at least 15-20 miles from the downtown area. If there is some type of coup or rebel takeover, the downtown tourist areas will be locked down first. It will take time for the rebel groups to shut down the outermost areas of the city. That additional time might provide enough of a cushion that you can arrange transportation to the international airport or catch a private car to a land border crossing.

If you have the ability to choose a hotel room, pick one on floors two to four on the back side of the building. Ground level rooms are accessible via windows to criminals outside. Rooms higher than the fourth floor may be difficult to evacuate in case of a fire or other emergency. Most non-American hotel rooms consider the ground floor as level zero. The first floor in a foreign hotel is often what we Americans call the second floor. It's always smarter to physically see the room to check location, electricity, and safety issues before you pay your money for the night. Try to get a room at the end of a corridor and farthest away from the elevator. Those rooms are usually closest to emergency exits and have the fewest number of people walking past them.

When forced to take a room on the ground or first floor, check your windows as soon as you get into the room. Look for ladders, tree limbs, balconies, or any other objects that could support the weight of a human. Some unscrupulous hotel staff members purposely leave accessible windows unlocked so that their sneak-thief friends can get into your room and steal your stuff. Make sure the windows are locked so you don't wake up to find a burglar going through your luggage.

Pick a part of the hotel that is as far as possible from the street below. Residents of third world countries generally use their car horns far more often than drivers in the United States. You don't want to be in a room right over the street if you want to get any sleep. In addition to the car horns, you will hear loud (or non-existent) mufflers and the voices of raucous partiers returning from the bars at 5 a.m. You will also smell the diesel fumes if you leave your window open.

If you can't pick your room, make sure you pack good earplugs. I use Mack's brand and find they work better than any others I've used.

When looking for a hotel or hostel on a very tight budget, you might not be able to find one in your price range in the "safer" parts of town. You may have to look around in some shady neighborhoods to find a hotel you can afford. If I don't have any recommendations from friends or internet sites, I usually do an internet search for the locations of each neighborhood's local police station. I try to book a hotel within sight of the police department. Even if the cops are corrupt, their presence usually keeps violent crime in the area down to a minimal level.

View from a hostel balcony in Cairo, Egypt. Rooms
overlooking streets like this will be loud, dusty, and
reeking of diesel fumes.

When checking into hotels in many foreign countries, you
may be asked to leave your passport at the reception desk
for a short time. This isn't a scam and happens in almost
every South American and African country. These
countries have laws requiring hotel owners to keep copies
of their foreign guests' passports for police inspection. The
hotel clerk will copy your passport and bring it to your
room in a timely manner. If this really bothers you, make a
few copies of your own passport and try to give one to the
clerk instead. They may or may not take it, but it's probably
worth a shot.

Just like at home, most third world hotels require that
you give them a credit card to hold as a deposit before
they will give you the keys to your rooms. Recognize that

in some countries, a debit card cannot be used for this purpose, even if it has a Visa or Mastercard logo. It's always smart to travel with a "real" credit card in addition to your bank's debit card. When you are choosing a credit card for this purpose, avoid picking either an American Express or Discover card. Neither is accepted in some third world locales.

It is also common for third world hotel guests to leave their room keys at the reception. The hotel does this as a way to keep track of guests and to avoid losing keys. I don't like leaving my room keys at the desk. I want immediate access to my room on my terms. I don't really like the hotel staff knowing I am out. If there is an emergency, I don't want to have to hunt down some sleeping hotel desk clerk to get my room key. As a more practical concern, as soon as you need your key, it is inevitable that there will be a busload of new tourists checking in at the same time. I don't like being forced to wait an hour to get my key. If the hotel asks you for the key when you are leaving through the front lobby, take the back door or emergency exit instead.

On the topic of keys, it's also a good idea to request two keys, especially if you are a solo female traveler. It's rare, but occasionally hotel desk clerks are paid by criminals to identify the rooms where young single females are staying. By requesting two keys it seems that you won't be staying alone. That may be enough to get "deselected" as a possible victim.

When registering at a hotel, you may also be asked for your occupation. If you work for the government, are a police officer, or in the military, don't tell them what you do for a living. Make up an occupation instead. I like using "teacher." It's innocuous and at least somewhat truthful for almost everyone. In the event of political unrest or rebellion, the rebel factions will be checking hotel rosters to see if there are any "valuable" hostages or potential sources of resistance. Government employees and men-at-arms fit both descriptions. You don't want to be the token representative of a rival government who is beheaded on live television as a publicity stunt. Keep things low profile.

Check your hotel's guest policy before you arrive. If you are planning on bringing any dates back to your room or are meeting a friend, be aware that some hotels' policies prohibit overnight guests. Some hotels don't allow you to bring guests at all, some won't allow it after specific hours and others will charge you an additional fee. Guests may also be required to show identification, even when they are accompanied by you.

When you check into your room, take a couple of minutes to explore the fire escape routes. Not only will that act save you time in the event of an emergency, but it's important to ensure that the fire escapes/exits are functioning properly. Budget hotel owners (especially in Asia) have been known to weld fire escape doors closed. The hotel owners don't want people using them to leave without paying the bill. It shouldn't be an issue in most of the mid-upper price range hotels, but for some of you budget travelers, it's prudent to check.

Many hotel locks will not be up to North American/ Western European standards. Supplement your door locks by traveling with a small rubber door stop. Wedge it under the door (from the inside) at night when you sleep. It won't keep out a determined attacker, but it will buy you a little time to act.

If your door locks appear subpar, place something in front of the door to prevent its opening. Anything you do that delays an attacker or thief will be beneficial. I've placed loaded backpacks in front of the doors and have even littered the entryway with empty beer cans to create noise if someone sneaks in. My friend Nick Hughes recommends carrying a couple sheets of bubble wrap in your checked bag. You can lay the bubble wrap on the floor inside the door for an improvised alarm.

Placing a chair and a couple of crumpled plastic bags in the entryway of a hotel room in Thailand. Someone might get into the room, but probably won't make it to where I'm sleeping without being heard.

Often, ensuite bathrooms are located right inside the main door. If the bathroom door swings out, leave it open at night when you sleep. The criminal breaking into your hotel room will likely make enough noise to wake you if the room door crashes into the open bathroom door.

Another makeshift "alarm" can be created with an empty beer bottle or water glass. Lean a chair up against the door to your room. Once it is in place, balance the water glass or empty bottle on the chair so that it will fall to the ground if the chair is moved. The glass breaking as it hits the floor should wake you up and alert you that your room has been compromised. If you don't have a chair, place the empty bottle directly on top of the door opening lever. If someone opens the door from the outside, the bottle will fall and provide you with an improvised burglar alarm

Building codes may not be up to American standards. If you stay in a place like this, you better

have an evacuation kit handy. Aguas Calientes,
Peru.

If you are staying in a higher class hotel that has electronic locks and fear that someone will gain access to your room, try this trick:

- Look at the outside (hallway) side of the door lock. At the bottom of the underside of the lock (facing the floor) you may find a small round hole. This is the access point used to bypass the room's electronic security.
- You need to plug this hole using anything you can. I like to use a strip of paper formed into a tightly fit roll that I then push into the hole. The roll of paper will gradually unravel and fill the hole, thereby slowing access. This technique is nondestructive and can be relatively easily removed by hotel maintenance staff.

One thing that many people forget is that in lower class hotels (and some nicer lodgings) there is a greater risk of theft from people you let into your room or hotel staff than there is from "outsiders." Be extremely cautious who you let into your room. Prostitutes, escorts, and "party friends" are notorious for stealing anything they can get their hands on. If you are worried about cleaning staff taking your property, lock it in the safe or in your luggage.

You can also play the TV or radio at a fairly high volume (but not high enough to cause complaints) when you are gone to deter people from entering the room if they have a key. I also always place the "do not disturb" sign on my door, regardless of whether I am in the room or not. That may give thieves a slight pause by creating the illusion that you are in the room when you are not. Likewise, leaving the "clean room now" sign out tells thieves that you are outside the room. Rather than use the sign, it's safer to call the housekeeping staff directly and request that they clean your room.

Instead of just placing the "do not disturb" sign on your door knob, actually shut the edge of the sign into the door when you close it. If the sign is hanging freely when you return, you know that someone has been in your room.

High walls don't always mean your hotel is secure.
Thief scaling a hotel wall in Cambodia.

On a side note, hotel staff should always leave the hotel room door propped open when cleaning a room. If you notice maids and staff entering guest rooms and closing the door behind them, go to another hotel for the remainder of your stay. There's only one reason staff would enter guest rooms and close the door behind them; they want to steal your stuff. Find another hotel.

Don't be afraid to improvise added security devices if your hotel locks are inadequate. Rubber door stops are great supplemental security devices when you are in the room. I've even tied sliding glass doors with paracord when I've found their locks didn't work. If you tie your only exit closed, make sure you have a knife handy to cut the rope or cord in an emergency. You may not have time to untie the knot.

Backpack blocking the door of my hotel room in Bogota, Colombia

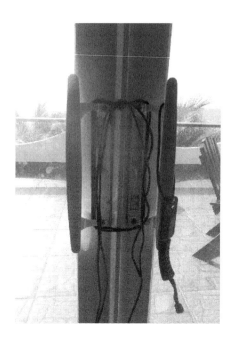

The sliding door in this Nicaraguan beach hotel
didn't lock from the inside. Problem solved with a
little paracord. Note knife hanging on door handle
in case I have to get out quickly.

If your hotel is located in a particularly hot and humid
location, it may have an in-room air conditioner. You will
see the same type of air conditioner in hotel rooms all over
the world. It's generally mounted on the wall above the bed
and is controlled via remote control. The numbers are the
temperature in degrees Centigrade. For Americans unused
to the conversion, 21 degrees C is roughly 70 degrees
Fahrenheit.

The in- room air conditioner may have a very strong odor of mold that spreads throughout the entire room and may cause headaches or allergy attacks. If mold odors bother you, carry a small spray bottle of Lysol and spray the inside of the air conditioner vents. You will have a much more comfortable stay. I carry some Lysol bottles on every trip I take to humid climates and they have proven very useful.

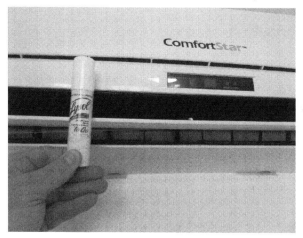

Air conditioner with trusty spray bottle of Lysol.
Spray the entire bottle up the air vents if you smell the odor of mold in your hotel room.

Hotels will occasionally program their room thermostats to keep temperatures within a certain range. Sometimes that range is too hot or cold for my comfort. If the hotel has a digital thermostat/controller on the wall, you may be able to change it to "VIP Mode" to disable the hotel's settings. Try this:

- Hold down the "display" button
- While holding that button, press "off"
- Release off, continue to hold down display, and Press the "up" arrow button
- Release all buttons

The display should flash "VIP" and you will be allowed to program whatever temperature you want. The VIP setting will also disable the room's motion detectors to maintain the temperature while you are asleep or not moving around.

If your hotel requires a room key to activate lights and air conditioning, you may be able to use an old credit card, membership card, or even a business card as an alternative. You can also ask the front desk for an extra room key card because you "lost" yours. Sometimes in very hot climates, I want to keep the air conditioning running in my room when I will only be gone for a short while. If that's the case, I try to use an alternate card in the power slot so that I can take my room key card with me. Most of the time it works. Occasionally it doesn't. It's worth a try.

When you are leaving your hotel, don't stand out in the street with all your bags. You become an easy target for anyone who wants to steal your stuff. If you have to wait outside for a taxi, leave your bags in the hotel lobby. Better yet, have the hotel staff arrange the taxi for you and wait in the lobby with all of your luggage under your watchful eye.

General Precautions

"Perhaps the greatest reason for bad travel experiences is the seemingly inherent egotistical attitude of being from the United States or some other "developed" country. Our unique reluctance to swallow our pride and our distinct ability to judge the rest of the world based on our set of values and laws have, without a doubt, caused more problems for Americans than any other."

-Jeff Randall

"People of good will frequently send one off with the injunction to "Have a safe trip!" There is no such thing as a safe trip. Safety is an illusion. It must always fail in the end. That does not mean that we should not consider safety, but never to cry "Safety first!" Safety, while something we should seek, must always be placed second to getting the job done. One who places safety first is, quite specifically, a coward. We do not go to war to be safe, neither do we climb mountains, or race cars, or hunt buffalo, to be safe. We hear commentators explain that we should not resist violent crime because we may get hurt. This is the advice of the rabbit people who live all their lives in fear and never know the joy of danger. There are people like that, and while we may feel sorry for them, we must never take their advice seriously."

– Jeff Cooper

I'm all for finding adventure in foreign countries. Go out and have all the fun you can. But if you want to maximize adventure while being as safe as possible, follow these two rules:

1. **Choose the safest mode of transportation possible** in every circumstance where there is an option. Most tourist deaths are caused by traffic accidents. Choosing a safe mode of travel is the most important thing you can do to stay alive in the third world.

2. **Get to your accommodation before dark**. That doesn't mean you have to lock yourself in your hotel room after dark, but when you are traveling between cities, it will be safer to make sure you get to your room before dark if possible. Arriving in town after dark will make your journey indescribably more difficult. Accommodation is harder to find and many places will be booked full for the night. If you arrive late enough, some smaller hotels or hostels won't even open the door. Everything looks different and there are far more predators cruising the streets.

Traveling in remote areas after dark is often significantly more dangerous than traveling during the day. At night, even the police officers are more dangerous. Every time I've been asked for a bribe or threatened by a third world police officer, it has been on the road at night. I've never been accosted at gunpoint during the day.

You should probably just say no if this driver offers you a ride. Honduras.

Assessing Local Safety- The relative "safety" of an area is a function of both the police/government structure and individual neighborhood crime characteristics.

Author David Andrew Brown compiled the best summary I've seen about of how governmental institutions affect traveler safety:

"There are a few things you should ask yourself before buying the tickets and boarding the plane. Here is my ABC for safe traveling:

A. Is by any chance the government of the country you plan on traveling to tyrannical? Are they oppressing people based on their beliefs or gender?

B. Are the army and the police the same thing, or are they two separate entities? In some countries, especially in communist one, there is not a clear distinction between the army and the police.

C. Does the region in which you will be staying have a noticeable problem with people being assaulted or kidnaped

If the answer to any of these questions is yes, then we can both agree that the region you plan on visiting is hostile. It can range from anything such as "let's rob this Gringo" to "slay the infidel". If you still have to go there, you should prepare accordingly. However, I must warn you that not even with all the preparation in the world, your trip is still a roll of the dice regarding personal security and survival."

Countries that meet Mr. Brown's description above will simply be more hazardous to your health than countries that are less tyrannical. If you travel to one of these "hostile countries" you must exercise more caution than if you are traveling in an area with a more benign government and police force.

Besides these broad concerns, the crime rate in the place you are visiting is likely to have a lot of neighborhood variation. Just like at home, if you can avoid some of the "bad" neighborhoods, you will be less likely to be victimized.

Given the massive differences in culture, customs, and income, how can you tell if the neighborhood you are visiting is safe or not? These guidelines may be pretty basic, but using them will give you a quick assessment of your relative safety in any neighborhood in the world:

1. Are there lots of armed guards?
2. Do the properties seem to be run down or uncared for?
3. Are people in the area walking in pairs or small groups rather than walking alone?

4. Is there a lot of graffiti present on the walls?
5. Are there obvious security measures (like broken glass embedded atop walls, electric fences, barbed wire, etc.) present?
6. Are there lots of people are aimlessly "hanging out" in the street?

If you answer "yes" to most of these questions, you may not be in the world's safest place. It's best to move on.

Broken glass atop the wall protecting a parking garage in Uruguay.

Beyond looking at these six factors, take a second and observe your environment to get a subjective "feel" for the location. Is there more order or disorder? Broken windows, graffiti, trash, fireworks, and items out of place are all signs of disorder. Numerous criminological studies have shown that there is a corresponding increase in crime as disorder increases.

One additional thing to notice is what has been called an "atmospheric shift." This term was coined in the book *Left of Bang* by authors who developed a system to teach soldiers to avoid potentially hostile environments. An "atmospheric shift" is when people change emotional and physical reactions in response to a specific stimulus.

Do people go about their business as usual when they detect the presence of an "outsider" or do they alter their behavior? When they see you, do they leave the area? Stop talking? Move away from you? Turn their back on you? All of these "atmospheric shifts" are negative. When you see them, you should recognize that your presence is likely unwanted in the area.

Conversely, if people start smiling when they see you, generally act the same as they were before, straighten up slouching posture, or approach you, those are more welcoming atmospheric shifts. When evaluating any location's potential for violence, avoid areas with uncommon amounts of disorder and/or those where you detect negative atmospheric shifts.

Of course, more obvious danger signs shouldn't be ignored either. It goes without saying, but if you value your life, you should probably avoid areas with armed protesters, militia roadblocks, gang members carrying machine guns, and burning tires in the roadway.

Passport safety- Keep your passport, the majority of your cash, and other important documents in a safe at your hotel whenever possible. Carry a copy of your passport around with you for identification purposes. You'll need it to use your credit card in some foreign countries.

Some experts will recommend carrying your passport on your person at all times so that it won't be stolen. I disagree. I've had numerous friends who have had passports pickpocketed on the street or who have accidentally left them someplace while out and about. I've never known anyone who has had a passport stolen from the safe or locked luggage in their hotel room. Play the odds, keep your passport locked up someplace safe and carry a copy of it on your daily activities.

The only time I would carry my actual passport on my person is if I was traveling to an area with potential for serious political unrest. If things got bad there, it's possible that you wouldn't have time to get back to your hotel before needing to escape on an international flight. A lost or stolen passport can be replaced in a couple days if you have copies, but you won't be able to leave the country without your actual passport. Thoroughly evaluate your travel situation and decide which passport carry option makes the most sense for you.

Money- Don't carry all your money in the same place on your body. Separate it into several different locations. That way, you can give up just a small amount (and not your entire stash) if you are robbed or asked for a bribe by a police officer. I generally carry a wallet that contains the majority of my cash attached to my belt and tucked down the front of my pants. It is well hidden and hard to access.

Public marketplaces like this world-famous "Black Market" in Ciudad del Este in Paraguay bring in lots of naive tourists for the local pickpockets. Be careful where you carry your cash.

I also carry a money clip full of about $50-$100 worth of local currency and a credit card in my front pocket. That's what I use for most daily expenses. When purchasing small items, it's never a good idea to "flash" large amounts of cash. Doing that sets you up for a robbery or theft. Using your small stash of local money ensures that your larger stash of money isn't revealed to any potential criminals watching. In addition to these two stashes of money, I keep

$200 American cash, a spare ATM card, and a spare credit card in my shoe for emergencies.

Money clip with local currency. The wallet has additional money, but is attached to my belt and thrust down inside my pants to prevent pickpocketing.

Many older travelers carry money belts under their clothes. I generally advise against that practice. While it may help protect against pickpockets, robbers know all about them. In every tourist robbery that I've heard about in a third world country, the robber has lifted up the victim's shirt to check for a money belt.

Pickpockets- Wherever you have large crowds of tourists, you'll have pickpockets. Generally pickpockets work in small gangs, with one or two people distracting the victim while another lifts the victim's valuables. Keep a zone of space around yourself when you can, and if you think someone's approaching you for a phony reason, trust your instincts and walk away.

Pickpockets also very frequently target tourists leaving bars late at night. They assume (most often correctly) that the traveler may be too drunk to notice the pickpocketing attempt. While you should never be walking around in third world countries wearing expensive jewelry or watches, you should make doubly sure you don't have any tempting theft targets visible when you leave a bar at night.

Before leaving a bar or restaurant, go to the bathroom and lock yourself into a stall. Remove all watches, jewelry, phones, or wallets and place them in your front pockets before walking outside. You'll want to do this in privacy (why I suggested the bathroom stall) because occasionally pickpockets will even employ "spotters" inside the bar to inform them where potential victims are carrying wallets, phones, or other valuables. Transferring all of your jewelry to your front pockets in full public view of everyone in the bar may provide the thief with all the information he needs to be successful   .

If you do carry a traditional wallet, carry it in your front pants pocket. If you insist on carrying a wallet in your back pocket, consider doing something that will give you some sort of notice if the wallet is removed by a pickpocket. One method is to wrap a couple large rubber bands around the wallet to increase friction between the wallet and the pocket to slow removal. Another technique advocated by Clint Emerson in his book *Escape the Wolf* is to place a plastic pocket comb lengthwise with the teeth facing up in the same pocket as your wallet. With the comb in place, the wallet can't be removed from the pocket without one of the comb teeth becoming hung up on the material in the pocket.

Even though many pickpockets who target bags or backpacks will use a knife to slice through the fabric, some still get in the old fashioned way, by opening the zipper. To prevent that on any pack or bag that has pull cords on the zippers you can simply interlace the pull cords. Pull the cord from the first zipper through the cord of the second. Then pull the second pull cord through the first. It should be fairly difficult to rapidly untangle. With every additional second the thief has to work to get your money, the chance of a successful theft decreases.

The other common way pickpockets operate is by generating a distraction. When you watch the scene they have set up, their partners are stealing your money. Fake fights are used very commonly. Two or more people will stage a verbal altercation or physical fight near you. While your attention is on that spectacle, the thief will take your wallet. Almost anything can serve as the distraction, even the natural scenery. Ever wonder why so many pickpockets operate in beautiful historic cities like Rome and Paris? They know tourists will be looking at the sights. When the tourists are paying attention to the beautiful buildings or historic sites, the pickpockets are getting rich.

One other distraction to look for is the deaf/mute charity worker scam. You will be approached by a couple of well-dressed girls with clip boards. They will indicate to you that they are deaf and mute and that they are soliciting for a charity. They will explain all this by writing on the clipboard. While you are paying attention to what they are writing, their pickpocket friends have time to plunder your belongings.

In Colombia, the residents have a very illustrative phrase to describe the concept of making a criminal's life easy by being a good victim. They call it "*dar papaya*," meaning "*to give (someone) papaya*." It signifies that you are making it so easy on the criminal it's as if you are giving him a sweet treat. Don't give your criminal attackers any papaya. Make them work hard if they are going to try to steal your valuables.

Everyday Carry– When you are walking around in cities or rural areas, carry a small messenger bag or sling pack to hold items that you might need to survive if you are stranded somewhere or encounter an emergency. I carry different supplies in each location I visit, but here is a basic list of items that I usually have on my person when I'm out in public in a third world country.

- City Map (or Google Maps on a smart phone with enabled data plan)
- Hotel Business Card
- Small first aid kit with materials to make pressure dressings and tourniquets
- Pill pack with broad spectrum antibiotic and anti-diarrheal medications
- Small packet of anti-bacterial baby wipes to clean your hands
- Two protein bars
- Bottle of water (and water purification tablets)
- Notebook and pen
- Small package of tissues
- Extra cash (hidden)
- Bandanna or triangular bandage

Everyday carry gear for third-world countries:
map, water, first aid kit, disinfectant wipes, protein
bars, notepad, and spare cash

In addition to your gear bag, you will want some additional items carried on your person. Carry local currency, some change for bathrooms, a pocket knife, your passport (or copy), and a flashlight.

Pocket carry gear in Colombia

Tips for Smoothly Navigating Daily Life in the Developing World

"If in doubt, just walk until your day becomes interesting."
– Rolf Potts

Safely walking around a new city– Are you are ready to go explore your new environs? When making plans about what to do or see in a city, take the time to use the resources available to you. If you don't have a good feel for the safety level of the city where you are saying, ask your hotel clerk for help. Show him a map and ask him to mark the areas that are safe and unsafe for both daytime and night. Some areas are perfectly safe by day, but extremely dangerous at night.

Taking a walk around the neighborhood where you will be staying as soon as you settle in to your hotel is a good idea. It's nice to scope out grocery stores, restaurants, and any potential problem areas to avoid during daylight hours. I find taking a short walk will help me overcome jet lag as well.

You may even consider booking a walking tour around your neighborhood on the day of your arrival. There are often such tours available free from English students wanting to practice their language skills or at a low cost from local tour guides in larger cities. In addition to giving you the lay of the land, local tour guides are a good reference to ask about areas of potential danger or neighborhoods you should avoid.

When walking down the street, face traffic to avoid being targeted for a bag snatching by a thief in a passing car or motorbike. This also allows you to dodge any crazy drivers who may not be paying attention to their surroundings. If you are carrying a bag, loop the strap over your shoulder and not around your neck. That way if someone grabs the bag, you will not be taken to the ground or hurt. To prevent bag snatching, carry the bag in front of your body rather than on your side or back.

Besides being alert for bag snatchers, you must also be alert for traffic. It does no good to keep your bag safe if you get run over by a car. Countless Western travelers are injured every year crossing the streets of foreign countries. Remember, traffic may be coming from the opposite direction than you are used to at home. Look BOTH ways before crossing the street.

Most crossings won't have this warning.

There is something else to consider with regard to walking etiquette. When a male/female couple walks down the street or sidewalk, the male should always be closest to the vehicle traffic. Most folks see this as a chivalrous way to protect the woman from cars hopping the curb, but there is also another reason. In some Latin American countries, the only women who walk outside the men on the sidewalk are working prostitutes. Avoid any issues or confusion if you are a man. Walk closest to the traffic.

When walking at night or through any area that might be dangerous, find a local family or couple to walk with. You are not likely to be victimized by a man out with his wife, especially if they have kids in tow. Don't walk right next to them in an annoying fashion; just follow them from a few yards away. Criminals tend to avoid larger groups of people. If you are traveling near a group of locals, the criminal may assume you are one of them and let you pass.

If you ever find yourself in an unsavory neighborhood, flag down a taxi or order an Uber and get out of there quickly. Your safety is worth more than the few dollars you will spend on a cab fare.

Just crossing the street in some countries can be
hazardous. Hoi An, Vietnam

If you get lost and need to look at a map, don't do it on
the street. It's a universal indicator signaling "lost tourist"
for any local criminals or scam artists who may notice.
Go inside a restaurant or convenience store to check your
map. If you do have to check it on the street, get your back
to a solid wall so that you can't be attacked from behind and
hold the map up just below eye level so that you can keep
your eyes on any danger areas.

All-Inclusive Resort Bracelets- If you happen to be
vacationing in an all-inclusive resort, you will likely be
given a non-removable wrist band that identifies you as
a resort guest. It also identifies you as a "gullible tourist"
if you leave the resort grounds. If you are staying at a
resort that uses bracelets as identifiers, ask them to place

the bracelet around your ankle instead. That way you can cover it with pants or socks if you go into a nearby town.

Hiding Spare Cash- One handy place to hide some extra money in your luggage is to use a hollowed-out box of dental floss. The dental floss container looks completely innocuous in your toiletries kit and is big enough to hold a few folded bills or a backup supply of prescription drugs. You can also store money in hollowed-out lip balm tubes or magic markers. Ladies can hide some rolled up bills inside an (unused) tampon applicator as well. Place the money inside the applicator and slide it back into the wrapper. No thief is going to open your tampons looking for cash.

Hide some cash in your toiletry kit by using a hollowed-out dental floss container

Another handy spot to stash a few bills is inside a hat. In all the robberies I've seen captured on surveillance video both here and abroad, I've never seen a robber check a victim's hat. Robbers will often pat down the victims' pockets and pull up their shirts to check for money belts. They never check the hat.

Put a couple larger bills inside a small Ziploc bag and use a safety pin to attach it to a nondescript location inside your hat. It's useful to have a little money stashed in a place like this in the event all of your other money is lost or stolen. Look ahead to the "beach safety" section of the chapter for some additional techniques for hiding your money.

Border Crossings-If you are making multiple land border crossings without pre-arranged visas, carry several passport sized photos with you. You may have to provide up to three different photos to get a single visa in some countries. There generally won't be services available at the border to take these pictures. Carrying a few extra photos is good insurance against getting stuck while trying to cross a border. I carry my extra photos taped to the inside of my passport cover for convenience.

If you plan on driving a car across the border, you will also want several copies of driver's licenses, vehicle registration papers, and insurance documents. Border authorities will usually require that you give them at least one copy of each of these documents. You may even want to make laminated color copies of your driver's license. Border agents in some countries have been known to hold your license and refuse to return it to you until you pay the requested bribes. If you give the border agent a laminated color copy of your license, you won't be as worried about having to pay. It gives you a little leverage in the negotiation process.

At the location of some land border crossings you will see a "no man's land" area after you leave one country, but before you enter the other. This stretch of land can be as little as 50 meters across or it could be several miles. The area will be dominated by unlicensed money changers, food stalls, smugglers, thieves, and taxi drivers. The area seems to be tailor made to victimize tourists. Move quickly through "no man's land" and get to your destination. Don't use the money changers and don't shop for souvenirs. You will find cheaper rates for both once you cross into the country you are visiting.

Beach safety- Third world beaches are prime hunting grounds for thieves. Beaches attract tourists. Tourists are regularly clueless about local customs and have lots of money. The thieves flock to the beach to victimize such easy targets.

Avoid taking anything to the beach that you are unwilling to lose. Visit with the assumption that everything you take there will be lost or stolen. Take the minimum amount of money and only the supplies you will need for your outing.. Recognize that third world thieves will steal virtually anything. Thieves stole a beach towel from me in Honduras when I ran back to my room to grab a bottle of water. In Brazil, I've had a $5 digital watch, a small first aid kit, and a paperback book taken from me at the beach. In fact, every time I've had something stolen from me personally during my travels, it's been at the beach. Let me restate that last point: 100% of my personal theft experiences in foreign countries have been at the beach. Don't bring anything there you aren't willing to lose.

Thieves will also occasionally use distractions to facilitate their crime. Take a look at the photo below. It's a beautiful Brazilian woman bending over in the water on Copacabana beach. What you don't see is the small gang of several teenage boys who are paralleling her progress on the beach. As soon as a guy is distracted by her provocative display, the thieves grab his stuff and run off. I saw the same girl and the same group of teens using this methodology three days in a row at the exact same beach location.

Enjoy the scenery. Her friends are stealing all your stuff.

When I go to the beach, I carry a small amount of cash on my person. I keep the cash in a Ziploc bag and store it in the pocket of my swim trunks. Having a waterproof bag allows me to take the money with me, even when I am swimming. I have a strap to wear my sunglasses around my neck. I won't even leave a pair of cheap sunglasses on the beach when I swim. If you do, they'll be gone as soon as you get into the water.

If you have to leave items on the beach while you swim, ask someone lying next to you to watch your stuff. This is very common. Even if you don't speak the language, you can get someone's attention, point to your stuff and then to your eyes with a questioning expression on your face. They'll understand your request.

As a last resort, you can hide valuables in fairly inventive ways if necessary. Bring an empty (and washed) sunscreen bottle or lip balm tube to hold your money. These items aren't as likely to be stolen. If you have no other options and can't get anyone to watch your stuff, casually dig a hole in the sand with your hand or foot. Bury your valuables in the sand and cover the hole with your towel if you have to leave your spot unattended.

Besides the threat of theft, you may have additional problems at third world beaches. Be careful of rip tides and rough surf. It's exceedingly rare to find beaches in third world countries staffed by trained lifeguards or emergency rescue personnel. You are on your own. If you are a poor swimmer, be cautious about entering the water.

In addition to dangerous currents or hazardous surf, beware of venomous marine critters, sharks, and water pollution. Consult a local guidebook before jumping in the water. It should have up-to-date information about particular hazards within the area you are traveling.

One other thing most tourists fail to consider when choosing a lounging spot on a third world beach is the proximity of overhead dangers. Often, the allure of sitting in the shade of the lone palm tree on a tropical beach seems irresistible. It's fine to enjoy the shade, but look up first. Ensure that you aren't reclining under a bird roost or a tree filled with mischievous monkeys. More importantly, make sure that there aren't any coconuts hanging above you. One researcher claims that fifteen times more people die each year due to injuries from falling coconuts than are killed in shark attacks. It wouldn't be cool to survive all the dangers of third world travel only to be taken out by a falling coconut.

Time- How residents of developing countries view the concept of time is difficult for many people to understand. I've seen residents of some countries stand in line for an entire day to pay a bill or to get a paper signed by some government bureaucrat. Time efficiency literally means nothing to some folks.

With that in mind, don't be frustrated if you can't get things done in third world countries. "*Island Time*," "*Manana Time*" or "*Africa Time*" are common phrases used to describe a lack of punctuality. If you get a dinner invitation in a developing country, it is often considered rude to be on time. Everyone is so chronically late that the host doesn't expect anyone to show up until at least an hour after the event starts. This practice has always been maddening to me as a "Type A" American. It takes a while to relax, go with the flow and not let tardiness and inefficiency bother me.

Patience and flexibility are key attributes for surviving third world travel. In most developing countries, efficiency and productivity are simply not the same priorities that they are in the United States. Sometimes even the simplest of transactions will be so encumbered by bureaucracy and inefficiency that it becomes painfully tedious. Rarely will anything turn out according to plan. As hard as it may be to do, just relax and go with it. Getting angry or complaining about how things work will not be productive. Remember that you are a guest in another country and behave accordingly.

Clothing- Fashion is likely very different in each country you visit. Outside of the USA and parts of Western Europe, males don't generally wear shorts unless they are at the beach or the gym. The quickest way to be identified as a "gringo" is to be seen wearing short pants. If you want to blend in, suck it up and wear jeans like everyone else. Note that I said "jeans" and not "North Face convertible nylon travel pants." Only foreign tourists wear those. If you choose them as a wardrobe staple, you will be quickly identified as an outsider and targeted for scams.

I've noticed that people in many other countries often take more pride in their appearance than Americans. Everyone will be wearing clean and pressed clothes. Women will generally be "dressed up" even when doing normal errands or shopping. You generally won't see people in public wearing track pants, sweat suits, or yoga pants (outside of Russia). If you are dressed in dirty or ragged clothes, you may offend the people with whom you interact.

Here's a prime example. I was once in a bar in Cartagena, Colombia with a female Colombian friend. The bar where we were drinking was infamous for being the location where the US Secret Service agents picked up some prostitutes. leading to an international scandal. We started talking about the incident and that conversation led to a discussion about how to tell the prostitutes from the "good girls" in the bar. Both groups were well represented.

My Colombiana friend gave me some good tips for identifying and avoiding the prostitutes. Using her tips, we watched the girls and attempted to classify them as either prostitute or "*good girl*." It made for a fun game after a few rum and cokes.

I was guessing pretty well when I saw a beautiful local-looking girl approaching a table of British guys. She matched all of my friend's identifiable prostitute characteristics. I pointed the girl out and said "*prostituta*." My Colombian friend immediately shook her head and said "No...*she's a gringa (white girl)*." I couldn't believe it. The girl looked like every other Colombian woman in the bar. I asked my friend how she knew this girl wasn't Colombian. She made a very intelligent observation, saying: "*That girl is wearing flip flops. No Colombian woman would ever wear flip flops to a bar. It's low class. That girl is a dirty gringa backpacker.*"

Sure enough, we spoke to the girl later. My Colombian friend was right. The girl in flip flops was from Colorado. It's a prime example about how locals pride themselves in the way they dress. As a traveler, you will be negatively judged by the locals if you wear clothing that is dirty, torn, or too casual. "Too casual" is often defined as wearing running shoes, sweatshirts, baseball caps, or logo T-shirts. Don't be surprised if you are refused entry to some locations if you are wearing these items.

Even though I advocate dressing smartly, it probably isn't worthwhile to carry a clothing iron with you when you travel. Rolling your clothes when you pack will eliminate a lot of wrinkles. If you need to press your clothes and your hotel room isn't equipped with an iron, call down to the front desk and ask if they have one there. Many hotels in developing countries won't have irons (or hairdryers) in every room, but they keep a small stock for their guests to use. If all else fails, consider hanging you clothes up in the bathroom as you take a hot shower. The steam will eliminate some of the worst wrinkles and make your clothing look a little more presentable.

Most foreign nationals have a poor opinion of the American military. If you are in the military or have served, don't flaunt this fact by wearing clothing with military logos or insignia. Avoid wearing military t-shirts, rings, or camouflage clothing. Consider covering up any military style tattoos. Young local "toughs" see members of the U.S. military as bullies, threats, or challenges. It doesn't matter to them if you are a supply clerk or a Navy SEAL. They'll still get bragging rights among their friends if they kick your ass. Wearing your Marine Corps T-shirt isn't worth the potential risk it creates to your personal safety.

Besides watching out for your clothing, you will also want to avoid carrying green, camouflage, or military style backpacks, duffel bags, or carry-ons. This is especially if you are planning on hiking in the woods, jungles, or mountains. Rebel groups hiding in the mountains or locals engaging in the drug trade may see your military backpack from a long distance as you hike and assume you are the police or military coming after them. Getting shot by a rebel sniper from 200 meters away will spoil your hiking trip.

Many sources recommend that travelers wear some sort of "photographers vest" with lots of pockets. The theory is that you can carry lots of survival gear in all the pockets and you will never be without your lifesaving supplies. To be honest, you will rarely need wilderness survival gear in the city. Wearing a vest like that marks you as a tourist, and maybe one with valuable photographic gear. The vest might even set you up for a robbery. In Latin America, photography vests are worn by black market currency exchangers and people who sell lottery tickets. Both groups have lots of cash and are easy marks for robbers. Leave the photographer's vest to the photographers.

You should additionally avoid clothing embroidered with a corporate logo. I regularly see American or European business travelers wearing clothing with the logos of the companies for whom they work. It's a bad idea. It clearly identifies you as someone who makes "a lot" of money, even if only by comparison to the locals. It also means that a corporation (with even more money) cares about your well-being. Both increase your risk of robbery or kidnapping. It's best to look unimportant. Dress neatly, but avoid any flash or flair. Most locals will notice your presence and will recognize that you are a tourist. Don't exaggerate your differences by wearing clothing that makes you stand out even more.

A couple of other things that keep Americans from blending in with locals in developing countries are our insistence on wearing sunglasses and baseball caps. Outside of North America and Western Europe, it is fairly rare to see people regularly wearing sunglasses. In most countries, only teenage boys and Americans wear baseball caps. Take a look at the local populace. If they aren't wearing caps or sunglasses, it may be best to ditch yours as well. Very few other clothing items (with the exception of wearing short pants) will identify you as an outsider more quickly.

Laundry– I rarely wash my own clothes while traveling. In most third world countries, laundry services are so inexpensive that it doesn't seem worthwhile to me to do my own washing. If I have to wash my own clothes I prefer to use a hotel shower. When staying in a hotel with adequate and reliable water pressure, I simply wear the clothes I want to wash into the shower. I get everything wet, and then lather my clothes with a bar of soap. I then rinse everything off, stripping off each clothing item and giving it a little extra attention upon removal if necessary. It's the fastest and best way I've found to wash my own clothes and is far superior to using a hotel sink.

After your wring the water out of your freshly washed clothes, hang them in the sun or in front of a fan to dry. If it's raining outside or you don't have a clothesline, roll the clothes up in a dry bath towel for a few hours. Squeeze or walk on the roll to transfer even more of the water from the clean clothes into the towel. This method will cut drying time in half as compared to simply hanging clothes in an area without adequate air circulation. If your clothes are still damp, the fastest way to dry them is to put them on your body. It will be unpleasant for a little while on a cold day, but it's the best thing you can do if you want dry clothes.

Other random tips-When you are eating or drinking in an open air restaurant, bar, or coffee shop, avoid choosing a table right next to the sidewalk or street. It's very easy for a thief to snatch your belongings off the table and be gone before you can react. If you are seated near any street pedestrian traffic, don't place valuables like phones or handbags on your table. Keep them attached to your body on the side farthest away from the street. To avoid a bag snatching, never leave any bag unattended. Get in the habit of looping your bag strap around your arm or leg whenever you sit down at a table in public.

In many countries, you will see nylon straps like this on the back of restaurant chairs. Use them to attach your bag and make it harder for a bag thief to grab it. Valparaiso, Chile.

You shouldn't generally expect that everyone queues up in orderly lines for service like they do in the USA. I've been in several places (like African airports) where service isn't provided to the person who has been waiting longest, but instead to the person who is most aggressive and pushes himself to the front of the line. I haven't found an adequate way to deal with this problem other than by joining in the scrum. If you step back and act politely, you will never be served.

Additionally, personal space in queues is different in other countries. Expect people to stand closer together and closer to you. It really makes you appreciate deodorant.

No matter how hard you try to fit in, your clothes, language, and mannerisms will quickly identify you as a foreigner. As an "outsider" you may be treated like a rock star, as someone unworthy of even the most basic human consideration, or anything in between. Good or bad, you will be noticed, despite your efforts to blend in. Recognize that in developing countries there is generally a much more pronounced racial and class consciousness than in North America. People are regularly judged on the basis of their race, skin color or ethnicity. You won't be able to change the system. Don't get frustrated. Do your best to embrace the local customs, smile a lot, be gracious, and laugh. Given enough time, that strategy will usually ensure that the locals will warm up to you.

Sporting Event Safety- Sports (especially soccer or "football") are a very big deal in most Latin American and European countries. The fans at these games are far crazier than any I've seen at a professional sporting venue in the United States. Not only do fans act crazy, they often become violent. In Europe, these violent fans are called "*hooligans*." They are called "*organizadas*" in Brazil. Whatever they are called in the country you are visiting, you should do your best to avoid them.

You might be surprised to note that during the last five years in Latin America, more than 30 people have been killed by these rabid fans either during or immediately following a soccer match. Fortunately, none of those killed was an international tourist.

Even for tourists, the games are still quite dangerous. Excessive drinking goes hand in hand with fans watching rugby or soccer games in Europe and South America. The presence of a lot of drunken spectators will heighten the craziness and potential for violence

Some of you will attempt to make yourselves safer by carrying weapons, but that won't work very well unless you are an exceptional smuggler. I've been searched or had a metal detector run over my body before entering every single one of the third world stadiums I've visited. Leave the blades at your hotel or read my tips about carrying undetectable weapons later in the book.

When entering the sporting facility, be alert for dangerous, stampeding crowds. Being overrun by a crazed crowd trying to gain entrance into a hotly contested game is a very real threat. Crowds are more likely to be deadly at the entrance of an event than at the event's conclusion. When crowds are leaving, there are generally multiple exits. On entrance, everyone is usually funneled through just a few entry gates, making it far easier to be caught up in a bottleneck and trampled on by the pressing crowd. If the crowd seems violent or surging, hang back. Don't be in a hurry to get in. If you know in advance that the event is going to be crowded, consider arriving at off-peak times, either very early or after the game has already started.

Be careful how you dress and where you sit at these games. You may be asked what team you are cheering for when you buy tickets. In most stadiums, seats are arranged in blocks designated for fans of certain teams. It's a bad plan to sit in the home team's block when you are rooting for the visitor or wearing visitor colors. I prefer to check out each team's colors before the game and then wear colors that don't match EITHER team. This is one instance where being an obvious "tourist" offers a little protection from the violence directed at fans of certain teams.

If there is any doubt about where to sit, choose the home side. There are more likely to be families and "non-combatants" there. There are likely to also be larger numbers for your protection against the other team's fans. You are essentially joining the biggest "gang."

You would be amazed, but in some stadiums, fans are allowed to set off fireworks in the stands. These fireworks are unpredictable and go everywhere. Change seats if you find yourself around anyone who is lighting them off. You may also consider wearing cotton clothing. Polyester and nylon blends melt and attach themselves to your skin when exposed to flames. The melting polyester will make your burn much more severe.

Fireworks being set off by fans in a Rio de Janeiro soccer stadium.

More violence occurs outside the stadium after the game than during the game itself. Be exceptionally careful leaving the event. It may be smart to leave a bit early so that you aren't out in the streets when the majority of the crowd exits the stadium. There also tends to be a racist/homophobic trend with soccer hooligan violence.

In Europe, most of the organized hooligan groups tend to be ultra-nationalist. Blacks and immigrants are targeted specifically for beatings. In South America, the focused violence seems to be directed more towards openly gay or effeminate men. If I were a member of any of the targeted races or minority groups, I would avoid the largest games and attend only smaller games with tame crowds. I might more favorably consider attending a larger game if I was able to attend with a large group of friends.

Be cautious using public transportation near large sporting events. Even if you don't attend the event itself, you may encounter sports hooligans, rioters, or drunken fans in the subway or on the bus before and after the big game. There are usually numerous bus stops, taxi stations, and subway entrances near any large sports stadium. Avoid those stations and stops when they are crowded with rowdy sports fans.

Money, Banking and Shopping Issues

*"As a tourist, you become economically significant
but existentially loathsome, an insect on a dead
thing."*
– David Foster Wallace

Credit cards are readily accepted in most areas, but less
so in others. It's always a good idea to have some extra
cash to pay for things if the merchant or restaurant doesn't
accept charge cards. Having cash, preferably small bills
in local currency, will also serve as an insurance policy if
you can't find a bank or ATM. There are some towns you
will visit that simply do not have ATMs. Many rural stores
and restaurants will not take credit cards. Having a backup
supply of cash will eliminate some potential hassles.

Don't bring traveler's checks from home. You will find
them very hard to redeem in most countries. No one
except elderly naïve American travelers uses them
anymore. There are ATMs available almost everywhere.
There's no need to carry a large amount of cash or use
the over-priced airport money exchangers. Just pull local
money out of the ATM as needed. This often guarantees
you get a good exchange rate, but may come with
additional fees from your bank. Before you leave, make
sure your ATM security code has four numbers. Some
travelers have trouble with foreign ATMs if they have PINs
with more or fewer digits. You should also let your bank
know that you will be traveling abroad and plan to use your

card so that they realize the charges you make are not fraudulent.

Furthermore, my recommendation that you use the ATM ensures that you will avoid going inside the bank to make a cash withdrawal. In third world countries, banks are frequently the place where all utility (phone, electricity, gas, water) bills are paid. Consequently, the lines are always very long and you will be waiting quite a while. It's better to use the ATM.

In dangerous neighborhoods, you may find that ATM machines are enclosed in lockable phone booth style huts. If you are using one, ensure that the door is locked. When you get your money, immediately stash it in a wallet or pocket before opening the door. Only use the ATM during daylight hours. If you have a friend with you, station him at the door to watch your back as you remove your money. Recognize that some foreign ATMs require the user to push an "exit" button after receiving their money in order to get the ATM card back. Don't forget. If you leave your card in a machine, there is a good chance the bank will destroy it before you have the opportunity to get it back.

You will want to be alert for ATM "skimmers." These are machines attached temporarily to ATMs by criminals in order to steal your bank card data. Look for bulky additions to the card slot. Another tipoff is if the machine advises you to "enter password slowly." Legitimate machines don't usually contain this warning, but the bolt on skimmers are not as technologically advanced as the ATM machines themselves and often record the keystrokes at a slower rate.

"Experts" often warn against using foreign ATMs because of the prevalence of these skimmers. I think their presence is exaggerated. In almost 20 years of foreign travel, I have never seen a card skimmer nor had my bank card data stolen in another country. If the thought of ATM skimmers truly worries you, stay away from the bank machines located near prime tourist areas. Those are most likely to be altered. Instead, choose an ATM located inside a bank, hotel, or airport where it would be more difficult for a criminal to install any extra machinery.

One additional safety habit to practice at the ATM is physically shielding your four-digit code with your other hand. Robbers will watch ATMs from a hidden location through binoculars in order to see the code you enter at the keypad. When you walk away, they hit you in the head, steal your card, and clean out your account using the passcode they saw you enter.

Covering up the keypad also helps defeat some types of skimmers as well. The crooks who steal the data on the magnetic stripe of your ATM card still need your pass code to get money. Most of the skimmers would be too large if they had to record both the data and the numbers punched in. It's hard to cover the whole keypad with some extraneous skimming machine and not be noticed. To avoid the problem, some thieves have installed a skimmer and then also plant a pinhole camera in a spot nearby to record what buttons you pressed when you used the keypad. Covering up the keypad with your other hand while punching in your withdrawal code is a prudent safety precaution everywhere, not just in shady third-world countries.

When you need to find an ATM, don't ask directions from a random person on the street. If you are looking for an ATM, that means you are going to withdraw money. That makes you a good robbery target. Go into a business and ask an employee for directions to the ATM. Try to do it in such a manner that others don't hear you.

Most ATM cash withdrawals will involve a transaction fee of a few dollars in addition to the exchange fee. Minimize the number of withdrawals you make. Taking out the maximal amount of cash each time you visit the ATM will reduce your overall transaction fees.

It would be a good idea to have at least two different bank accounts with separate ATM/debit cards. Carry one card with you and keep the other one locked up in a safe place in case your wallet is lost or stolen.

If you must acquire local money, ATM withdrawals will provide better exchange rates than most money changers, especially the money changers who hang out at international land border crossings. If you do have to exchange currency, avoid the currency exchanges near the border. Their rates are high and it's generally not a safe environment to display any money in public. There is also a significant risk that you may be given counterfeit currency by a scam artist money changer looking to exploit your lack of knowledge about the appearance of his country's currency.

A common scam used by shady border money changers is to tell you that there are no bank machines in the country you are visiting. Countless clueless tourists fall for this hustle every day. As you are crossing the border, you will hear the money changers yelling: "This is the last ATM to get money. Get as many dollars out as you can and we will convert it to the local currency for you." Don't fall for this ruse. You're probably not traveling in a country that doesn't have ATMs. Certainly you may visit towns or neighborhoods that don't have them, but you will generally be able to make a withdrawal almost everywhere in the world. Don't pay the inflated exchange rates charged by the money changers at the border.

Be especially cautious of any money changers who want to exchange currency in some back alley or take you anywhere out of public view to perform the transaction. Currency exchange scams are extremely common, and some of the scam artists may be violent robbers trying to prey on naive tourists.

I avoid money changers, but if it is necessary to use them, take your time and count the money thoroughly. I would advise using only female money changers as well. In my experience, they have been less likely to be criminals or scam artists than their male counterparts. Make all transactions in places that are within public view. It's tough to balance the need to be safe from the money changer and not to flaunt your currency in the street where other criminals may see it. That's why I prefer to use an ATM inside a bank instead.

The two on the left are unlicensed black market money changers working the border between Bolivia and Brazil. Stay away from people like this. There are too many scam artists trading counterfeit currency at international borders. Get your money from an ATM instead.

Be aware that when changing money in some countries there are two different exchange rates. There is always the "official" exchange rate. You get those exchange rates when you pull money out of an ATM or charge something on a credit card. In countries with unstable currencies or economic problems, there is often a second, "black market" rate that usually pays a higher amount for foreign currency than the "official" rate.

Trading money at the black market rate on the street is usually a violation of the law, but I've never known a tourist to be prosecuted for doing so. The black market generally exists because the local currency is unstable and/or the local people are prohibited from buying dollars at the "official" rate. That leads to competition for available dollars and thereby drives the value of your dollar upward on the currency exchange market.

Guidebooks will note which countries have a black market currency exchange. Rather than trading your money with potentially shady black market dealers and risking prosecution, it's best to use the "official" money exchanges and their formal rates. If you do want to trade money at black market rates, avoid dealing with street money changers. There's too much of a risk for robbery. Instead, look for businesses called "jewelry exchange" or "gold exchange." These places often deal in black market currency as well.

The safer way to get black market exchange rates without actually changing money is to simply pay a merchant directly in American cash. Any merchant with an IQ above 50 will gladly take American dollars if his own country's currency is in a downfall. Negotiate the price in the local currency and then ask offer to pay for the items in American dollars at the black market exchange rate. The merchant will usually accept your offer.

If you are visiting a country that uses American dollars or are planning to convert American money to local currency on arrival, be aware that many stores or money changers will not take any American bills if they are torn, ripped, wrinkled, or defaced. Get fresh new bills from the bank before your trip. You may also need your passport for bank assisted money transactions. Be prepared and have it with you when going to the bank to save yourself the hassle of being denied service after a long wait in line.

Recognize that occasionally all the ATMs in a neighborhood (or even a city) will be out of money at the same time. This happens quite frequently on weekends in large South American cities (Rio de Janeiro is the worst). No matter how many ATMs you visit, you won't be able to take out any cash. They are all empty. In these situations, it's prudent to have additional ways of facilitating a cash transfer from friends or family members. Many money transferring services like PayPal, Xoom, or Venmo work in foreign countries as well.

If you visit the bank, you may realize that it is common in many Caribbean or Latin American countries to see guards carrying shotguns or rifles standing outside of banks or currency exchange locations. These guards wear plate body armor and are present for a reason; there are enough robberies to justify their presence. If you don't speak the language, be cognizant of your appearance. The guards will want you to take off hats or sunglasses before entry. They will also want to check your bags. Expect this and comply before they ask, especially if you aren't going to understand what they are saying. It's generally not advisable to argue with men who are wearing body armor and carrying shotguns.

No matter how you get your money (from a bank, by withdrawing it from an ATM, or by using a currency exchange) thieves may try to set you up for potential criminal victimization. In Peru there is a saying: "*Hay sapos*." It means "*There are toads.*" Peruvians use the term as a caution to people handling money in public. There are always "toads" watching for easy victims. You may not see the *sapos*, but rest assured that they will be present. Exercise caution.

Tipping– Different countries have varying customs with regards to both tipping and haggling (or bargaining). The smart traveler will do some research in guidebooks or on the internet to figure out the local customs before arrival. With regards to tipping, service providers in some countries do not expect a tip. In other countries, the common tipping custom is to merely round up to the nearest whole unit of currency. Some countries will automatically include the tip on your restaurant bill.

Tipping customs for services like restaurant meals or taxi rides vary greatly depending on the country you are visiting. For a quick tipping reference, download the Global Tipping App for your smart phone.

Bargaining/Haggling– A general guideline for haggling with merchants is that most brick and mortar stores have fixed prices where haggling isn't really encouraged. Most haggling is done in markets and in tourist shopping areas. If you are in doubt, ask the merchant for "a discount" when you make the purchase. Even in a lot of stores where haggling isn't the norm, the merchant will frequently knock a little bit off the price.

Before you start bargaining at a local market, take a look at how you are dressed and what you are wearing. If you have $1000 worth of North Face travel clothes and are wearing a $20,000 diamond engagement ring, it's going to be hard to convince the local merchant that you can't spare another dollar. These merchants size up customers every day. They get good at it. Dress down and shop with a local if you want the best bargains.

Before you buy anything, get an idea of the going local price. Ask a local how much something should cost. Even better, if you see a fellow traveler carrying a similar item, ask him or her how much he/she paid.

If haggling is commonplace, go into it with the attitude that it's a game. Remember, the twenty cents you save by aggressive bargaining probably won't affect your life in the least, but may mean quite a lot to the local merchant. In most tourist areas, you'll see similar items in every store or market stall. Don't buy the first thing you see. Bargain to get the best price several times with different merchants so that you get a realistic idea of what the item is truly worth.

In many places, the first price quoted by the merchant will be double or triple the item's actual worth. He will want you to counter with a lesser price. He will then move upwards from your counter. It's better that you do not make the responding offer. Instead, without giving him a price target, tell him it's too expensive and you want the "real price' or the "discount price". The merchant will then drop maybe 20% off the price. That's your new starting point for negotiation. Now it's time for your counter. The games are beginning.

When you finally get to your best price, walk away. The price will then likely get even better and you'll know the item's true value for the next stall you visit. The best quoted price given by the first merchant should be what you use to get a better price at the next stall. The power of walking away sends a clear message about what you are willing to pay and what you are not. It is one of the best negotiating strategies to use when bargaining in local markets.

As you bargain, it's important to smile and be friendly. Don't be angry or insulted. Remember, it's just a big game. Be realistic in what you expect to pay as well. While it is a game and the fun is in the playing, a dollar doesn't mean much to you but may be quite significant to the merchant. Be fair and respectful of their livelihood, the time they spend, and what you can afford. Be committed to purchasing what you have negotiated for and don't just play the game for the rush of the gamble.

I think the best description of the bargaining/haggling process was written by Christopher Blin in the book *Swimming to Angola.* In that book, he wrote:

"1) *Think of what they want you to pay- eye level*

2) *What you want to pay- chest level*

3) *Where you are after bargaining- somewhere around the neck*

4) *What the locals would pay- knee to ankle level*

5) *What they would charge if you forgot to ask the price beforehand -above the top of the head*

You win the game if you can keep your transaction within the "strike zone"- from knees to chest."

When you are shopping in local markets, it's generally a better idea to do business with adults rather than children. The merchants know that tourists will respond well when a cute kid tries to sell them something. Thus, they pull their kids out of school and force them to work at a young age. The kids rarely go back to school and are doomed to take over whatever is left of the family business when they grow older instead of learning new or marketable skills in school. Do your part to help developing countries improve. Don't buy things from children. Ensure that they go to school instead.

Even though the children are cute, you shouldn't buy anything from them. They should be in school rather than selling things at the local market. Roadside market in Cambodia.

In addition to seeing children being exploited by selling things to tourists, you will also see begging "mothers" with bundled up babies looking for your spare change. You seldom see a begging woman without a "baby" in her hands. Do you find it interesting that you never hear the baby cry? The babies are ALWAYS asleep. Kind of odd, huh? That's because these "babies" are really just bricks or chunks of firewood wrapped up in blankets. They are a prop to play on your sympathy so that you are more likely to give money to the "mother."

Other Money Traps- Be careful of the "gringo aisle" in foreign supermarkets. In larger cities, big supermarkets will have an aisle full of American, British, and Australian food items. They are all imported and will be VERY expensive, often two to four times the cost of the same items at home. If you do shop in the imported foods section, pay very close attention to prices.

Also be cautious when evaluating prices of big-ticket items, especially in upscale stores. As a general guide, imports, electronic items, computers, and vehicles will be significantly MORE expensive in third world countries than they are at home. When you see a price that seems obscenely low, it is likely the monthly payment for the item rather than the total price. In South America (particularly Brazil) this "pay-by-the-month" pricing is more commonly listed than the total price on big ticket items. The only place you won't see this pricing structure is on grocery items or in small corner markets.

If you have problems understanding the local language or have difficulty communicating with a vendor, use a small calculator (or the same function on your phone) to help you. Simply type in the amount of money you want to pay and then hand the calculator to the merchant. He will either accept your offer or clear out your number and make a counteroffer of his own. Negotiations can continue indefinitely in this manner without either of you speaking a word of each other's language.

Pirated videos and music– It's common to see small stands or independent merchants selling pirated or copied DVDs in the developing world. They only cost a couple dollars each and usually work fairly well. Selling pirated DVDs is a huge industry in the developing world.

If you do decide to buy any of these copied DVDs, only purchase items at a fixed location stand. Don't buy from some guy selling the DVDs off of a bed sheet on the sidewalk. If you purchase a DVD that doesn't work from a seller in a fixed location, you can always return it. You'll never find the sidewalk seller again and you'll never get your money back if you get scammed.

Recognize that buying such goods may be tacitly tolerated by authorities even if you are technically breaking the law. The authorities' toleration can change at a moment's notice as soon as they receive orders from superiors to "crack down" on foreign lawbreakers. You don't want to be thrown into jail over a couple DVDs. Besides this fact and the copyright issues involved, selling pirated DVDs also provides funding for criminal or terrorist organizations. You will often find that large criminal syndicates are the groups that make the copies to sell to the individual retailers. That's an enterprise you may not want to support. It's best to avoid pirated or counterfeit goods.

Merchants selling stolen and counterfeit goods on
a busy city street. The goods are paced atop a
blanket with ropes attached to each corner. When
the police come, these guys pull the rope, which
then converts their blanket into a bag. The thieves
quickly run away. Be careful who you buy from.

Eating and Drinking (Without Dying)

Sanitation in many countries won't be up to your normal standard. The red flag (actually a plastic bag) in front of this Peruvian house signifies that the owner has home-brewed beer for sale.]

Food

> *"Travel for the swag, for the direct connection to your animalistic side. Go for the food, for the booze, for the exotic women, and the mystery grub. The view, the smell, the stench of the city, the cold rain. Tragically, you will need to battle long and hard for*

a profound experience, one untouched by the
profiteering mentality that seems to follow tourist
hordes around like a bad smell"
– Chay Blythe

It had been a 10-hour bus ride on my first solo trip to a third world country when the driver finally stopped at a roadside restaurant in the mountains of Peru. I was starving. I had no idea that the bus drivers wouldn't stop on a regular basis and hadn't packed any food for the ride. As I stiffly disembarked from the bus, I was happy to see a sign that said "Buffet" near the restaurant door. I paid some ridiculously low price for access to the buffet and grabbed my plate.

Well used to American buffets, I was ready for a huge spread of food. Nope. Buffets in the Andes Mountains aren't quite the same as they are at home. The "buffet" had a grand total of three items: Boiled potatoes, baked alpaca meat, and stewed beef hearts. That's it. Nothing else. It tasted even worse than it sounds. It was one of my first encounters with third world dining and I will remember the foul taste of that alpaca meat for the rest of my life.

I've learned a lot since my early days in the mountains of Peru. Now, eating in foreign countries is one of the most interesting aspects of traveling for me. You can enjoy a wide variety of new flavors and combinations of foods. Additionally, a lot of new protein sources are available, as people in foreign countries will eat animals that may not be considered edible at home. Keep an open mind and try new things. If you are not willing to try a new food, avoid being openly disgusted by someone else's dinner. It's all a matter of taste.

General Restaurant Tips-When evaluating a restaurant, look for where the locals eat. With a lack of formal government sanitary inspections, the only way you can tell if a restaurant is safe or not is by the number of locals eating there. Locals won't return to a place that makes them sick.

Along the same lines, try to avoid American chain restaurants in other countries. Places like KFC or McDonald's sometimes cater to risk-averse tourists, but in my experience, I notice a lot more inconsistency with the foreign chains. They really aren't any safer than the local places, so why eat there? If you shun fast food in your home country, you shouldn't start eating it in third world countries because it's "safer." The food in the local versions of American fast food restaurants is still sourced locally and is likely to have the same hazards as the family-owned restaurant down the street. Save the McDonald's visits for times when you need to take advantage of their free Wi-Fi. Order a coffee and avoid the food.

Why would you eat McDonalds when whole
piranha is on the menu?

In many locations, the cheapest and safest meal to eat is the "set menu." Local establishments will often have a daily meal special for lunch or dinner. It usually involves a cut of meat, some rice, and some potatoes. Most set meals are very cheap and quite filling. They are also less of a risk for acquiring a food-borne illness because they are in high demand and haven't been sitting out long. They may not always be the most flavorful items on the menu, but I've never gotten sick after eating one.

Travel guides will recommend that you avoid "street meat" or food served from temporary roadside carts or stalls. I disagree. I've never had any issues eating street food. I think it's often safer than food served in established restaurants. The roadside stalls will often be cooking the food right in front of you. The food is fresh and is served hot, unlike some of the restaurant food that has been sitting around without refrigeration all day. The street carts don't have cabinets or storage rooms that can become infested with rats or bugs like many restaurants.

"Street meat" in Ecuador. Grilled guinea pig.

Like my advice for other restaurants, look for a line of locals. Make sure that the food is hot, there are no insects around, and that it doesn't appear to have been cooked a few days earlier. Avoid buying your food from the dude selling meat from a Tupperware container with no heat source within miles. Don't choose uncooked meats (like steak tartar), sushi, or any meats that have been pickled. If you follow those guidelines, eating at a roadside stall will be at least as safe as any restaurant you are likely to visit.

While I heartily recommend eating food from vendors on the street (if they meet the criteria listed above), please exercise caution when consuming items other than food from a street vendor. The homemade drinks the vendor is selling probably taste great but they were made with local tap water. Any sauces sitting out for your food likely contain unpurified local water as well. Eat the food that's hot and fresh, but avoid any drinks or sauces unless they come pre-packaged.

You should also be careful with regards to the cutlery a restaurant or street vendor gives you. If your fork and spoon are metal, chances are that they have been washed in the local tap water after their last customer. Sometimes restaurants in the developing world don't even have an adequate water supply to properly clean the plates and silverware. Without water, the restaurant owners simply wipe the silverware down with a towel and send it out to the next customer.

Dirty dishes or silverware that has been exposed to local bacteria in the water supply may be a greater danger than the food itself. You can stick to plastic utensils or bring your own silverware, but that might be a hassle. I just carry extra anti-bacterial wipes with me everywhere I travel. If the silverware seems the least bit sketchy, I will disinfect it with a cleaning wipe before eating.

Tanzanian butcher shop with no refrigeration.
After seeing the hanging beef, I chose to eat the
freshly killed chicken instead.

If you are on a budget and looking to eat at a real restaurant rather than a street side stall, move away from the tourist areas. Look for a restaurant without English signage or menus. Often just walking a few blocks outside the town's tourist area leads to a 50% reduction in the price of your meals. Also look for restaurants near colleges or universities. University students are poor all around the world and a cottage industry has grown up around most campuses to provide cheap meals for the students.

Finding vegetarian meal options in third world countries is not extraordinarily difficult, as long as you don't mind bland food. The basis of the majority of the developing world's diet consists primarily of rice, beans, and potatoes. If these foods suit your fancy, you'll never have problems finding vegetarian options. If you are looking for more specific or exotic vegetarian dishes, try the Happy Cow App for your phone. It will help you find and sort vegetarian restaurants around the world.

If you have Celiac disease or just prefer to eat gluten free, check out the Dine Gluten Free travel app. It uses crowd-sourced information and is searchable for worldwide gluten-free dining options. People with different dietary restrictions are likely to find other similar apps or online guides to help them conveniently choose restaurants while traveling.

If you have other food allergies, use the Allergy Food Translator App. If you are in a French, German, or Spanish speaking country, the app can translate more than 60 different food allergies into the native language so that your food vendor can read it.

You can also save money by preparing meals yourself. You'll have to shop like a local in the grocery store and have a refrigerator, but it is often much cheaper to prepare your own foods, especially breakfasts and lunches.

You may have some strange food options in third world grocery stores. Diagram of the different cuts of alligator meat at a Brazilian butcher shop.

Dairy Products– Dairy products may not be safe in developing countries. Ice cream and local cheeses are often the worst offenders. In addition to simply ingesting bacteria from unpasteurized dairy products, third world cities often experience power outages. There is a higher than average chance that a power outage has contributed to storage temperatures that are too high to prevent bacterial overgrowth in dairy products. If you have an ice cream craving, try to pick a sorbet instead. The more acidic sorbet provides an inhospitable environment for lots of bacteria.

Fruits and Vegetables- General guidelines about eating fruit involve avoiding unwashed, unpeeled, or uncooked fruits of any kind. That's generally good advice, but travelers must also be aware of "clean" fruits like melons or gourds. When fruit sellers price their produce by weight, occasionally they will poke small holes in the fruits and let them soak up water from roadside drains in order to artificially increase the weight. I don't eat any fresh melons purchased at fruit stands, only peeled and sliced melons served in reputable restaurants.

Even if the fresh fruits look amazing, remember that they have likely been fertilized with human or livestock waste and washed in the local polluted water.

Water- The tap water in most third world countries is not potable. Don't worry about that. Every corner store in the world sells bottled water very cheaply. When buying water, make sure that the seal is still on the cap. Also, be careful when opening any water bottles you buy in Asia. They will be filled to the very top. If you squeeze the bottle at all when opening the lid, you will spill water all over yourself.

You may also see water sold in small plastic bags. They are cheaper than bottles and usually come with a straw. Just poke the bag and suck up the water through the straw. I find them to be a pain and I generally spill about half of the bag trying to drink it. I don't think the cost savings is worth it, but your mileage may vary.

Bag of water sold in a Colombian corner store.

In addition to bagged water, you will also see vendors selling fruit juice or soft drinks in plastic bags. They are especially popular with the vendors who work in bus or train stations. I won't buy them because I have no idea what's really inside the bag. I'd advise you to avoid them as well, but I would say that the juices are popular amongst the locals and I've never actually seen anyone get sick after drinking from one.

In lieu of buying bottled water, you can carry a water filtering bottle, a Steri-Pen or purification tablets and purify the water from your hotel's tap for drinking. I will often carry one of these options as a backup water treatment method in case I get stuck somewhere where I can't buy bottled water.

Be cautious about ice in your drinks as well. Most commercially purchased ice is made with purified water and won't be a problem. Homemade ice cubes are a different story. Commercial ice cubes are usually cube-shaped and have a hole or indentation in one side. If the ice is oblong and doesn't have any type of hole, it is likely homemade. Avoid ice if you are at all concerned about the water safety. If you are exceptionally fearful of the local water supply, you should also avoid using tap water to brush your teeth. Take extra care not to swallow any water while showering as well.

Ice cubes that look like this (from a Nicaraguan restaurant) are probably made with local tap water. Be careful.

And speaking of ice, don't be surprised when the drink you order is served warm without ice. The reason could be that ice is expensive and the restaurant doesn't normally put it in drinks. It could also be that the ice is made from local tap water and the restaurant staff knows that you, as a tourist, would likely get sick if you consumed it.

On the other hand, it's common in some countries to put ice in the beer that they serve you. That's usually because their refrigerators don't work very well and the beer won't be cold enough for enjoyment. Give it a try. I thought it would be horrible, but I quickly grew used to it.

Condiments- Table condiments are a regular and unexpected source of bacterial contamination. Limit the use of any condiments (like ketchup, mustard, mayonnaise, and salsa) that appear the least bit suspicious. Up to 60% of condiment sauces in one study (out of Mexico) were contaminated by an unhealthy concentration of E. coli bacteria.

Insects– Rural people in developing countries have a long history of eating insects. Most bugs are very safe to eat and are far less likely to make you ill than eating unwashed fruit, poorly cooked meat, or dairy products stored at room temperature. Before eating, ensure that you have removed any venom sacks or poisonous parts. If you aren't sure what's poisonous, ask the local who sold you the bug. They will show you how to eat it and what parts to avoid.

I've tried lots of insects in Southeast Asia and Africa. Most of them tasted pretty good. The majority were fried in oil. They tasted kind of like uncooked popcorn kernels, crunchy, but tasteless beyond the taste of the oil in which they are cooked. If you see bugs on the menu, give them a try. Even if they don't taste all that good, you'll have a great photo to show your friends.

If you can't remember any of this advice or have any last minute questions, download the CDC's Can I Eat This? app for your cell phone. You plug in the country and what you want to eat; the app tells you if it is safe.

Third World Toilet and Restroom Issues

"Living is about adventure and adventure is about elegantly surfing the tenuous space between lobotomized serenity and splattered-bug terror and still being in enough pieces to share the lessons learned with your grandkids. Adventure is about using your brain, body, and intellect to weave a few bright colors in the world's dull, gray fabric. And, hell, man, it's not about you surviving; it's about helping others to survive...and doing it in style."
– Robert Young Pelton

The toilet pictured below was my very first experience using a squat toilet. I camped quite a lot as a kid, so crapping in a dirty latrine or behind a tree wasn't a foreign concept for me. Despite my experience defecating in non-traditional places, I truly wasn't prepared for the grotesque level of disgust I experienced when trying to use the squat toilets hiking the Inca Trail in Peru.

That first toilet was the cleanest one I used over the five days I spent on the trail. To make matters worse, I had pulled a leg muscle water skiing just before I left for the hike. With the torn muscle, I couldn't support myself while squatting. I resorted to taking large amounts of Immodium so that I didn't have to use the disgusting toilets. That strategy worked, but made my experience at Machu Picchu somewhat less stellar than it could have been. I've learned a lot since that first third-world toilet experience. Pay attention to my tips in this chapter so you won't have to suffer like I did.

Typical third world squat toilet...better bring your own paper and have some strong leg muscles.

Bathrooms may be significantly different from those you use at home. You may have to use a squat toilet even in larger cities. It takes a little practice to perfect your aim and not soil your clothes in the process. If the floor is exceptionally dirty or you are not practiced in the art of squatting, it may be easier if you completely take off your shorts or pants. If you are a female wearing a skirt, it is a much easier process; just lift the skirt up and tuck it into your bra strap

Squat toilets like the one pictured above tend to be the most difficult type for tourists to use. They are similar throughout the world. The ones you'll see on the Inca trail in Peru work the same way as the ones in the Cairo airport. The secret is to squat deeply. You should be flatfooted when you do this, not up on your toes. Many Westerners lack the flexibility to do this. If you plan on traveling to an area where squat toilets are common, it would be worth your effort to spend a few minutes a day before your trip practicing getting into a deep, flat footed squat position.

If you are truly dedicated, I would advise practicing your squatting using your toilet at home in the weeks before you leave for your trip. Lift up the seat and squat over the bowl without sitting down when using the toilet. You'll actually want to squat deeper than this when using a real squat toilet, but the "hovering" simulation at home will help train your muscles so that when you get to a third world country it won't be quite as traumatic.

If there are no foot markings or outlines, no matter if you are male or female you should generally face the hole when urinating and put your back to the hole when defecating. When there is something more than a simple hole, squat toilets will often be shaped like a keyhole. When defecating, you will want to be facing the narrow end of the keyhole shape. Use the bucket of water nearby to wet the pan of the squat toilet before you use it. This makes "flushing" your mess away much easier.

If you choose not to remove your pants, you will want to pull them down farther than usual. Be careful when doing so. Occasionally this results in dumping the contents of your pockets down the toilet. I generally place the contents of my pockets into my carry bag when I have to use a squat toilet in public. Taking the time to do that is far better than fishing around in a pit toilet to find your wallet or pocketknife.

I've spent a lot of time explaining how Westerners should use a squat toilet. In rural areas of the world, you'll see signs like this explaining how to use a "normal" toilet to people who may not have ever experienced indoor plumbing.

In bathrooms without running water, you will generally see some type of large bowl filled with water near the toilet. Sometimes there will be some type of ladle or pitcher for pouring water out of this bowl. This water is used for both "flushing" the toilet and as a primitive bidet. Pour the water into your left hand and then use it to wash your backside. Dump more down the toilet to flush away your waste.

Most squat toilets won't have toilet paper, only a hose or a nearby bowl filled with water. If you bring your own toilet paper or baby wipes, you'll be fine. Just use the hose to wash them down the hole or place them in the trash bin beside the toilet. If you don't have toilet paper, you'll have to do like the locals. Wet your left hand in the water bowl and use it to clean yourself up. Now you understand why I advise carrying some toilet paper with you.

Sign outside restroom in rural Thailand. I can't explain.

If you do have to use a toilet that requires a bucket for flushing, the secret for washing everything down the hole is to throw the water into the toilet in a single powerful rush. Allowing the water to slowly trickle into the toilet will ensure that your waste remains stubbornly plastered to the porcelain sides of the toilet bowl.

Even if you are in a country with Western toilets, you may see a waste bin right next to the toilet bowl. That's for your used toilet paper. Really. In many third world countries, the plumbing isn't robust enough to handle toilet paper. If you flush the paper, you will clog the toilet. If there is a waste bin next to the toilet, discard your used toilet paper there.

Good advice for any third world toilet. If you see a small trash can next to the toilet, dispose of your used toilet paper there.

You may also find that the Western toilet you encounter might be absolutely filthy and/or missing the toilet seat. If you don't have the thigh muscles necessary to "hover" over the toilet as you do your business, consider using a plastic garbage bag. Cover the entire toilet with a trash bag and then cut a hole directly over the bowl. The trash bag covering will serve as a barrier to keep your bare behind out of contact with the filth.

Some third world toilets have two flush buttons on the top. One is a low powered flush for urine. The other is a higher powered flush for solids.

On the other end of the scale are the Asian toilets that have buttons that do everything from flushing to washing to air drying. Some even have buttons that heat the seat or activate a fan. All of these are different. If you start playing around, you may flood the whole bathroom. Most of these toilets have an emergency stop switch. Find that one first, before you start pressing any other buttons.

South Korean toilet. This toilet is more complex
and has more services than a smartphone. It's
safest not to press any buttons!

Public restrooms may charge a fee for use. Carry some
small change in the local currency for that purpose. You
will also want to carry your own toilet paper or baby wipes.
Many public restrooms don't provide toilet paper.

Restroom customs will also vary in many third world
countries. Don't be shocked if the restroom is unisex. Also,
don't be surprised if a cleaning person of the opposite
gender walks in while you are using the facilities. It's quite
common for that to happen in South and Central America.
Some restrooms in South East Asia employ restroom
attendants to massage men's shoulders as they use the
urinal. One Thai bar I visited had a chiropractor who
adjusted men's necks as they stood at the urinal.

It's common for third world restrooms to have cleaners who are of the opposite sex. Occasionally you may even get a warning sign like this.

Most folks are so happy to find a Western toilet in a third world country that they forget about more obvious bathroom safety concerns. Restrooms worldwide are frequent locations for crime of all sorts. Robbers, prostitutes, and drug dealers all use the relative privacy of public restrooms to ply their trade. Restrooms in very remote areas or in bars or restaurants that serve alcohol are the most likely places to encounter a criminal when you are just trying to use the toilet.

Crime in women's restrooms tends to often be some type of petty theft. Thieves snatch purses, backpacks, and camera bags from an adjacent stall or while those items are hanging from the hook on the back of the toilet stall door. If you are taking valuables into the toilet stall with you, don't hang them on the door hook or place them on the floor. As uncomfortable as it may be, it's safest to place the items on your lap when you do your business rather than putting them anyplace else. Better yet, have a friend outside watch your stuff while you use the toilet.

Crimes that occur in men's restrooms are occasionally more violent. Guys who are under the influence of alcohol or drugs are often attacked while using the toilet and robbed of their personal valuables. Most people are distracted, embarrassed, and in a vulnerable position when using the restroom. Those facts make for an ideal distraction to allow the robber to attack. It's common that robbers will initiate the confrontation when a male victim is using the urinal. The robber will walk behind the victim and then quickly smash his face up against the wall several times before stealing his wallet. Think about where men's hands are located when using a urinal. They are not usually in a position to block a strike or to prevent his head from impacting the wall. It's a particularly vulnerable place to be.

Rather than using a urinal, I advise men to use the toilet in a restroom stall if at all possible. The stall's door lock won't be substantial enough to forestall a serious attack, but it will provide enough of an obstacle to give you time to access a weapon or prepare yourself to fight as the door is being broken down.

If you are forced by circumstances to use a urinal, adopt the "drunk man peeing" posture. You've all seen how extremely intoxicated men stand at the bar urinal. They place their forearm up against the wall about eye level and use it to support their weight so they don't fall down. It almost looks like they are trying to hold the wall up. Occasionally they will be leaning so far forward that they are resting their foreheads against the forearm leaning up against the wall. As funny as that sounds, it's actually one of the more defensible positions one can use at the urinal. The bracing forearm prevents an attacker from slamming your head up against the wall or the top of the urinal from behind. It's also in a great position to fire a rearwards horizontal elbow strike into the attacker's face

Choose either a stall or urinal that is farthest away from the door. The last stall or urinal in the line will have less foot traffic around it. People shouldn't be walking outside the stall or behind you while you are at a urinal. If you chose the first toilet option you see, you would expect other folks in the bathroom to walk past your location to access a free toilet, thus someone walking behind you wouldn't be perceived as a warning sign. It should be. Don't allow anyone to hang around aimlessly outside the bathroom stall or walk behind you at the urinal.

In rural areas all over the world, there seems to be no shame about urinating or defecating in public view. Where there are no public toilets (and sometimes even where there are) people will squat along the side of the road and do their business. Men, women, kids, it doesn't matter. They'll just squat down wherever it's convenient without even trying to shelter themselves behind a building or tree. You often see people urinating along roads as they wait for public transportation. Sometimes there will be whole lines of people all crapping just off the dusty road. Don't act shocked or alarmed when you see it. Everyone poops.

The concept of "privacy" is a little different is other countries. These are male urinals on the public street outside the Sambodrome for Carnaval in Brazil.

Some of the third world toilets I've seen have been so repulsive that I chose to do my business outside in the woods. When you have to use nature as your bathroom, avoid urinating on any hard surface (like a road). The splash back will be unpleasant no matter if you are a male or female. Find a place with soft ground and a little privacy, shuffling your feet and making some noise as you approach so as to scare any snakes or vermin away. Speaking of snakes, you should also avoid squatting under any low, overhanging branches in a snake-infested area. Snakes like to lounge on these low hanging branches and may drop down on you if disturbed. You should also look around to make sure there are no fire ant hills or mounds in the immediate area. Peeing on a fire ant mound will cause the resident ants to become very upset. They will climb your legs, stinging as they go.

Try to find a slight grade or slope. Face uphill when letting go. If you are squatting, gravity should carry your waste away from your bunched up pants. If you are standing, you can direct the stream so that it flows downhill between your legs so that your shoes don't get wet.

Don't assume you'll have running water in the bathroom....

If you happen to be traveling in a war zone, you may want to drop your trousers in public. Rebel armies have been known to place land mines in areas that are attractive as outdoor toilets. If you are hiking or driving through a clear landscape, don't pick the only tree or rock around to hide behind. That prime bit of privacy may be mined.

When using any outdoor toilets, especially at night, make sure you use a flashlight to look down the hole and under the seat. Spiders, snakes, rats, and other critters take up residence in these buildings quite frequently. Sitting down without first looking can result in a nasty bite to an area on your body that you really would rather not have bitten.

Restrooms in a high end Peruvian restaurant.
Which would you choose?

You should also be cognizant of the fact that different languages have different words for "male" or "female." Spend a couple seconds studying which restroom is the correct choice for your given gender. Take a look at the photo above. The M stands for "mujeres" (women), not "men." The H means "hombres" (men). I almost went blindly into the restroom bearing the "M" label before recognizing my ingrained perceptions and automatic actions may not serve me as well in a foreign country.

Third World Bathing

Many third world showers have electric water heaters directly in the shower head. These "suicide showers" conserve energy and usually work well, but they can be slightly dangerous. DO NOT adjust the water temperature switch while the water is flowing and you are standing in the tub. It can lead to a very nasty shock. Turn the water off and get out of the tub before you adjust the switch.

The easiest way to operate one of these death traps is to move the switch to the middle position before you even turn on the water. As mentioned above, leave it there and don't mess with it while the water is flowing. Turn the water on. Some of these shower heads only operate within a certain range of water pressure. Start with the water turned all the way on and wait about two minutes. If the water isn't warm, turn the pressure down a bit and see if that works.

The whole process seems incredibly dangerous, but in the hundreds of showers I've taken with electric showerheads, I've only been shocked once. It was just a minor tingle that happened when I was being stupid and adjusting the temperature control while the water was running. Since then, I've followed the procedures I listed above and haven't had any more shocking showers.

"Suicide Shower" electric shower head in Costa
Rica. The temperature is controlled by the switch
on the front of the unit.

When you encounter a shower with an unreliable water
supply where the water stops flowing or you randomly lose
water pressure (which commonly happens in more remote
locations), employ the technique called "partial washing."
Instead of lathering up your whole body and head and then
rinsing everything off, wash and rinse one body part at a
time. Start with your head and work your way down. That
way you won't get stuck with your whole body covered in
soap when the water suddenly stops flowing.

I've found that it is most convenient to pack liquid body wash rather than a bar of soap. If you prefer to travel with a bar of soap, take a beer bottle cap and push the serrated edge into the bottom of the bar of soap. Set the bar cap down on the edge of the tub. Since it sits on the cap, air can circulate around it and dry the underside much more quickly. You can also pack a small mesh bag and place your wet bar of soap in that. Hang the bag up from the shower curtain rod to allow the soap to dry faster.

The hot and cold water control knobs on the sink may be reversed depending on which country you are visiting. In some countries, hot is on the right and cold is on the left. Even though it is plumbed in this manner, the right side knob might have a "C" on it and the left knob an "H". It's completely random. If you aren't getting hot water, try the opposite knob. Don't be surprised if you don't have hot water in many low budget accommodations. When you pay $7 a night for a hotel room, what do you expect?

A common third world sink. Move the dangling rod
right or left to get hot or cold water.

In Southeast Asia, you may encounter large water tanks
in bathrooms. These tanks are used for bathing, but you
shouldn't climb in or wash your feet in the tank. There will
be a large cup or ladle. Use that (or your hands) to pour
water onto your body as a primitive shower. Using the tank
as a bath tub contaminates the water for everyone else.

Just for Female Travelers

According to USA government statistics, the number of U.S. women traveling overseas increased by an incredible 98.7% between the years 1993 and 2012. Female travelers ages 18-24 now outnumber their male counterparts by three to two when comparing visits to foreign countries.

Unfortunately, with the increased number of solo female travelers comes an increased number of crimes against women. While female travelers rarely experience crimes other than petty theft, violent crimes do occasionally occur. All travelers, especially women, should take measures to protect themselves.

The most important advice I can give any person, male or female, is to trust your instincts. As a solo female traveler, you WILL attract attention. In most third world countries, women traveling solo are a rarity. Men will talk to you not only out of sexual attraction, but because you are a curiosity. If anyone seems a little TOO friendly or ingratiating, it is usually because they are grooming you for either a scam or a violent crime. Trust your gut. Being "nice" is a criminal tactic, not just a personality trait.

If you think the attention that you are getting from the local men (or other travelers) is more than just curiosity, get away quickly. Don't be afraid to be rude. Don't be afraid to lie. It's smart to have a pre-planned story about meeting your husband or boyfriend later in the day or in the next town. That might be enough to discourage unwanted male attention.

Some of my female friends have gone as far as buying a cheap costume jewelry wedding ring and wearing it on the ring finger of their left hands. Women who are perceived as "taken" or married are less likely to experience the aggressive come-ons that are common in chauvinistic cultures.

Contrary to expectation, it is often the "tourist" areas that are most dangerous for females traveling alone. Although the areas catering to tourists in developing countries often have a greater police presence, they also provide a huge naïve victim pool for the serious predator. Don't think you are safe just because you are in the "civilized" part of town or have other travelers in the vicinity.

In most third world countries, it is actually the rural areas that are safer for solo female travelers. Despite the relative isolation, people in the area all know one another and depend on each other for safety. That courtesy is often extended to travelers, who are treated as valued guests.

In either urban or rural areas, it is best to get the advice of locals, especially local women. If you have questions about the area or concerns about your safety, asking a local woman for advice will be highly valuable. The local women will know what is dangerous and be familiar with local customs and social mores. They will likely give you the best advice you can get.

Earlier in the book, I wrote about one of the most important safety practices to follow was to make sure you arrived in any new town during daylight hours. This holds especially true if you have not yet booked your accommodation. You don't want to be wandering around in the dark in an unfamiliar city trying to find a place to stay.

The advice is even more important for females traveling alone. Besides all the concerns that any male traveler would encounter, the female traveler has an additional problem: the total lack of women in public places. In many traditional cultures, you just don't see unaccompanied women out after dark. The only women on the streets are prostitutes, thieves, and addicts.

The lack of "normal" women means that there will be fewer people who will be willing to help you. If you are lost, hurt, or abandoned in the daytime, chances are good that any passing local woman will help another woman in need. With no local women around, it becomes more difficult to find trustworthy assistance.

Besides the lack of available help, if you are on the street after dark local men may assume that you are a prostitute or addict and treat you as such. You will get a lot of unwanted attention that might eventually become dangerous. It's safer to avoid the whole problem and arrive in a new town while it's still light outside.

Dress- Female travelers should dress conservatively. Depending on the country you are visiting, very short skirts or shorts are not often seen outside of beach towns or on prostitutes. Capri-style pants or long skirts are generally a pretty safe bet for any location. I often see female travelers carrying a large scarf or cover-up. They can use it for warmth if heating isn't adequate or it can be used to cover any offensive exposed skin if you choose to visit a place (like a church or temple) with a very strict dress code.

That same scarf or wrap can also be used in transitional areas when you travel. That cute little black mini dress may be perfectly appropriate in the big city nightclub where you plan to go for the evening, but it might draw a lot of unwanted attention in the bus or subway you take to get there. Carrying a simple lightweight cotton wrap or scarf can provide some instant token "modesty" if you find that your outfit is bringing more unwanted attention than you desire.

Tank tops and shorter sundresses are likely to be commonly seen and accepted in larger cities or beach communities. Use caution if you are wearing sleeveless shirts or short dresses in rural or agricultural areas. The rural populations tend to be more traditional and may look down upon women who they perceive are dressed too casually or in a revealing manner.

In the regular tourist attractions where formal dress is required, the attraction will often have extra clothing to lend or rent out to female travelers who are "inappropriately dressed." As distasteful as it may be to don a sweaty cover-up that some other tourist just took off, it may be worth the sacrifice if the attraction is something you really want to see. If you are refused entry, ask the attendant if they have a place where additional clothing can be borrowed.

Other items can also be used as an alternate type of covering for your body. One trick I often see female travelers use is carrying their backpacks or day packs in the front of their bodies rather than on their backs. This position makes it harder for pickpockets to access the bag. It also covers the breasts, reducing men's stares or "accidental" touches.

Speaking of packs, recognize that there are backpacks that are specially made for females. These packs have a shorter frame and are designed to be worn lower on the back. Some also have narrower shoulder straps. If you plan on carrying a backpack as your luggage, it will be worth your money to buy one that actually fits your body.

Attitudes toward female travelers– Chauvinism and machismo are alive and well in many third world countries.

It isn't at all unusual for women to be whistled at, cat-called, or groped in public. If you are a female traveler, decide in advance how you are going to deal with such annoyances. Be cautious in your interaction with groups of aggressive men. Domestic violence laws haven't reached some parts of the world. In some places, men feel perfectly justified in striking a woman if he finds her actions offensive.

Besides having to adapt to a culture steeped in machismo, you must also acknowledge the way locals may stereotype "Western" women. Because of the ready availability of both Hollywood movies and online porn, the men of many third world countries have a skewed perception of North American women. American and Canadian women are viewed as "easy" as compared to the local women. Because of this perception, third world men may be even more aggressive when pursuing you romantically.

Be cautious if you are alone and drinking in a bar or restaurant in a predominantly Islamic country. In that environment, "good" women don't drink alone in bars. If you choose to drink alcohol as a woman in an Islamic country, do so in the privacy or your own hotel room or in a bar only when accompanied by other people. If you are seen drinking in a bar alone, it may be assumed that you are a prostitute or are "easy." You don't want to deal with the hassles that assumption might create.

Another way the Western women unintentionally help to propagate the myth of being "easy" is by having their photos taken by local guys they don't know. A North American women will be approached by a local man who wants to "take a photo" with her. Even in developing countries, nearly everyone has a phone with a camera.

The young local guy will politely request that you pose with him for "just one photo." He will use that excuse to get very close to you and/or cop a feel as his friends take the photo. He will then typically show your picture to all of his friends the next day, describing in great detail the fictional amorous adventures that you "shared" the night before.

It's a good reason to avoid having your photo taken with young local men you don't know. It just further reinforces the reputation of Western women as being "easy" even if you never sleep with a single person on your trip.

Even worse is that when you agree to pose for one photo, all of the guy's friends will then request that you pose with them as well. At best, it's a waste of time. At worst, it's an opportunity for a sexual assault or pickpocketing. Politely avoid such requests. If you feel that you absolutely must pose for a photo, tell your amateur photographer that you will only pose for one photo and it will be with the entire group, not one-on-one. Anyone who wants your photo to commemorate a legitimate occasion will be happy to have the group picture. The guys who just want your picture to create a lurid story for their buddies will suddenly lose interest and put their camera phones away.

Packing- You ladies have some special concerns when it comes to packing. I'll never have to worry about packing pretty jewelry or hair products for my adventures. Most of my female readers wouldn't be caught dead without looking their best, even in a third world hellhole.

Since you all tend to pack some different items than my male audience, I will give you a couple female specific packing tips:

Sometimes schedules get hectic when traveling and you won't have a whole lot of time to get ready in the mornings. If you use a curling iron or hair straightener, wrap it in a cooking pot holder before putting it in your luggage. That way your clothes won't be singed or catch on fire if you have to pack up quickly before your hair appliance has a chance to properly cool.

To keep your necklaces from getting tangled up with one another, thread each necklace through a drinking straw before packing it in your bag. Earrings can be kept neatly paired up by storing them on a small button. Just put each earring in one of the holes with which the button would usually be sewn on to a piece of clothing. You can also use daily pill containers to neatly organize rings or other small pieces of jewelry.

Necklaces threaded through drinking straws to prevent tangling during travel.

If you have stinky or dirty shoes, wrap them up in the hotel's complimentary plastic shower cap. The shower cap should help keep the rest of your clothes from getting contaminated. To further combat the stench of dirty clothing in hot and humid third world environments, toss a couple of scented fabric softener sheets in your suitcase. Your clean clothes will keep their clean smell.

Most hostels and budget third world hotels will not have enough clothes hangers to keep your clothing wrinkle free. If you are concerned about such things, you can buy foldable travel hangers to hang up your clothes. Another solution is to use an old fashioned wire hanger. They are much thinner than plastic hangers and can be stuffed in your luggage without taking up too much space. Some serious business travelers will put one or two of these wire hangers alongside their computer in their laptop bag. It's an easy spot to store a couple of hangers without adding weight or bulk to your main piece of luggage.

When you are traveling with makeup, there is no need to carry each bulky package. Contact lens cases make great travel containers for small amounts of makeup or creams of any sort.

Feminine Hygiene Products- A constant complaint from female travelers is the lack of availability and/or quality of tampons in foreign countries. You will be able to buy almost any cosmetic or toiletry needs in foreign drug stores. Tampons may be the exception. Pack plenty of extras from home if you think you may need them.

You may want to consider packing tampons without applicators. They are smaller, so you can pack more in the same amount of space. The lack of applicator also simplifies disposal issues when you cannot flush anything down the toilet and the waste cans are missing from public toilets. Make sure to diligently wash your hands before inserting your tampon. Bacteria from your hands can easily cause a urinary tract infection, especially when you may be dehydrated and stuck in sanitary conditions that aren't as clean as you are used to at home.

Even if you don't normally use maxi pads or panty liners, you may want to pack a few for your trip. They work well for large bleeding wounds. Friends (both male and female) have also used them as additional "protection" when they contracted illness with particularly explosive diarrhea. An additional layer will prolong the cleanliness of your underwear. There's nothing worse than dirtying all of your underwear and having to find a place to do laundry when you are ill.

You should also include a few extra Ziploc bags because you may have to pack out your used tampons or pads. If you are in the back country or have to change your tampon alongside of a road on a long trip, there won't be any trash cans.

Male Religious Figures– In several Southeast Asian countries, you will see monks in colorful robes out in public. They may be begging for charity, eating at a restaurant, or riding public transportation. Some of these monks have taken vows to avoid the temptation to have sex. They may be forbidden to speak to, look at, touch, or sit next to women. Expect to be asked to change seats in a bus or plane if you are a woman and find yourself seated next to a monk. Be careful not to initiate conversation or touch a monk lest you commit a huge cultural faux pas. Even the monks who are willing to talk to females will likely be unable to touch them in any way, including accepting an object directly passed from a female. If you have to hand an object of any type to a monk, it is always safer to hand the object to a male and let the male pass it to the monk.

Date Rape Drugs-There is an epidemic problem of men drugging female travelers' drinks in tourist area bars all over the world. It's very important that women who drink keep a close eye on their beverages. Many of the date rape drugs used are colorless, odorless, tasteless liquids that rapists carry in small bottles (often eye drop bottles). A rapist can drug your drink in seconds and you will never know until you start to feel the drug's effects.

Women should not accept drinks from anyone they don't know well. They also shouldn't leave drinks unattended. If you begin having strange or unusual side effects that aren't consistent with the amount of alcohol you have consumed, get a friend's assistance and get home immediately. Do not accept a ride with any strange man from the bar after you notice the drugged feeling.

Even these precautions, however useful, may not stop all drugging. The bartender may be in collusion with the rapist and he may be the one drugging your drinks. It's much tougher to catch when the bartender mixes the drug quickly with the rest of the ingredients in your drink.

This bartender-assisted drugging has happened to me personally. In Jamaica, my girlfriend went to a bar and ordered drinks for both of us. She came back and we began sipping them. Very soon after finishing my drink, my head started to spin and I was unable to walk. My body felt like Jell-O and my girlfriend had to help me to bed where I passed out and didn't wake up until late the next morning. When I awoke, I didn't remember the previous night. I had only consumed one other beer before the drink and I never left the drink unattended. The only way my drink could have been drugged was if the bartender did it. My girlfriend was fine. We surmised that the bartender was attempting to drug her and got my drink by mistake.

In another experience, a female friend of mine was drugged in a bar in Quito, Ecuador. My friend was not a heavy drinker and I had never seen her inebriated. I was surprised when I looked across the dance floor and saw her collapse on the floor. The man with whom she had been dancing scooped up her unconscious body and carried her outside. By the time I got through the crowd and out the door, the man was attempting to put her in his car. I "persuaded" the man to leave her in my care. He did and quickly drove away. Another friend and I carried her back to our hotel.

She vomited several times during the trip home and was in and out of consciousness for the next six hours. When she awoke, she had no recollection of what happened after she had accepted a drink from the bartender. It was only her second alcoholic drink of the night and she passed out shortly after finishing it. She got the drink directly from the bartender and never left it unattended. Again, it was likely the bartender who drugged her drink.

These bartender-assisted date rape druggings are difficult to prevent. The best way to avoid being drugged is to order beer in a bottle. Order it "to go" with the cap still on and uncap it yourself. Otherwise, you must watch closely when the bartender opens it for you. Make sure he doesn't pour the beer into a glass (which may already have the drug in it) or add ice (that has the drug mixed in).

Female travelers may have some different concerns than their male counterparts, but that shouldn't discourage any adventurous females from traveling through the developing world. A little common sense and pre-planning will reduce most of the dangers, even if you are a woman traveling alone.

Taxis, Motorbikes, and Automobile Transportation

> *"Risk is something you have to understand to measure. Never confuse what will kill you with what you are afraid of. At the end of the day you are more likely to die in the taxi from the airport than on the front lines."*
> – Robert Young Pelton

My plane touched down in Belize City, Belize. I had been warned about this place. Safety conscious friends had informed me that it was one of the most dangerous cities in the world. I was only staying there one night before starting a sea kayaking trip off the coast, but I was a little worried. I was a fairly well-seasoned traveler and could take care of myself. My concern was that I was traveling with my girlfriend and it was only her second time outside the country.

We breezed through customs and immigration and worked our way to the taxi queue outside the airport. It was a sweltering tropical evening. As I looked at the taxis waiting to pick up passengers, I was surprised to see that none of them were the familiar yellow color I was used to. In fact, it just looked like a long line of cars. Not a single one looked like a taxi. *Are we in the right place?*

I looked around and saw that we were in a line marked "taxis." A porter was calling up each of the "taxi cabs" and assigning all of the passengers to a driver. The voices in my head were saying: *"Don't worry. It's a third world country. Just go with it."*

My taxi turned out to be a late 1980's model Ford Crown Victoria. It was spray painted white in color and had more dents and scratches than I could count. The driver was quite friendly and explained that there weren't many "real" taxis that operated in Belize City. The cars that I saw were all "gypsy cabs;" independent drivers in personal cars trying to make a little extra money. It was essentially Uber before Uber was even a concept.

We cruised along the dusty roads heading towards the city with the windows rolled down. The air conditioning didn't work. The driver was listening to a children's gospel radio show on the AM radio. Kids were singing hymns and answering the host's Bible trivia questions.

The radio host asked another question and our driver hurriedly dialed his cell phone while saying *"I know that! I know that!"* He got through and soon we heard his voice both in the front seat and playing on the radio. Apparently Belizean gospel stations don't have a seven-second delay.

The host seemed confused that a grown man was calling in to what was obviously a children's show. The host asked *"How old are you?"* Our driver answered *"I'm 59, but I'm still a child...a child of God!"*

We had barely left the airport and we already had some stories to tell out amazed friends back home. The taxi ride was getting surreal. I started looking for the hidden cameras.

As we entered the city, I began to see why my friends cautioned me about it. Shabby houses, lots of barbed wire, stray dogs everywhere, and lots of hard looking men standing around. They all were watching us like hawks.

There was nothing we could do to blend into this environment.

The driver drove us through progressively worse neighborhoods. By now he had turned the radio off and was no longer speaking, even when we asked him questions. He was pissed that the radio host had rebuffed him because of his age. He just drove silently in a simmering rage. I made sure our doors were locked and casually put my hand on the knife in my pocket.

Suddenly, without warning, the driver stopped in the middle of a dark alley. He threw the gear shifter in park, grabbed the keys and jumped out without saying a word. He ran into a nearby building.

> "Oh shit! We're about to get jacked! I yelled at my girlfriend, "Get out! Get out!"

I didn't know where we would go, but I wasn't going to be carjacked or kidnapped. If someone wants a fight, I'd rather do it right here in the street than be taken someplace where there aren't any witnesses. My brain was operating in warp speed. Questions were coming faster than I could come up with answers:

> "How could this trip go from answering bible trivia to a kidnapping attempt in five minutes?"
> "Do I try to get our bags from the trunk, or do we just run?"
> "Where the hell are we?"
> "Where is our hotel?"
> "Fuck, my girlfriend is wearing flip-flops."

All of these thoughts are running through my head as I opened my folding knife and hid it under my bandanna.

I did a quick scan and didn't see anyone approaching. I told my girlfriend to watch and yell if she saw anyone while I fished around in the driver's compartment looking for a spare key or the button to open the trunk.

As I was rummaging under the seat, our driver came out. He had a heavy bundle in his hands. *"Here we go"* I think as I tighten my grip on the knife and start maneuvering myself between our driver and my girlfriend.

The driver saw the determined look on my face and recognized what I was thinking.

> *"Oh, no! I'm not going to hurt you! I just had to stop at my friend's house and pick up my boat motor. He had been working on it for me and his house was on the way to your hotel. Get back in. Your hotel's right down the street."*

Our hotel was just down the street and the remaining two-minute ride was uneventful. No more bible questions. No more kidnapping attempts. Welcome to the roller coaster ride of third-world public transportation.

Travel Risks– Naive travelers often misunderstand the true risks they are facing when they engage in third world travel. Fears of murder and concerns about fatal infectious diseases are what worry the greatest number of Americans considering traveling abroad. These concerns are largely unwarranted. Less than 1% of all American deaths overseas are related to infectious disease. Homicide was the cause of death for approximately 17% of the American overseas fatalities according to one Peace Corps study.

But even that number is misleading. In the country with the highest murder rate for American tourists (the Philippines), the murder rate for American tourists is less than 22 homicides per ONE MILLION visits. That means you have a roughly 0.002% chance of being murdered when visiting the most dangerous country in the world for Americans.

When we look at the average murder rate in overseas travelers, we see it is in the neighborhood of 0.7 homicides per one million visits abroad. That means that your chance of being murdered is literally less than one in a million. In contrast, the murder rate in the United States hovers around 0.5 homicides per million people per year. When you look at these statistics you'll see that your chance of being murdered on a foreign vacation is roughly the same as the chance you will be killed at home in any given year. It's really not a huge concern.

The real danger to Americans abroad is not disease or homicide, it is motor vehicle accidents. The median rate of American motor vehicle deaths in foreign countries is approximately 4.0 per one million visits, making deaths by vehicle travel roughly five times more common than homicides.

Tourist deaths in foreign countries are most commonly caused by traffic accidents. Vehicle and road safety standards may not be the same as you are used to at home. City street on the outskirts of Phenom Penh, Cambodia. Note approaching overloaded truck on the left.

Choosing a safe mode of automobile transport might be the single most important thing you can do to reduce your chances of accidental death in a third world country. Here's what you need to know:

Vehicle Safety– Vehicle safety standards, traffic law enforcement, and driving styles will likely be very different from home. The single largest cause of death for foreign tourists in almost every country is motor vehicle accidents. I generally find that it is worth a little extra money to hire a car and driver rather than renting a car and driving myself in most countries. You don't know the driving customs and are likely to have some problems that you never anticipated. It's easier to let someone else do the hard work. An additional plus is that your driver can probably give you great travel advice and steer you away from the dangerous areas. Give it a try. You'll be surprised how cheap it is. I've hired cars and drivers in Africa and South America for a whole day for less than $50.

Before traveling, look up your destination country on the Traffic Death Rate Wikipedia (https://en.wikipedia.org/wiki/List_of_countries_by_traffic-related_death_rate). If the country you are visiting has an unacceptably high rate of fatalities, you are better off relying on public transportation instead of driving yourself.

Rental Cars- Despite the craziness inherent in using public transportation, I don't usually drive in developing countries. It's far easier and less hassle to hire a driver, use a taxi, catch an Uber, or hop on a bus. If you do choose to drive, try to avoid driving at night. Roads rarely have adequate light. Sometimes the locals will drive without headlights, thinking it saves gas. Recognize that most roads will not be up to the same standards as your home country. Sidewalks are rare. Potholes, uncovered manholes, and animals in the roadway are all common hazards.

I've had some pretty miserable experiences renting cars in third world countries. One thing I've learned is to always avoid any pre-payment when reserving a rental car. On one occasion, I prepaid for a rental car. When I arrived in-country, the rental car company had gone out of business. In another instance, the company I prepaid for the car did not have a representative at their booth in the airport (where I was supposed to pick up the vehicle). I had to borrow a cell phone and call the company. They sent an employee, but it took more than an hour for him to arrive. If I hadn't prepaid, I could have rented a car with another company and been on my way. It's fine to make car reservations online before your travel, just don't pay for the car in advance.

Cows in the road in rural Costa Rica

If you are driving a third world rental car, add 25%-50% to the drive time given to you by whatever mapping website or app you use. Poor road conditions, construction, and unforeseen emergencies are guaranteed to make your drive time considerably longer than what Google estimates.

When driving a rental car, know that different countries require different types of emergency equipment to be carried in every car. If you are stopped at a police road block, you may be detained for a "safety inspection." Some countries require that you carry fire extinguishers, flares, or reflective triangles in case of a breakdown. If you don't have these items, you can be ticketed by police. Check the laws for the countries you are visiting before you drive.

Contrary to popular belief, if you do rent a car, you won't need an International Driver's License. The International Driver's License is commonly purchased in AAA offices in the USA. It looks like a small passport and is merely a translation (in several languages) of your current driver's license. I'm not aware of any country that requires the International License for car rental. The driver's license from your home country will be enough. The only time I would personally get an International Driver's License is if I was renting a car in a country that used a completely different alphabet (like Russia or China) where translation of my original licensing document could be quite difficult.

Some countries (especially in Latin America) have special procedures to insure that rental car drivers pay any parking tickets they may collect. The cops remove and confiscate the license plates of the rental car upon issuing a parking ticket. You must go to the local police station and pay your ticket before getting your plates back. This practice causes confusion for lots of tourists. If you find a ticket on your rental car, check to make sure your license plates are still attached. If they are not, you'll have to track them down at the local police station before returning your car.

Overall, rental cars are a big hassle. When visiting locations with cheap cabs or good public transportation networks, it's almost always better to avoid renting your own car.

Third world road hazards: The Nicaraguans who
painted the speed bump didn't have any traffic
cones to protect the paint until it dried. They used
rocks instead.

Taxi Cabs- Cab drivers like to mob tourists in arriving third
world countries. You will likely be swarmed and have
numerous taxis and drivers from which to choose. As you
are considering your transportation options, take a couple
seconds to look at the tire tread (make sure the vehicle has
some tread left on the tires) and ensure that the vehicle
has seat belts before haggling over the price or choosing a
vehicle. You will be surprised how many vehicles you will
disqualify using these two criteria alone. Third world taxi
drivers don't have enough money for "unnecessary" vehicle
repairs.

Although it may seem absurd to suggest, make sure your
driver isn't drunk. Drunk driving laws are not enforced

in developing countries the same way they are at home. I've seen many taxi drivers (especially in Brazil) drinking 40 ounce bottles of beer while waiting for fares. If your driver smells of booze, find another one. Drunken taxi drivers and poor vehicle maintenance will seriously increase your odds of being killed in a car crash.

Most taxi drivers will not speak English. When you arrive at your hotel or hostel, pick up a couple of the hotel's business cards from the front desk. The cards will have the hotel's address and phone number on them. If you get a taxi driver who can't understand you, hand him the business card and he'll be able to get you home. Taking a photo of the front of your hotel or the street signs at the nearest intersection and showing it to your driver may also communicate where you need to go if you can't speak the language.

After a couple hours riding in this Thai songtaew
taxi, I was grateful for $7/hour Thai massages.

If you speak any of the local language at all, speak it as soon as you get in the cab. Cabbies are less likely to overcharge or scam you if they think you may be a resident or familiar with the city. Speaking even just a little of the local language will make the taxi driver think you may know what's going on and keep him honest. You may also consider taking a photo of the cab driver's licensing paperwork as soon as you get into the car. The photo will help the authorities identify the driver/taxi cab in the event that you are scammed or robbed.

I only take a photo of the cab license if I really start feeling strange about the ride. I usually attempt to be extraordinarily friendly instead of being outright suspicious or rude. I practice my foreign language skills with the driver by asking his name, where he grew up, and about his family. Usually, I've found that tactic tends to "personalize" you a bit to the driver. He sees you as a friendly person, curious about his life and country, not just merely another tourist dollar. A simple friendly conversation like this will do wonders to prevent you from being overcharged, scammed, or victimized by a driver's criminal friends.

One other tactic I use is to ask the driver for his phone number on the pretext of hiring him again later in the week. I may or may not ever use it, but it's always good to have a taxi driver you can call if you get lost or stranded. When you ask for his number, the driver is less likely to scam you because he sees a repeat business opportunity.

If your cabbie speaks English, he will commonly ask you if it is your first time in the city/country. Always answer with a "no." First time visitors don't know how things work and get the "long ride" so the driver makes some more money. If you make up a story about having been to the city before, the cabbie is more likely to take a direct route, figuring you know where you are going.

If you have a smart phone with an activated foreign data plan, consider pulling up Google Maps as you ride. That way you can see where you are going and will know if the driver is taking you out of the way to boost his fare. Keep the doors locked and the phone down low as you use it because it can be a sought-after target for criminals when you are stopped in traffic.

Firmly refuse any offers from your driver to take you to a "couple places" on the way to your destination. The places where the taxi drivers stop pay him a commission on anything you buy. If you stop at all the places your driver suggests, your 10- minute trip will turn into a three-hour ordeal.

It is generally a good practice to avoid allowing anyone else to get in the taxi with you. Occasionally drivers will stop and allow other passengers to ride in the cab in order to make some more money. Usually it's legitimate, but occasionally those "other passengers" are robbers who are in collusion with the driver. In a big city if someone else gets in the taxi, get out and don't pay the driver. Tell him that you are going to call the police.

In smaller towns and especially in rural areas, it may be more commonplace to share taxi rides. On one of my trips to a small island in Nicaragua, the taxi driver picked someone else up in nearly all of my rides. That was just the way things worked down there. For a 70 cent cab ride anywhere on the island, I couldn't complain much. When visiting areas like this where ride sharing is commonplace, offer your taxi driver a little extra money if you want to ride alone and stay safe. He'll usually accept the offer and avoid picking up other passengers.

Horse-drawn taxi (calesh) in Luxor, Egypt

Never put all of your luggage in the trunk of the taxi. Take your carry-on bag or backpack into the passenger compartment with you. If you have to flee the cab in a hurry, you will at least be able to keep control of some of your possessions and valuables.

Watch the cab driver to ensure that he places all of your larger bags in the trunk. A common taxi scam (especially at crowded airports) is perpetrated by the cab driver and an accomplice. The cab driver escorts you into his cab.

After you get in, he loads most of your bags into the vehicle trunk. He leaves one or two on the roadway behind the car where you won't see them. When the cab pulls away, a previously unseen accomplice runs up and snatches the bags the cabbie failed to load into the trunk.

In the same vein of luggage protection, always wait for the cab driver to get out of the car at your destination before you do. While direct luggage theft from cab drivers is uncommon, it does happen. You don't want to get out of the cab only to have the cabbie speed away with your luggage. If your destination isn't in a dangerous location, it may even be best to wait until you get your luggage to pay the taxi driver.

Make sure your doors are locked and your windows are up. Thieves on foot, bicycle, or motorbike drive between lanes of traffic stopped at intersections and will reach in through open windows to steal purses, wallets, shopping bags or cameras. They get away easily when the taxi cab is caught up in gridlocked traffic. Make sure you don't have any valuables visible in your hand or lap. Some criminals on foot will break your window, reach in, and steal your stuff while the taxi is stuck in traffic.

Leaving your windows open about one half inch at the top takes away some of the window's stability in the frame and makes it much harder to break than a window that is fully closed. Consider cracking your windows in dangerous areas.

Determine how to lock and unlock the door immediately upon entry. Do you have to hit the unlock button in order to open the door or does it open automatically? Figure all this stuff out so you won't waste any time in a crisis situation.

If you are alone, sit in the rear seat on the passenger side of the car. If you have to escape from the driver, you will have a slight head start (or a little cover) as the driver has to run around the car to reach you.

Hiring a taxi driver as a tour guide usually works well, but don't hire one if you want to tour an exceptionally poor neighborhood. Poor people don't use taxis. They walk or ride the bus instead. A taxi cab occupied by foreign tourists driving through the ghetto stands out. It makes a very tempting target for the robbers and thieves who live in the area. It's generally a good policy to avoid touring the ghettos, but if you must, hire a driver who isn't in a marked taxi cab. Uber or Lyft is a better choice when traveling in a sketchy neighborhood.

Horse-drawn calesh, motorcycle, and old car all
vying for the same lane in Luxor, Egypt.

Driving styles in other countries often vary considerably from what you may be used to at home. Don't criticize your driver's abilities. It may appear that he is driving crazily, but he knows the roads better than you do. If you have to keep your eyes closed, do so, but don't open your mouth.

I've had drivers turn off their headlights (because it supposedly increases gas mileage) on curvy Ecuadorian roads in the dark. Taxi drivers in Rio de Janeiro don't stop for traffic lights at night so that they are less vulnerable to car jackers. Driving lanes are generally a suggestion rather than a requirement almost everywhere. It seems insane, but in all my years of travel, I've only been in one minor traffic accident. Relax and let your driver do his job.

In general, it is safer to flag down a moving taxi than to approach one sitting at the curb. Moving taxis aren't generally waiting for a victim.

If you take a taxi to visit some location or attraction in a third world city, take a look around at your destination. Are their taxi cabs readily available for the ride home? Many local markets that you may want to visit are in the poorer parts of town where people ride the bus instead of taking taxis. There may not be a reliable source of transportation back home. Ask your driver where to find a taxi to get back. If he can't give you a location to find another cab, you may want to pay him some extra money to wait around and take you home. Negotiate the deal before you leave. I usually pay the first cab ride in full and then give him a few extra dollars (in good faith) toward the waiting fee before leaving. I pay the rest of the waiting fee I've negotiated and the cab fare home when I get back and see that the cabbie is still waiting. Don't pay the whole round trip fare upfront. There is no incentive for the cabbie to stick around once he has all your money. He may just leave you stranded as soon as you walk away.

You will undoubtedly end up visiting some fairly dangerous areas by taxi. Take a look at the environment on your arrival. If the place looks dodgy or you see lots of people loitering about, it may be safer to settle your fare inside the taxi, before you get out. That will prevent potential criminals from seeing where you keep your money hidden. I generally pay my fare inside the cab on all of my trips except when I'm going to or from my hotel and the airport. If you have luggage in the trunk, it may not be best to employ this technique. If you pay the driver and get out, he has the opportunity to speed away with all of your bags.

Finally, you should look out for "copycat cabs." These are vehicles driven by criminals that are painted up to look like taxis in an attempt to victimize tourists and clueless locals. When you get in one of these "cabs" you will be robbed or kidnapped instead of being taken to your destination. When you arrive in your city, take a close look at the cab's appearance. There will usually only be a couple cab companies operating within each city. Familiarize yourself with what those cabs look like so that you may be able to spot an imposter.

The easy "tells" are mismatched paint jobs, magnetic door signs instead of painted logos, a lack of numbers, or poorly wired roof lights. If the taxi roof light appears to be stuck on with a magnet and powered by a cord running to the car's cigarette lighter, you might want to pass it up for a taxi that appears a little more authentic.

If you abhor taxis at home and prefer to use services like Uber or Lyft, there is an equivalent service in some other countries as well. The Easy Taxi app (www.http://www.easytaxi.com/) works similarly to Uber but is active in much of South America and a few countries in Southeast Asia. I've never personally used it, but it appears to be a safe and successful concept that keeps you from having to hail a taxi in an unfamiliar part of town. The Taxi Finder App (http://www.taxifinder.com/) is also a useful one to download. It allows you to find the closest and most reliable taxi company in more than 600 worldwide cities.

An additional benefit to using an app to get a cab or using a radio dispatched taxi is the fact that there is a "paper trail" that is created. If the cab driver scams you, he is easier to track down. It also makes it easier to get property back if you accidentally leave something in the taxi. If you are using an app or dispatched taxi, there will be some record somewhere of which particular cab came to pick you up. In the worst case scenario, this information can also be used by investigators if you are kidnapped or otherwise victimized by the taxi driver.

Overall, using an app like Uber or the local equivalent is probably the best public transportation advice I can give you. I recently used Uber in Peru and was amazed at both the cheap prices and easy availability of the drivers. There are no scams to worry about. No cash money changes hands. Most important of all, you won't pay the "gringo tax" of inflated tourist fares when using a ride sharing app. If the country I'm visiting has a ride sharing app, I will now preferentially use that in lieu of flagging down a taxi on the street.

Moto-Taxis– In some Asian countries "moto-taxis" are more common than cars. These are motorcycles that look like a cross between a scooter and a dirt bike. They are cheap and plentiful, but riding them will be quite an adventure. Just beware that many ex-pats living in Asia call these things "death scooters." Remember, the exhaust pipe is on the right side of the bike. It's hot and will give you a nasty burn. Get on and off the moto-taxi from the LEFT side only.

You should also be careful when getting off a motorbike parked next to a bunch of other bikes. While using caution to avoid being burned on your exhaust pipe, don't accidentally back into the hot exhaust pipe of the bike parked next to yours.

Riding moto-taxis in Vietnam

When riding as a passenger on one of these motorbike taxis, you should definitely be wearing eye protection, even if it is just a cheap pair of sunglasses. A bug going into your eye at 50 miles per hour will ruin your day. You should also be a good passenger so that your driver doesn't crash. Don't suddenly grab a hold of the driver's body, even if you are scared to death. Hold on to the back of the seat behind you.

If either driving or riding as a passenger, it is better to store any bags or purses in the compartment under the motorbike's seat rather than slinging them across your body. Some bag snatchers will forcibly grab your bag in an effort to steal it. If it is attached to your body, that grab may cause you to crash the bike or fall off of it and land in a busy roadway. Either of these events can cause serious injury. It's best not to tempt the thieves. Keep your bags hidden if you are able to do so.

If you rent or purchase your own motorbike, be especially cautious as the drivers of parked cars exit their vehicles. People getting out of cars parked on the side of the road regularly fail to look in their mirrors before they open their car doors. On several occasions, I've seen these drivers open their doors directly into the path of an oncoming motorbike, occasionally causing serious injuries. Ride defensively and look out for opening car doors.

Motorbike Thieves– Be especially alert if you see a motorbike occupied by two younger men cruising slowly in your vicinity. While multiple people on a motorbike is far from unusual, you won't often see two younger guys riding on the same bike. This is a very common set up for a robbery. The bike pulls up; the passenger hops off and sticks a gun in your face. He steals whatever he wants and then hops back on his handy getaway vehicle.

In Brazil, this same tactic is how the criminals will steal running motorcycles at traffic lights. The gunman hops off the back of his bike, pulls his gun and then rides away on your motorcycle.

Motorbike bag thieves also work in pairs. One person controls the motorbike while the second commits the crime. These robberies are so common in most third world countries that you should be suspicious anytime you see two young men riding together on a single motorcycle, especially if they are wearing helmets. Helmet use isn't quite as common in many developing countries. Robbers don't wear the helmets to protect themselves in the event of a crash, but instead to hide their identity from potential victims.

Keep your taxi windows up to avoid the "snatch thief". Sign on the street in Bangkok, Thailand.

Buses, Trains, Subways and Other Transportation Options

"...and what is a bus but a failure crystallized into the form of two stories of metal, painted red, hurled out into the world to hoover up losers from the streets of London?"
– Douglas Coupland

The bus trip wasn't supposed to be too bad...only about six hours. Even though we were going through the Ecuadorian Andes, the roads weren't too steep or winding. No barf bags issued. There was plenty of room. I had no complaints.

Then the rain started. It never stopped.

Even though we were traveling on a national highway, at times the road alternated between pavement and dirt. High mountain dirt roads, heavy buses, and rain make for a bad combination.

You guessed it. We got stuck. The dirt road turned into a muddy quagmire. The wheels on the right side of the bus quickly became buried axle-deep in the thick mud, dragging the bus to a stop.

The stuck bus...

The driver tried rocking the bus back and forth to no avail. His assistant yelled at us in Spanish "*Everyone off the bus!*" Did I mention that it was pouring rain? Like most passengers, I didn't expect to have to get off the bus in a rain storm. My rain gear was in my backpack in the luggage storage compartment. So was everyone else's. There was a collective moan as we all exited into the storm.

There were no large trees for shelter, just jungle scrub. We stood under these small bushes and tried to stay dry as the driver tried to break the bus free.

It didn't work. The next call in Spanish was "*Everyone get your bags off the bus!*" Apparently, the driver thought the bus would move easier if they removed some weight. All of us trudged across the muddy road and grabbed our bags. I was able to get my rain gear out, but all my other clothes in the bag quickly became saturated with water. I don't know if it was a good trade.

Even after removing the bags, the bus remained buried in the mud. The driver's assistant called out again; "*All the men to the back of the bus to push!*"

This was a big bus, like a U.S. Greyhound. About a dozen of us male passengers tried pushing as the females without rain gear held banana leaves over their heads to try to stay dry. Pushing didn't move the bus an inch.

My friends trying to stay dry under an improvised umbrella...

We were in real trouble. The bus had no radio and there was no cell phone reception up in the mountains. The driver said we may have to spend the night.

Traffic on the mountain highway was starting to back up as the vehicles on the road behind us couldn't pass the stuck bus. As the bus driver was being screamed at by all the motorists stuck behind him, a truck carrying a bulldozer pulled up. Without saying a word, the truck driver backed his earth mover off the truck's trailer. He swiftly plowed down the jungle scrub on the side of the road, making an expedient detour around the buried bus. All the traffic behind us took the new "road" past the bus without incident.

The bulldozer making a new road around the stuck
bus

Once there was no stopped traffic in the way, the bulldozer driver turned his machine on the bus. He pushed the bus right out of the mud and quickly loaded the dozer back onto his truck.

We were cold and wet, but we got back on the bus and continued our journey. We made it to our destination a little late and a lot soggier than expected, but we didn't have any more problems.

For the rest of the ride, I couldn't help but think about how this situation could not have happened in the USA. The bulldozer driver couldn't just destroy a section of the high mountain "rainforest" to create a new road without being sued by the property owner and found guilty of dozens of EPA legal violations. He would have never pushed the bus with his bulldozer blade out of fear of being sued if he damaged something. It would have taken forever in the USA to summon a heavy equipment tow truck and get the bus out of the mud. A little third world ingenuity got the problem solved in about 20 minutes. It made me grateful for the resourcefulness of the Ecuadorian people, but I've never again taken another long third world bus ride without having extra clothes, rain gear, food, and survival supplies.

"Chicken Bus" in Panama

Local Buses– The "chicken bus" or "collectivo" (minivan taxi) will almost always be extremely crowded. Undoubtedly, the local sitting next to you will not be wearing deodorant. If you get hot easily, do anything possible to get a window seat. It will be the only way you can control fresh air for the duration of your trip. If you do pick a window seat in order to control airflow, try to pick one on the side of the bus that isn't in the direct sun. Even with the window open, the tropical sun in some countries combined with the greenhouse effect of the window is sure to make for an uncomfortable ride.

If you choose to go cheap and ride the "chicken bus" you will learn very quickly that there is no such thing as a full bus. People will be crammed two or three in a seat and the aisles will be filled with standing passengers. It will be so hot, crowded, and so smelly that you would do anything to get off. You should have picked the Deluxe Bus. It's worth it to pay a few extra dollars to ride in comfort.

View from inside of one of the less-crowded chicken buses in Panama. It actually got more crowded later in the trip

"*Collectivos*," "*Matatus*," and local mini buses will assuredly NOT be anywhere near on time. You will need a lot of patience to use these forms of transportation for anything more than a few minutes' drive. There will be multiple unscheduled stops, they will never arrive or leave on time, and you will never be on one that isn't packed far beyond full.

Avoid these mini buses unless you are being very budget conscious or unless you want to experience more of the local culture than you have ever imagined. You will be packed so tightly that it is commonplace to find your seatmate's head on your shoulder as he sleeps or his hand in your lap as he stretches for more room. The locals don't think twice about using each other as pillows, so you shouldn't be shocked if your seat mate ends up drooling on your shoulder.

Depending on the city you are visiting, bus and collectivo fares can be taken at either the start of your trip (by paying the driver), during your ride, or on exit. If you don't know how the money is taken in your individual city, have the money ready when you get on the bus. Exact change is always best, as drivers get mad when they have to take time to make change. If your money is refused, then you will pay on exit. Some buses have a driver's assistant to collect the money. This guy will be standing at the front of the bus and will come back to collect your payment after you get seated. He won't be uniformed or have any identification. If no one is taking your money when you get on, expect someone to approach you at your seat. It's legitimate and is common in many countries.

On some buses, the driver doesn't want to wait long enough to collect money. The bus will start moving as soon as you set foot inside. On those buses, it is commonplace to pass your fare (via the other passengers) up from the back of the bus to the driver or the driver's money gathering assistant. If people are handing you money, just pass it forward

Deluxe or Long Haul Buses– Third world long haul buses are usually very cheap (only a couple US dollars an hour) and are surprisingly comfortable. You can certainly find the stereotypical "chicken bus" but it's worthwhile to buy a ticket on a "first class" or "deluxe" bus. Some buses have in-seat entertainment like an airplane and may even have free Wi-Fi.

Long haul buses don't have regular stops. The bus only stops when the driver is hungry or has to use the bathroom. I once did a 26 hour bus ride in Brazil that only had three stops. Another 12 hour ride in Colombia had a single 20 minute stop at a roadside restaurant. The stops that are made aren't in the best locations. They are usually determined by which restaurant gives the driver free food. Prepare for anything. It may be a long while before you get to stop for anything to eat. Bring your own food. You will see the locals bringing everything from watermelon to whole cooked chickens to eat on the trip.

If the driver or his assistant is passing out "barf bags" as you board, take one. They are being passed out for a reason. I don't generally get motion sickness. I haven't thrown up in a vehicle since I was a small child. When the conductor wanted to hand me a bag as I was boarding a bus through the mountains of Colombia, I laughed and waived his offering aside. What a mistake. Three hours later, I was throwing up into a plastic grocery bag from my backpack that I had been using to carry my dirty laundry. I'll never pass up a barf bag again. More importantly, I'll never board another third world bus without bringing my own bag to contain my vomit.

Be careful about eating too much food. The toilets on these buses often don't work. Intentionally going somewhat hungry and thirsty could prevent an embarrassing incident.

If you are taking a long distance deluxe bus, bring a sweater, jacket, or light blanket. These buses are often air conditioned to near-Arctic levels. If you want to stay comfortable and avoid hypothermia, bring something warmer than a T-shirt to wear. You may also want to remember to pack some insect repellant in a handy location. On many buses, the only climate control is an open window. When driving through jungle areas, open windows equal a certain mosquito infestation. A little bug spray can mean the difference between a pleasant night's sleep and spending hours scratching and swatting on the bus.

On deluxe buses, there will be carry-on luggage storage in both overhead compartments and under your seat. Only use them if you plan on remaining awake and alert. As soon as you fall asleep, the thieves will take anything you leave unattended. If you plan on sleeping, keep your bag on your lap. If you want to place your bag on the floor of the bus, place it between your feet and loop the bag's strap around your ankle.

Be cautious if any other passenger offers to help you stash your bag in an overhead compartment. Sometimes thieves will use this ruse to covertly slash your bag with a razor and remove its contents. More brazen thieves will take the bag from your hands, toss it to an accomplice at the front of the bus, and then block the aisle so that you can't give chase as the accomplice runs away.

I talked about your carry-on bags, but where do you store your sheep? On top of the bus! This bus zoomed past me in the highlands of Ecuador.

Don't be surprised when buses take on additional passengers who sell food, beg for money, or provide entertainment. These people pay the driver a small fee in order for access to the passengers for a short time. They will ride for a short while selling food, giving impassioned speeches for money, or singing songs. It's generally safe to give these folks a small token tip for the entertainment value, but feel free to ignore them if you choose.

It's always comforting to see a bullet hole in the windshield of the bus you are boarding.

If you are traveling by bus, it makes sense to have waterproof luggage or a waterproof cover for your bags. When luggage compartments fill up, your bags will be placed on the roof no matter what the weather conditions are outside. I also generally attach a carabiner to the outside of all of my bags so that I can have a little additional security by locking it to a luggage rail, rope, or another bag when my stuff is strapped to the outside of a bus or van.

Luggage on the roof of a "chicken bus"

It is usually safe to check bags in the compartments under the bus. Some luggage handlers will expect a "tip" in order to make sure your bag is stowed properly. Watch what the locals do when loading their bags. If they are paying a tip as well, you aren't being charged a "gringo tax." You will not have access to these bags at any stops. Make sure you bring all of your valuables and any items you might need on the trip inside the passenger compartment with you.

Pay attention to which side of the bus your luggage is loaded. It's best to sit on the same side of the bus as your luggage. That way, if there is any delay in disembarking the bus, you will be able to keep an eye on your luggage as it is being offloaded.

When your bus arrives at its destination, get outside quickly. Luggage handlers often throw all the bags out into the street as soon as the bus stops. Make sure you can grab yours so thieves don't walk away with it or someone who accidentally picks it up thinking it is theirs. Some bus lines will require your checked bag ticket to claim your luggage. Don't throw it away.

In some countries, if you look like a traveler, you will get mobbed by hostel peddlers as soon as you step off the bus at the bus station. Each one will be trying to get you to stay at "his" hostel. If you don't have your accommodations sorted, use these guys to your advantage. If you don't mind staying in a hostel, there isn't likely that much difference between the different options in town. Negotiate with these guys and tell them you'll stay in whatever hostel provides you free transportation from the bus station. The touts will take you there in their own car if it means a commission from the hostel. Yes, you're probably getting screwed, but at least you didn't have to pay an inflated price cab fare from the bus station to the hostel.

Bus Security Procedures– Depending on the country, you may have to undergo additional "security" screening. Some bus stations have walk through metal detectors and x-ray machines like American airports. They are also common in subway stations. If you are carrying a weapon, don't check your bag until you are certain that you won't have to go through one.

Police may also stop buses and either search luggage or examine your identification documents. Expect to be targeted if you look like a "foreigner." If you are young, male, foreign, or dressed in ragged clothing, the cops will likely want to see who you are and search you for drugs.

Bus Safety- In terms of being protected in the event of a car crash, sitting in the middle of the bus is best. Passengers sitting in the front or rear are more likely to be injured in a crash where the bus hits something or a vehicle rear-ends the bus. Sitting in aisle seats keeps you away from any flying glass if a window is broken during the crash,

Finding a bus route- If you don't speak the language, the multiple ticket windows at a local bus station can be daunting. Instead of being confused and ending up on the wrong bus, check out the listings on Bus Bud (https://www.busbud.com/en). That site lists bus routes and ticketing information for nearly 100 different countries.

Rome-2-Rio (https://www.rome2rio.com/) is worth checking out as well. It bills itself as the world's most extensive repository of train, bus, airplane, and ferry routes. It's simple to use. Just enter origination and destination cities. The website or app will tell you the easiest way to get there.

Rail Travel- Trains are also a cheap way to travel. They generally don't move too fast, so expect to be on them a long time. If you are riding the train for a short trip, choose a seat close to the conductor or where any other railway employees are stationed. You are less likely to be a victim of crime if you are in a location visible to the train employees.

For longer travels, you'll want to buy a sleeper cabin. It's worth the money to have a bed rather than a hard chair for a 15 hour train ride. Most are fairly comfortable and include bedding. Check the mattress for bedbugs or fleas before you lay down. Signs of bedbug infestation are detailed in the medical conditions chapter later in the book.

Many sleeper trains have seats that can be converted into beds. They won't be set up for sleeping as soon as you arrive. If you want to sleep early, tell your porter and he will arrange the bed. Otherwise, at a set time (usually between 9 pm and 10 pm) the porter will come around and change all the seats into beds. In some countries, you have to pay a small amount extra for clean linens. The price should be included in the ticket price, but it often isn't. If the porter asks you for a couple dollars for sheets and pillows, it's not a scam. That's just how the system works.

My bunk on a Vietnamese sleeper train.

Most train sleeping compartments will not have locks. If you happen to be sleeping in one alone, or you know all the travelers sleeping with you, you may try placing a large strip of duct tape along the inside door crack for security. It's not the same as a door lock, but it makes it harder to open the door from the outside and will make an audible sound if the door is opened when you are asleep. The conductors won't like it, but it will keep you a little safer if you aren't able to lock the door of your cabin or compartment.

It's best to bring your own food on a sleeper train. Food options for sale are usually limited to local stuff that you probably don't want to eat. On one trip on a Vietnamese sleeper train, the only food available for sale was fertilized eggs with the chicken embryo still inside. In Thailand, the sleeper train fare consisted solely of crackers.

> "Aiming one's bodily refuse on a shifting train is like hunting for a deer while drunk."- Kaitlin Solimine

Most train toilets empty directly out onto the tracks. Don't use the bathroom while the train is stopped at the station. Wait until you start moving. No one at the station wants to smell your excrement for the next few days. In addition to having sub-par bathrooms, many third world sleeper trains will not have any running water. Make sure you bring hand sanitizer or wet wipes with you to the toilet. I promise that you WILL want to clean your hands after you've visited the train's overcrowded bathroom.

Train station in Vietnam. Don't use the toilets while
the train is stopped. The toilet empties on to the
track and your private business becomes publically
shared for all to enjoy in the days to come.

I've ridden trains in lots of third world countries, but I
would do whatever possible to avoid riding the train in
India. Indian trains have the reputation as being the world's
worst. The trains are so crowded that up to 3500 people
a year are killed after being crowded or pushed out the
doors of the moving trains. People also ride on the roofs,
looking for some space and air. The roof riders regularly
get decapitated by power lines crossing over the tracks. If
you ride the trains in India, use them for short trips only
and buy the best ticket you can afford. Having a "cultural
experience" may be fun, but it isn't worth being run over by
a train to acquire.

The least comfortable train that I've ever ridden.
This one was in Ecuador. I wouldn't ride on the
roof of a train in India unless I wanted to lose my
head.

Foreign rail travel can be difficult to schedule at times.
Fortunately, if your destination is Europe, there is a free
phone app that does all the heavy lifting for you. Check
out the Rail Planner App for complete timetable and
connection information for all of the trains running in
Europe. Another great resource for European train travel
is Seat 61 (https://www.seat61.com/)

Ensure that you check the operating hours of any of the
train stations where you might be making a connection.
In some third world countries, train station services close
at night, even though trains may still be running. When
the stations close, they become fairly desolate places. If
you are a solo traveler (especially a female solo traveler),

disembarking into a remote and unstaffed train terminal can be a threat to your safety. When few people frequent any public space, you'll see criminals start to congregate looking for victims. Don't provide them an easy target. If your train is scheduled to arrive at the station at an odd hour, check and make sure that the facilities remain open for 24 hours in order to have the safest experience.

Something else to note is that, depending on the country, smoking cigarettes and/or drinking alcohol may be prohibited on the train. It's prudent to check out the rules before you book the ticket.

One other caution: Some foreign rail tickets are purchased based on what stop you plan to use as your disembarkation site. Conductors may randomly spot check your tickets to ensure that you are not riding the train longer than the distance you purchased. Save your train ticket until you have completely left the train station at your arrival. If you don't have a ticket when the conductor asks for it, you may be forced to purchase a new one. In other locations (mostly in Europe) tickets have to be validated before travel. When you buy the ticket, it is essentially an open ticket for the route selected, not for a specific day and time. You need to find the validation machine near the ticket counter and get your ticket stamped. Otherwise, the conductor may think you are trying to ride for free when he checks your ticket onboard.

When you board a train and are still waiting to depart the station, be alert for a common train scam. Someone from the outside of the train will tap on your window, show you a badge of some sort, and then motion for you to get off the train. As soon as you do, the "officer's" accomplice will steal your carry-on luggage and both people will run away. It's best to ignore any activity going on outside the train.

If it is a real cop who needs to talk with you, he will board the train to do so. Whatever you do, don't leave your bags unattended any time the train is stopped.

Subways- Subways are a remarkably easy way to get around urban areas. I've found that the easiest way to decipher subway or metro routes is by using the MetrO phone app. MetrO gives precise instructions for navigating the subway systems in more than 400 different cities. Most subways I've used have been remarkably clean and efficient. The few subways available in the USA could learn quite a few lessons from these "backwater" third world metros.

One caution about using subways is that they are often fertile grounds for pickpockets. The close proximity and constant jostling of people in a subway car or on a platform provides pickpockets with plenty of victims from which to choose. Make sure all of your valuables are well secured and move any backpacks/purses to the front of your body for more protection.

One especially dangerous pickpocket scam is regularly used against travelers (especially elderly travelers) who don't understand how the subway system works. Two pickpockets work together. One will stand immediately in front of the victim. The second will stand immediately behind the victim. The first pickpocket acts as a "blocker," slowing the victim's ability to board the car until the doors are about to close. The blocker then steps into the car, but doesn't leave enough room for the victim to enter too.

The second pickpocket (the "pusher") then pushes the victim forward. The victim is trapped between the blocker and the pusher while the subway doors close. The fear created by the jostling combined with the closing doors provides all the distraction that the pickpockets need to steal a wallet or purse.

Pushing is commonplace on entry into third world subway cars, but people purposely blocking your path are not. Most people want to board the car with as little contact with fellow travelers as possible. If you find yourself being excessively jostled, herded in a certain direction, or purposely trapped in the closing doors of the subway car, recognize that you are being targeted. Move aggressively forward or backwards while yelling loudly. You need to either disengage from the pickpockets or create such a stir that all the other passengers take notice of the situation. Either technique works well but both require some significant assertiveness. If you are unable to muster the courage to be that assertive, it is best that you avoid riding the subway in peak hours. When crowds are much smaller, pickpockets have a harder time working this scam.

Because of the close proximity of the passengers, subways are also a frequent site where women are groped or sexually assaulted by strange men. Usually, these men won't approach their victims face to face. Instead, they will come up behind you and place their hands on your buttocks or try to push their fingers between your legs. The subway car might be so crowded that you can't even turn around to confront your attacker. That's what they are counting on.

If you feel hands groping your body, make a scene. Often yelling the word "thief" will get more attention than merely screaming at the man who groped you. In any event, making a strong verbal scene will likely stop the groper in his tracks. To avoid the hassle entirely, get your back to a wall if possible. Molesters don't tend to operate in areas where victims can see their faces.

One other thing to note is that when riding third world subways, I rarely see people smile. Even in countries with a reputation for friendliness, most subway passengers have facial expressions ranging from detached boredom to a rage-filled scowl. Seldom will you see a smile. Smiling on public transportation isn't common because it invites unwanted contact.

Females who smile will get approached by many more local men. Besides wanting to avoid unwanted social attraction, in many cultures smiling at random is viewed as being insincere. It's considered a waste of energy to smile at people you will never see again. Thus, you'll see lots of stony faces in subway cars. It's probably best that you adopt the same mask that the locals have. They are acting that way for a reason, even if it isn't immediately apparent to you.

It goes without saying, but you should work to maintain your situational awareness at all times when riding the subway. Don't close your eyes or fall asleep. Avoid wearing headphones as they both diminish your ability to hear a potential threat and signal that you may be carrying a valuable iPod or phone. Traveling with another person is almost always safer than traveling alone.

Tuk-Tuks- Tuk-tuks or "moto-taxis" are three-wheeled auto rickshaws. They are basically motorcycles with a passenger cabin designed to hold between two and four people. They are used in developing countries as taxi alternatives. In most countries the Tuk-Tuk is a cheaper option for local transportation than taking a taxi. They are open air, so they should generally be avoided in bad weather. They also have difficulty negotiating muddy or mountainous terrain. Don't hire a tuk-tuk if you have a long journey or are traveling on poor roads.

You should generally avoid hiring a tuk-tuk in Thailand. They are extremely popular there with tourists, but you'll rarely see locals using them. Thailand is one country where taxi cabs are actually far cheaper than auto rickshaws. Don't waste your money on Thai tuk-tuks. You'll arrive at your destination faster and cheaper in a taxi cab.

Thai tuk-tuk in Bangkok

Hitchhiking- I covered travel safety on planes, trains, automobiles, tuk-tuks, motorbikes, buses and subways. There is one other way of getting around as well...hitchhiking. Hitching rides is much more common in third world countries (especially the poorest ones) than it is in the USA. I'm hesitant to give advice on this mode of travel because I don't think it's very safe, especially for female travelers. I also have absolutely ZERO experience with hitchhiking. I've never hitched a ride in my life, either here or abroad.

If the idea of hitchhiking does appeal to you, I would suggest that you check out the HitchWiki (http://hitchwiki.org/en/Main_Page) website. It is a collaborative website filled with the experiences of other hitchhikers around the world. Wikis are sorted by country. I would look here for information first before I even considered sticking out my thumb.

If you do decide to hitchhike, critically evaluate the person stopping to offer you a ride. Nervous, anxious, or drunk drivers should be avoided. You should also avoid anyone who has a weapon visible in the car. Don't get into a car with anyone with whom you can't win a street fight. Avoid getting into cars with large groups of men or even a single driver who is significantly larger than you are

Water Travel– No third world travel adventure is complete without some kind of boat trip. Whether it's a sea kayak, dugout canoe, or motorized ferry boat, you may be spending some time on the water. Be very cognizant of the location of such items as life jackets and emergency inflatable rafts. I've seldom been on a third world boat of any type that had enough of these. It may sound selfish, but I'm going to ensure that if I'm traveling by boat, I get whatever safety equipment is available. If that means arriving early to get to the head of the line, I'll do it.

Inside the crowded ferry traveling between islands
off the Belizean coast. Note a lack of obvious
safety equipment.

Ocean passages between the mainland and outlying islands
can often be rough. I rode on one ferry to Utila Island in
Honduras that was nicknamed "*The Vomit Express.*" If you
have ever gotten seasick, dose yourself with an anti-nausea
medication before you board any boat.

Most over the counter anti-nausea meds have a side
effect of sedation. That might be useful on a very long boat
ride, but is often detrimental. When I don't want to sleep
on the boat I take a prescription (in the USA) anti-nausea
pill called ondansetron (Zofran). It works very quickly and
does not cause drowsiness. If you get sea sick, ask your
doctor to prescribe it for you before your trip. If he won't,
you'll probably be able to purchase it without a prescription
in most third world pharmacies. If ondansetron is not
available,   look   for   over-the-counter   anti-nausea
medications like Gravol or Dramamine. Some people also

report that eating foods containing ginger works exceptionally well for preventing motion sickness.

An additional remedy for nausea described in medical journals is to inhale the smell of rubbing alcohol. I keep alcohol wipes in my first aid kit to disinfect cuts. The same alcohol wipe can be held under the nausea patient's nose and inhaled. No one has discovered the mechanism by which this alcohol-smelling treatment works, but it often works very well in a fraction of the time it takes to digest a prescription anti-nausea pill.

You should also do your best to sit near a door or window. Besides providing a source of fresh air, the doors and windows will serve as escape routes in the event of a capsized boat. Third world boats are notoriously overloaded and prone to sinking. Looking back at past boating disasters, it is clear that passengers nearest to the exits had a much better chance of surviving the emergency.

No matter the size of the boat, one rule of thumb is to never have your luggage strapped to your body at any time. If the boat capsizes or you fall out with a full backpack, you'll sink to the bottom. Hand carry all your bags rather than strapping them to your body when on any vessel on the water.

If the boat strikes another object or begins to sink, follow the directions of the crew. They know best how to keep passengers safe. Stay on the sinking boat as long as possible. Even if you want to jump free to avoid being trapped, resist the urge. Only flee the vessel when you absolutely have to. Staying on the sinking boat as long as possible allows you to avoid hypothermia and the exhaustion that will eventually occur when you are swimming or treading water for an extended time period.

The Captain might give an "abandon ship" signal. The signal is seven short horn blasts followed by one long one. Jump overboard if you hear that cadence of blowing horns. Be sure to carry a life preserver and whatever type of emergency gear you can have on your person without causing you to sink. You might need that survival gear once you make it to land or in the event you are picked up by a life raft.

The sign outside the Thai ferry station encouraged wearing "jacket life" but there was no safety gear actually available on the boat.

Technology

"Suddenly you are five years old again. You can't read anything, you only have the most rudimentary sense of how things work, you can't even reliably cross a street without endangering your life. Your whole existence becomes a series of interesting guesses."
– Bill Bryson

I started my travel addiction relatively late in life. I first left US soil was when I was 29 years old. I went to Jamaica to attend my sister's wedding. Even though I was staying at an all-inclusive resort, it was still a decent experience. This was before the days of smart phones, text messages, or laptops that people actually carried with them. The resort didn't even have a computer that guests could use to send email. The only way I knew how to make contact back home was by using an old fashioned voice phone call from my cell phone, a cell phone that pre-dated even the "new" flip phone styles that were soon to come into favor.

Now keep in mind that I had never ventured outside of the USA before. I actually thought that cellular call charges were based on the distance between the two callers. I knew it was cheap to call home from Florida. Jamaica is only about 100 miles from Florida, so I figured that those calls would be cheap as well.

I called my girlfriend at home three times while I was in Jamaica. None of the calls was long. Each one probably averaged around 10 minutes. When I returned from the trip and opened my cell phone bill, I almost had a heart attack. I still remember the amount of the bill to this day: $973.00.

That was an expensive lesson learned. Now I've learned how to communicate in ways that won't break the bank. Read on for my tips on the cheap use of technology in third world countries.

In the last five to ten years, technological advances have made life much easier for travelers. The ubiquitous smart phone has virtually replaced paper guidebooks and city maps. Advances in computer reservation software internationally have made it simple to book hotels and flights without speaking to a reservation clerk or travel agent. In fact, most travel arrangements can now be made with smartphone apps. You no longer even need to visit an internet cafe to make your reservations. With a couple of button presses on your phone, you can accomplish in seconds what took days for your parents and grandparents.

The following are my recommendations with regard to using technology to plan your travel and while you are traveling. Like any technological advice, things change quickly. Prices change. Features are frequently added or removed. The advice I provide is accurate and useful at the time of this book's printing, but don't be surprised if the situation changes in the near future.

Phones – You will likely to be able to use your current phone plan in another country, but charges for minutes and data might be obscenely high. It is almost always better to get a local number when you travel. In most countries, you can buy replacement SIM cards for your phone. The cards cost $5-$40 and some come with minutes and data already included. You can add minutes to your card at most phone shops and occasionally at grocery stores. This will likely be the cheapest option if you are going to be in the country for a while.

In order to do that, you will need a phone that has a removable SIM card that is also "unlocked." If you bought a cell phone in the USA with a service plan, most likely it is "locked" and won't function with another carrier's SIM card.

If your phone is older or beyond its contract expiration date, most phone companies will unlock it remotely. It only requires filling out a form on your carrier's website or a phone call to customer service. When I got my most recent phone upgrade, I kept my older iPhone and had it unlocked so that I can use it with a local SIM card for international travel.

You can also buy unlocked cell phones that will accept foreign SIM cards on both Amazon and eBay.

You can get cell phones and SIM cards
anywhere...even places where there are more goats

in the road than cars. Note cell phone store in
background. (Egypt)

In some countries, it's illegal for foreigners to buy SIM
cards. Other countries require a national ID or voter
registration card to activate a new phone. If you go to a
store that won't sell you a SIM card or phone, go down the
street to a smaller "mom and pop" operation. For a couple
dollars extra, a lot of merchants are willing to overlook
some of the more burdensome government dictates.
Others will even register the phone in another person's
name for you for an extra charge.

Some countries will sell SIM cards to foreigners but may
require photo identification to do so. There are even some
locations that require two separate forms of identification
(like a passport and a driver's license). Until you know
the requirements where you are, it's a good idea to carry
your passport with you in your attempts to get your phone
working. It's a horrible feeling to spend 45 minutes trying
to explain what you need to a convenience store clerk who
doesn't speak English only to find that you can't complete
the transaction because you forgot your passport. Even
if they are breaking the law by illegally registering your
phone in someone else's name, they'll still ask to see your
passport. I don't understand the system, but that's how
most places do it.

Other countries (India, for example) even require that
you provide a 2"x2" photograph in order to purchase a SIM
card. It's always useful to have a couple of these photos
with you for border crossings, but you may need them for
telephone privileges as well.

There is one downside of purchasing SIM cards illegally.
The sometimes unscrupulous sellers may refuse to

properly register the cards with the government (if that is required) and your phone will suddenly stop working a day or two later. Don't buy your SIM cards from anyone on the street who you might not be able to find again if they scammed you. Buy only from legitimate brick and mortar (or tin and tar paper) buildings.

In some Latin American countries, SIM cards are sold attached to small plastic cards. The plastic card will have a code written on it. Don't throw away the card. You'll need that code every time you add additional minutes to your SIM card.

When you don't speak the language, purchasing a local SIM card can be a daunting task. I would recommend trying the mobile phone shops at a nearby airport or in the convenience stores located in the tourist sections of town. You are more likely to find an English speaking clerk in those places.

If you've decided to buy a local SIM card for your calls, take a quick look at the Too Many Adapters (https://toomanyadapters.com/buying-local-sim-cards/) blog. That website has a regular series about buying local SIM cards in third world countries. The articles provide all the possible options and discuss which work the best, are the easiest to purchase, and which cards provide the best value. It's well worth your time to do a little homework here before you attempt your purchase.

With an unlocked cell phone you can also purchase an "International SIM Card" here in the USA in advance of your travel. These cards work in up to 60 countries. Rates are not as good making local calls in country, but are likely cheaper than using a local SIM card when calling back to the United States. I think the local SIM card is the better option for the traveler who is planning on making the majority of his calls within the country he is visiting.

The international SIM card is good for anyone who wants to avoid paying extravagant roaming and long distance charges through their home cell company when making international calls. It is also a good option for the traveler who is visiting numerous countries in one trip and who doesn't want to spend extra time and money getting set up with a local SIM card in every different country he or she visits.

Troubleshooting SIM Cards- Depending on the type of cell phone you have and the country you are visiting, a local SIM card can generate lots of spam text messages that are both annoying and will quickly deplete your phone's battery. You may be able to change the settings on your phone by using the "SuperSim" menu to reduce the frequency of these messages. If this doesn't work, talk to the employees at the phone store where you bought your SIM card and they should be able to fix the problem for you.

In some countries, you will be asked for a security code to activate your new SIM Card. If the code isn't included with the card's packaging material, try "0000." That is the default code that many providers use.

If you have any additional problems, a quick visit to a mobile phone store will usually get the problem sorted out fairly rapidly.

If you don't want to go to the trouble of buying a new phone or SIM card, you can enable the Wi-Fi on your smartphone and use a service like Skype to call for free using the Wi-Fi available in most hotels. Wi-Fi is far more abundant (and almost always free) in third world countries than it is back in the USA.

Renting a local phone is an option as well. In many countries you can rent a new smartphone for somewhere in the neighborhood of $50 a week. That's a great option for people who currently carry locked cell phones or for folks who are only traveling for a short time. It's also the method used by high level business travelers who are visiting destinations (like China) where espionage is a serious problem. Rather than take the chance of getting their own smartphones infected with viruses, bugs, or tracking software, they will simply rent a local cell phone and use it exclusively when traveling.

One additional option for American travelers is the T-Mobile "Simple Choice" plan (https://www.t-mobile.com/optional-services/roaming.html).This plan extends your current minutes and data plan to more than 120 additional countries without any additional long distance, roaming, or data charges.

The plan isn't any more expensive than the options you may already be using and seems like an easy choice for the frequent traveler. I haven't used the service, but I have several friends who use it regularly. In Europe, Asia, and South America, data speeds are significantly slower than what you may be used to in America, but not so slow as to be annoying. Everyone I know who travels extensively and uses this cellular plan loves it.

For most American cell phones, you will have to dial 00, then the country code, then the local number you want to call to connect.

Preventing Phone Theft- Avoid using any expensive cell phone while walking down the street. Stop in a safe place if you need to use it. Snatching cell phones from distracted tourists is a very common tactic used by third world thieves.

If you are concerned about theft, make the screen saver/ sleep image on your cell phone a photograph of a piece of paper with your name, Email, and other contact information. Write "*Return to xxxx for a reward if found.*" Make the same photo the first one taken on your camera memory card as well.

Some of my traveler friends also rely on the free app/ program Prey Project (https://www.preyproject.com/). Prey is an anti-theft tracking software for your laptop, phone and tablet that lets you remotely locate, lock, and wipe your device if it is ever stolen, You do this by logging into a web platform where you can also trigger actions like sounding an alarm or show an onscreen message to let the thief know you're after him.

Travel Applications (Apps) for your Smart Phone or Computer– Apps like FourSquare, Yelp, and Around Me work in other countries. You can use them (with your hotel's free Wi-Fi to avoid data charges) to get good restaurant recommendations or directions.

You will definitely want to download the Google Maps App to your smartphone. The only downside is that it requires internet connectivity or Wi-Fi in order to work. While at your hotel (on free Wi-Fi) find a map of the area you would like to explore. Once you have it, tap on the 'info sheet' for any location and choose "*Save map to use offline.*" As long as you're logged into your Google account the map will be saved as an offline copy to your phone so that you can use it even when you aren't connected to the net. The copy will even sync across different devices.

If you prefer guided tours to reading maps, the Pocket Guide App (http://pocketguideapp.com/en) is what you need. This app uses your phone to provide professionally narrated audio walking tours through the most popular sections of major cities worldwide. You can download each city tour from home before you arrive in country and then just play them on your phone without needing an internet connection.

If being part of a tour isn't your idea of a good time, you can use the Kamino App (https://www.gokamino.com/) instead. This app crowd sources "urban hikes" from a team of contributors, giving a wide range of self-guided tours in cities around the world

Whats App (https://www.whatsapp.com/) is a popular application you will want to download as well. It is very popular in Asia and South America. It allows you to send chat messages and photos to your friends using free Wi-Fi. Text messages are the cheapest way for Americans to communicate overseas, but at $0 .25-$0.50 each, they can still get pricey. Whatsapp allows you to text and send pictures for free. Highly recommended.

Also remember that texts between two iPhones are free if using Wi-Fi and the iMessege system included on IOS 6.0 or later. To ensure you are using iMessage, verify that the texts you send between you and the other iPhone user are blue instead of the usual green in color. If you plan on only using free Wi-Fi to text other iPhones, turn off your SMS data because if you lose Wi-Fi signal, your phone will send the message as a text and you will be charged.

If you arrive in a foreign city and can't find anything to do, try looking for activities on the Viator phone app (https://m.viator.com/mobileapps/). Viator shows you the best deals for locally operated tours and activities in more than 800 locations worldwide. You will be amazed at all the fun options you may be missing.

Privacy Issues- Although the government of the United States has a miserable record with regards to spying on innocent people and intercepting both email and phone conversations of virtually every citizen, many Americans don't take notice. If government agents aren't knocking down their doors, they assume they are not being monitored.

That's not a good assumption either at home or in a foreign country. Especially as a foreigner in Communist countries, formerly Communist countries, and totalitarian regimes you should assume that your cell phone and computer are being constantly monitored. Don't give the governments of other countries an excuse to arrest you or solicit you for a bribe. Make sure you don't have any porn on your computer or phone and don't try to access porn websites in the countries you are visiting. That is illegal in many countries and possessing it isn't worth getting arrested. I shouldn't have to say it, but don't make any references to doing anything illegal over the phone or email. Even if you are joking, you could be arrested. A life sentence in a third world prison would ruin your vacation.

Some countries may ask to examine your computer at the airport before customs officials approve your visa. If you have exceptionally sensitive data on the computer, encrypt it with a password that you are unable to remember. Don't write the password down anywhere. Instead, email it to a friend. Delete the sent email from your email program.

When you cross into a hostile country and they demand the password, you can honestly say "I *don't know*." Tell them it is your company's computer and they have not yet given you the password. In the worst case scenario, the customs officials will seize your laptop, but without the password, they won't gain access to the data.

If you make it through customs without incident, email your friend using another device, get the password and then change it to one you will remember.

Even if you lock your computer up, you shouldn't expect that it will remain unmolested. In some countries, it is commonplace for hotel employees to give the country's secret police unlimited access to travelers' hotel rooms and safes. If you bring a computer, you should assume that it will be compromised. Although it probably isn't necessary for the common traveler, high level business travelers might consider bringing a cheap, essentially disposable, laptop computer on travels to totalitarian countries. The "disposable" laptop shouldn't have any trade secrets, new product designs, or sensitive communications stored on it in any location. It should be completely "clean" and contain only the information the traveler needs for the specific trip.

Travelers who employ this strategy recognize that the $200 cost of a cheap laptop computer is merely the cost of doing business in a country that will steal trade secrets in a heartbeat. Since viruses and malware can be so easily installed on an unattended computer, savvy business travelers will never connect their "disposable" laptops to company networks, instead selling them to locals for a reduced price just before leaving the country.

One other thing to note is that some websites will be completely blocked in the countries you visit. Social media sites like Facebook are often targeted for blockage, so are any sites that may be overtly critical of host country government policies. There are workarounds to this problem (like using VPNs or proxy servers), but the technology changes so rapidly that any recommendations

I make will likely be out of date in a matter of months. If your Facebook page won't open, use Google to search for a solution particular to your individual country. Or just go without Facebook for a while. I promise you won't die.

If social media sites are not blocked, you should assume that they are being monitored. Do not make any posts critical of the country you are visiting or any of its governmental officials. It is a huge security risk.

In June of 2014, an American citizen was arrested in Indonesia after making a remark critical of the government via his Twitter feed. One tweet got him jailed. In March 2015, an American citizen was jailed in the United Arab Emirates for a Facebook post he had made while in the United States calling his employers "filthy Arabs." When he returned to work in the UAE, he was arrested for "cyber slander" charges. Most recently, an American woman was arrested for "subversion" in Zimbabwe after calling the president a "sick man" on Twitter.

In a foreign country, you do not have the same freedom of speech that you do in the USA. The US Embassy won't be of much assistance when you are arrested for violating a local law.

In many former Soviet-Bloc countries, you will find "public phone charging" locations in tourist hotspots. They are places where you can plug in your smartphone to give it a quick charge. NEVER use these services. I have good information from a high level employee of an American three-letter agency that most of those sites will install surveillance malware on your phone.

Internet Access- If you can't find reliable free Wi-Fi access, head to the closest McDonalds restaurant or Starbucks coffee shops. I wouldn't normally advise you to patronize either of these American restaurants, because local options are almost always better, but both are known for having free fast WiFi all over the world.

You'll want to be careful about connecting to random Wi-Fi networks, especially in tourist areas. Identity thieves and computer criminals will often set up Wi-Fi networks just to steal tourists' identity information. Other criminals will attempt to steal your data from an already established Wi-Fi hotspot. Before connecting to any public Wi-Fi networks, check out the SkyCure Threat Map (https://maps.skycure.com/). Enter your location on the website and it will alert you of any known Wi-Fi threats in your area.

Another common scam for identity theft suspects is to name their scam network the same name as the hotel you are using. When you open up your browser you will see an open connection for something named "*Holiday Inn Guest Wi-Fi.*" Naturally, you click on it. It isn't really the hotel's Wi-Fi router. The hacker intercepts all the data transferred through the connection. Ask the hotel the name of the router to which you will be connecting. Take an extra second to verify that your connection is truly your hotel's network and not a hacker's creation.

While Wi-Fi access is very prevalent (and increasing daily) in most countries, in some places you'll still find that the only internet access in your hotel is through a wired connection. Look at your laptop before you leave. Newer laptops may not be equipped with an Ethernet port for a wired connection. If that describes your laptop, pick up a cheap USB to Ethernet adapter and Ethernet cord to throw in your laptop bag.

If you can't find Wi-Fi, don't despair. Most third world countries will also have internet cafes. Rates vary depending on the location, but are generally less than $1 an hour. You can check email or use Skype right from the public computer very cheaply. Most of the internet cafes have VOIP phone booths for very cheap international calling as well. The easiest place to find these internet cafes is to look in a city's large shopping malls. Almost all malls will have one.

The @ symbol is often difficult to find on Latin American keyboards. It's especially difficult to see on public internet cafe computers with worn off lettering on the keyboard. Try pressing the "alt" key and then the numbers 6 and 4. That usually works. If not, ask the attendant in the internet cafe. They will be used to having the same question from lots of other clueless tourists.

Don't forget that your Kindle reader (depending on the model) might have 3G internet browsing capabilities as well. Mine is pretty slow and the touchscreen keypad is horrible for typing long messages, but it will work fine for emergencies or occasional use. The Kindle is great for traveling because you can carry hundreds of books in the same amount of space that a single paperback book takes up in your pack. The internet access is just a bonus. The Kindle will work in most urban areas with cell coverage except a large part of Africa and a couple of countries in Central America.

The Kindle Reading app (https://www.amazon.com/kindle-dbs/fd/kcp) is also a useful addition for your smartphone or tablet. It's a handy backup location for reading downloaded guidebooks if you find yourself turned around or are looking for a nice place to eat or drink.

If you choose to carry a laptop computer during your travels, leave the laptop case at home. Your laptop is likely worth several months' salary for the residents of most developing nations. That makes it an attractive target for theft. Instead of using an obvious laptop case, carry the computer in a small backpack instead.

Make sure that you can access your bank account information online. You will want to periodically check on your accounts/credit cards from a trusted computer while you are overseas to guard against theft and fraud. ATM "skimmers" are endemic in some countries. Be alert and conscientious to check your account balances periodically to proactively ensure that your credit or debit cards haven't been used fraudulently. You can read additional ATM safety tips in my chapter on banking and money issues.

One other tip if you are traveling with your computer/tablet/phone: As of July 2014, certain foreign airport security may require you to power up your electronic devices before boarding international flights. Ensure that all your electronics are fully charged when you leave for the airport. If you can't show the security agent that your electronic device will power up, you may risk its confiscation or miss your flight. I personally wouldn't purchase any electronic items in the airport itself unless I was sure that the device came at least partially charged right out of the box. It wouldn't be a bad idea to pack a portable electronic charger as a backup plan if you have the space.

Cameras and Photographs- Expensive cameras are frequently targeted by thieves. Don't walk around with a high-dollar camera hanging around your neck. Besides being a tempting target for thieves, it also clearly identifies you as a tourist. Camera bags are also an obvious indicator. Carry your camera in your daypack or sling bag instead. Only pull it out when you need it. Be cautious about your camera strap as well. Often, camera straps will have the brand name of the camera to which they are attached embroidered on them. That's an ostentatious sign of wealth that some thieves can't resist. If you have an expensive camera with the brand name advertised on the strap, either cover the letters with tape or replace the strap with a generic model without any lettering.

Store your camera in a Ziploc plastic bag or dry bag when you are outside your hotel room. The bag will help protect it from an unexpected downpour as well as reduce condensation on the lens if you are transitioning from an air conditioned building into the hot weather outside. Adding a silica desiccant packet (like the ones that come in vitamin bottles) to the bag will also help reduce the condensation even more.

Always ask the locals for permission before taking their photographs, even if in a public location. Some indigenous cultures consider photos to be highly offensive or even in conflict with their religious beliefs. It's better to be safe than sorry. If you are in a tourist area, don't be surprised if the local you ask for a photograph demands a cash payment for the privilege. Some of the locals get asked for photos so often that they have turned to "modeling" as a career. Decide in advance if, and how much, you are willing to pay a local in order to get a photograph.

It's also very important to remember that police officers, the military, checkpoints, and government buildings should NOT be photographed without permission in third world countries. The military and police officers get very annoyed when you take their photographs. Cops have been known to steal your memory card or even your entire camera if you photograph something "sensitive." Don't do it.

Take extra caution to avoid taking photographs when police, military, or governmental officials are in the area.

Government employees are sensitive about potentially embarrassing infrastructure deficiencies and don't want you taking pictures of buildings, roads, or bridges in poor repair. The cops or government officials often use your camera as an excuse to extort a bribe. They see you taking photographs and then tell you that you need to buy a "camera permit" for your "illegal" camera. This is almost always a scam and an extortion attempt. Resisting paying the tax or fine may be a tedious or dangerous prospect. It's better to avoid the problem in the first place. Don't take photos of "military areas" or when obvious governmental employees are in the area.

Take time to frequently back up the photos that you take onto a web-based storage service or use multiple memory cards. Thieves like cameras. It's bad enough if your camera is stolen, but far worse if you lose all the photos you have taken of your trip.

If you don't have an e-reader and rely on old fashioned heavy paperback guidebooks, you may not want to carry the books around with you on your daily explorations. In addition to the book being bulky and heavy, it instantly identifies you as a clueless tourist when the locals see you reading it. Instead, use your camera or phone to take photos of the relevant guidebook pages. If you need to find some information about the part of the city you are exploring, just use the camera's zoom feature to read the photo of the guidebook page.

Parents traveling with minor children or people traveling with aging family members who might become lost or confused should take a picture of the child or parent in their care every day before leaving the hotel. Having a current photo documenting appearance and the clothing worn by the person will help immeasurably in the event your child or elderly relative becomes separated from you during the day.

Filing a missing person report with a police officer who doesn't speak your language is a difficult proposition. If you can show the police a current photo, say the word "lost" in the host country's language, and tell the cops where the person was last seen, it will make it much more likely that local emergency services will locate your missing relative.

Power Adapters and Chargers– Electricity will often be delivered through different kinds of plugs. You can buy travel adapters very cheaply. Research which plug your destination uses and then buy the adapter you need, ideally before you leave home. There are universal adapters that will fit every outlet in the world. To avoid the hassle of carrying numerous adapters with me while I travel, I find it easier to buy a single adapter that will work everywhere. Occasionally, hotels have adapters available to lend to their guests. If you forget your adapter, ask to borrow one at your hotel front desk. You can also purchase power adaptors (for a much higher price) at airport electronics stores.

The power supply in the United States is 120 volts. The rest of the world can vary anywhere between 100 and 240 volts, with the majority being in the 220-230 volt range. All electronics are sold with a label describing the type of power they can use. It's important to check this label because if you plug your 120 volt electronic gadget into a 240 volt power outlet in another country, you could damage the device, trip a breaker, or start a fire.

Most newer electrical devices will function with any type of power between 120 and 240 volts with the conversion being conducted within the device itself. The easiest travel solution is to only pack these types of devices. If you want to take some other gadget with a limited range of power functionality, you'll also need to pack a voltage converter so you don't blow it up.

If you are staying in a nicer hotel, don't forget to look at your TV for an emergency charging source. Newer TVs can have USB ports on the side. They can be used for charging phones, IPods, and tablets without needing an electrical adapter.

Health Issues in the Developing World

"The only society I like is rough and tough, and the tougher the better. There's where you get down to bedrock and meet real people."
-Robert W Service

Health and Medical Insurance- Travel medical insurance is a good idea. In fact, in my mind it is essential. Especially if you are traveling in remote locations, emergency evacuation insurance will ensure you can get to an adequate hospital relatively quickly without going bankrupt. Your US- based insurance coverage may not be valid in other countries. Even if illness or injury during travel is covered by your insurance company, foreign hospitals won't accept your insurance card. They will demand cash payment and you'll have to seek reimbursements later. Get a receipt for everything! I generally get my travel medical insurance from Insure My Trip (http://insuremytrip.com/)or Worldnomads (http://www.worldnomads.com). Medical coverage is generally quite inexpensive.

Recognize that many of the fun things that you'll want to do on your trip (like scuba diving, snorkeling, and mountain climbing) might not be covered by your travel insurance policy. Read the small print and make sure you are covered in case you are injured having fun during one of these "dangerous" activities.

Is water buffalo riding covered by travel insurance?

You should also check what insurance your credit card provides. Many cards offer theft protection, medical coverage, or trip cancellation insurance if you purchased items using the card. If your credit card already provides insurance coverage, you can save some money by not purchasing duplicate coverage

Prescription Drugs

"You can buy anything over the counter...if you choose the right counter."- Rachel Jones

Bring an extra supply of any prescription or over-the counter drugs that you regularly use. You want to ensure you have enough medication in the event you get delayed or stranded someplace without a pharmacy. Split the pills up so that if one of your bags is lost or stolen, you still have enough pills to get you through. Write down the generic names of all prescription drugs. Many foreign pharmacies do not use the same brand or trade names that are used in the United States.

Along with your list of prescription drugs, also write down a list of any drugs to which you might be allergic. It would be even better if you could write the local names of the drugs and the word "allergy" in the language of the country you are visiting. You can show this list to any medical personnel treating you or to any pharmacist from whom you are buying drugs to reduce the chance of any dangerous health complications.

I've never had any difficulties finding the drugs I need in foreign pharmacies as long as I had the generic name. If you are concerned about not being able to communicate with pharmacy staff about what drug you need, download the World Drugs Converter App to your phone. The app is usable offline and provides the local name for most drugs after you enter the USA brand name and the country where you are trying to find it.

Most drugs are sold without a prescription in third world countries. Each country has slightly different regulations and different drug formularies, but most pills can be obtained by merely asking the pharmacy counter clerk. No prescription necessary. Most pharmacies sell the drugs by individual pill and will just give you a small plastic bag or blister pack full of pills when you ask. Because of this practice, lots of Americans go to third world pharmacies to buy opiate pain pills or anti-anxiety pills like Valium or Xanax that are difficult or illegal to acquire at home without a prescription.

Be careful who is watching you make your purchase. Even in a narcotic naïve population, some criminals know the value of opiate pain pills on the street. They won't hesitate to rob you of your newly purchased drugs as you walk out of the pharmacy.

I learned this lesson a few years ago in Bolivia. I was in a pharmacy buying some altitude sickness medications and started to walk out with the bag in my hand. The pharmacist had a look of horror on her face as she stopped me. She told me in Spanish to hide the bag under my shirt. A gringo walking out of the pharmacy in a sketchy neighborhood in La Paz carrying pills is likely to get jacked. I avoided a potentially dangerous mistake due to a kind and street smart pharmacist.

The purchasing procedures in some larger pharmacies in Latin America are completely baffling. You stand in line and make your request to the clerk. She then writes your request down and gives it to another person who finds the drug and brings it to you for your inspection and/or approval. If you want it, the second clerk gives it to a third person, who then gives you a number and delivers the drug to the cashier. You get in line again at the cashier's station, give her your number and then she finally sells you the drugs. It always seems like about three steps too many for me, but that's how it works. If all of this is too confusing, just visit a small pharmacy with only one person working.

If you wear glasses, get your optician to write down your prescription for you. Take the prescription with you so that you can get glasses replaced quickly in a foreign country in case of breakage. Especially if you are traveling in Asia, optometrists can quickly make you a new pair of glasses while you wait. Prices will be far cheaper than they are at home as well. In some countries you can buy contact lenses in vending machines at larger grocery stores if you know your prescription.

Just like when buying food, go to pharmacies where you see lots of locals shopping. Avoid pharmacies that are on cruise ship docks or those who obviously cater to tourists. Those establishments are more likely to be selling counterfeit medication. In a tropical environment you should also look for a pharmacy that has air conditioning. Pills degrade more quickly in high temperatures. You don't want to but a drug that has been sitting on a shelf in 100 degree temperatures for six months before being sold.

In all larger third word cities, you will likely be able to find an English speaking doctor or hospital. Most guidebooks list these medical resources. Your embassy might also be able to help you locate an English speaking doctor. If all else fails, ask your hotel desk clerk for a recommendation. Larger hotels will have a doctor available or on call for hotel guests. You can also try to find a good hospital before you leave at the Hospitals Webinfometrics (http://www.hospitals.webometrics.info) website.

Basic First Aid Kits– I carry an extensive medical kit when I travel, but I also carry a smaller kit that I can throw in my sling bag when I'm doing something more adventurous than shopping. All the items inside my mini-kit are TSA-legal and small enough that they don't take up much room. Mine is carried in a small nylon pouch. Inside, I have the following:

  – A "snivel kit" with Band-Aids, steri-strips, over the counter meds (loperamide, ibuprofen, diphenhydramine) antibiotic ointment, and disinfectant wipes to clean out small cuts or scrapes
    – C.A.T. tourniquet.

– A Triangular bandage, carabiner, and key ring. The bandage can be used for many conditions. When I put the three together, I can make another tourniquet (http://www.youtube.com/watch?v=47yDBpyDCyM#t=15).

– Duct tape (longer lasting than medical tape)

– Petrolatum gauze (for dressing a sucking chest wound)

– Pressure Dressing

– Quick Clot Hemostatic Gauze

– Prescription pain meds, anti-nausea meds, and broad spectrum antibiotics

– Safety pins

– Gauze pads

-Water purification tablets

-Blister treatment or moleskin

– Caffeine pills. For those of us who are addicted to caffeine, it's useful to pack some Vivarin or No-Doz tablets into the medical kit. If you get stranded in a place where your morning coffee isn't available, taking a caffeine pill will eliminate all of the caffeine withdrawal symptoms you would otherwise be forced to endure.

Pre-packaged first aid kits purchased at a store or online are usually almost useless. They seldom contain the gear you need for a serious emergency and are often filled with superfluous items that you will never use. It's almost always more cost effective to make up a kit yourself.

Take a look at where you are traveling and what the likely risks are. If you are staying in towns or cities, you will be able to buy any first aid supplies you need at the drugstore. You may not have to carry anything at all (except diarrhea pills, you may not have time to get to the store to buy those). A small kit like the one mentioned above will be more than enough to handle any of the common emergencies you might encounter in an urban environment.

Advanced Medical/Trauma Kit- If you are traveling to a violent city or in an area far away from medical attention, it would be prudent to put together your own more advanced medical kit. If you are constructing your own kit, rather than buying a fancy medical bag, consider using a small Tupperware container. It is crush resistant, durable, waterproof, and cheap.

You'll want plenty of extra bandaging and wound cleaning supplies. Common lacerations and abrasions are the most likely injuries you will experience or treat. Band aids, gauze pads, roller gauze, tape, and co-flex will be used often. You'll want something to clean the wounds before covering them as well. Pack some antiseptic wipes or alcohol prep pads for this purpose.

A topical antibiotic is extremely useful. Get the ointment rather than the cream if possible. It stays on better in tropical conditions. More information about topical antibiotic selection is available under the "wound care" subheading in the "Medical Conditions" chapter.

You will want to pack at least one broad spectrum oral antibiotic in your medical kit. In travel medicine, we generally want to do the opposite of what is done in the doctor's office at home. When you are at home, the doctor will perform a culture to specifically identify the bacteria present. With that information, the doctor can prescribe the best antibiotic to kill the individual type of bacteria without causing additional damage to your body or contributing to antibiotic resistance.

In an austere environment where lab tests are not available, and there is no definitive medical care, it makes the most sense to carry a single antibiotic that will kill almost everything so that you don't have to rely on bacterial testing that you won't be able to obtain in the jungle of a foreign country.

Most travel doctors will prescribe an antibiotic from the fluoroquinolone family for this purpose. Most commonly prescribed oral fluoroquinolone antibiotic is ciprofloxacin (Cipro- 500 mg two times per day) or levofloxacin (Levaquin- 750 mg one time per day.) Both antibiotics are prescribed for up to three days to kill any traveler's diarrhea of bacterial origin. They also have coverage for skin, urinary tract, and respiratory bacterial infections. In some South East Asian countries, azithromycin (500 mg one time per day) is substituted for the ciprofloxacin because of local resistance to the antibiotic.

One of those antibiotics should form the basis of your travel drug supply. The only gap in their coverage is a type of bacteria called "anaerobic bacteria." Ciprofloxacin and levofloxacin do not work well on anaerobes (bacteria that live without oxygen, often in the digestive tract.) In the case of an anaerobic infection (Dysentery, Giardia, penetrating abdominal trauma), most doctors prefer metronidazole (500 mg three times per day.) Don't drink alcohol if you are taking this medication.

With a fluoroquinolone and metronidazole, you should be well equipped to handle about 90% of the infections you may encounter in your austere travel. Do some research before you leave. Talk to your doctor about dosing and possible allergies. There are side effects when you take these drugs and they can make some conditions worse.

Know exactly when they are appropriate and when they are not before you take anything.

Vaccines- Immunizations can be important to remain healthy, but they won't protect you against all diseases. Furthermore, they won't do anything to protect you against the most common cause of traveler death: traffic accidents. I must admit, I'm rather cavalier about getting my recommended vaccines. I've obtained some, but I certainly don't follow most doctors' recommendations.

I can't give medical advice; I can only share my own experiences. I've never had any problems with any of the diseases that most travelers get vaccinated for. You should research the issue yourself and make an informed decision. Read some books and talk to your healthcare provider before you follow my (or anyone else's) lead.

Remember, if you do choose to get vaccinated, some vaccines require a certain period of time to allow your body to build up immunity. Some vaccines require multiple injections over a longer period of time. Plan ahead. Get your vaccines at least four to six weeks before your departure date. Some may take even longer to be effective. Again, research each vaccine before your trip.

The CDC Travelers' Health Website Tool (http://wwwnc.cdc.gov/travel) is a handy, one-stop location to find out exactly what prophylactic medications and/or vaccines you will need for each country you visit. Simply enter the country name and a few other details about your trip from a drop-down menu and the CDC will provide its medical recommendations.

The Vaccinations App by Medicus 42 GmbH is an easy way to keep track of the vaccinations you've received and when you got them. If you are exposed to a disease in a foreign country, the local doctors or hospitals will need this information to make the best treatment decisions.

American Society of Tropical Medicine provides an online directory of tropical medicine and traveler health clinics if you need to find a travel doctor in advance of your trip.

Specific Medical Conditions

The advice given in this chapter is based on my personal experience, the advanced medical training I've received, and evidence from current medical literature. Application of the information I provide is at your own risk. Use common sense and discuss the issues with your personal medical advisor if you have any concerns. Don't do anything stupid that will have a lasting effect on your body or brain.

One of the more challenging aspects to managing your health in a third world country is deciding when you need real medical attention and when you can get by with self-treatment. No one wants to go to the doctor in a foreign country or navigate a completely different health care system. I get it. But sometimes you may have to suck it up and see a professional.

I have given specific recommendations for a variety of ailments below, but I can provide some good general guidelines as well. If you experience any of the following, seek professional medical treatment:

- A fever lasting more than 48 hours, especially in areas where Malaria or Dengue is present
- Shortness of breath (beyond lack of altitude acclimation) or chest pain
- Bloody urine or diarrhea
- Orthopedic injuries with severe or untreatable pain or notable deformity

This is by no means an all-inclusive list, but it covers the basics. Having accompanied numerous traveling companions to third world hospitals and medical clinics over the years, I have been pleasantly surprised at the professionalism and inexpensive treatment my friends have received. Get medical care if you need it.

The rest of the chapter provides more in-depth medical advice about a variety of common ailments suffered by travelers. It is organized alphabetically by condition.

Allergies

If you have allergies at home, you are likely to have them just as bad (or worse) when traveling. Try to avoid any specific allergen and pack the antihistamine that works best for you. I prefer the non-drowsy, longer acting antihistamines like loratadine (Claritin), but diphenhydramine (Benadryl) works well and quickly. The only downside is that most people get drowsy using it. That side effect can be useful in other situations however. If you have insomnia because of time zone changes, a couple of Benadryl pills at bed time can help you sleep.

If you have severe allergic reactions that lead to anaphylaxis, you should carry an epinephrine auto-injector with you. Your doctor will be able to write you a prescription for one. The most commonly prescribed brand is the "Epi-Pen." No matter which brand you get, you'll want the two-dose model. In a significant number of anaphylaxis cases, a second dose of epinephrine is necessary. Standard dosing regimens are one dose as soon as the severe reaction is noticed, followed by a second dose five minutes later if symptoms aren't reduced or get worse.

Along with the epinephrine, military field medical protocols call for 50 mg of diphenhydramine (Benadryl), 10 mg of dexamethasone (Decadron), and 150 mg of ranitidine

(Zantac). Each of these drugs helps to control a different part of the anaphylactic reaction. If you are in an austere setting and lack epinephrine, try any combination of the drugs above. It may not work, but it's worth a shot. Anything is better than dying with an obstructed airway due to an allergic reaction. Even if you get yourself or your patient stabilized using an Epi-Pen and/or a combination of the drugs listed above, you'll still want to get him to a hospital as soon as possible for evaluation.

Altitude Sickness

If you are traveling in mountainous country above 10,000 feet of elevation, you should be prepared for altitude sickness. Susceptibility to altitude sickness is mostly genetic. Age and fitness levels have little effect on whether or not you get sick. Most altitude sickness is caused when you ascend too fast for your body to acclimate. General guidelines to reduce the chance of altitude sickness above 9,000 feet (2,750 m) are to increase sleeping altitude no higher than 1,600 feet (500 meters) per day, and plan an extra day for acclimatization every 3,300 feet (1,000 meters). Most people will be acclimated to high altitude in three to five days.

Some of the symptoms of altitude sickness may be caused by dehydration. When there is less oxygen in the air, your respiration rate increases. That means you will lose more water by breathing more rapidly. You have to drink additional fluids to replace the water lost by increased breathing.

The first indications of altitude sickness are often a headache, lack of desire to eat, and a general feeling of malaise. The altitude sickness can progress to creating uncontrollable nausea and vomiting, confusion, and lack of coordination. If you notice these symptoms, descend.

The symptoms will disappear within a few hours at a lower altitude.

If descent isn't an option, there is evidence that taking Ginko Biloba or ibuprofen (Advil or Motrin- 600 mg. every eight hours) can reduce altitude sickness. Locals in South America will chew coca leaves or drink coca tea to prevent or treat altitude injuries. I've tried it and it worked pretty well for me. Chewing the leaves or drinking the coca tea is not the same thing as using cocaine. There is no euphoria caused by the unprocessed leaves. At best, it provides a stimulant affect that is similar (for me) to drinking a cup of coffee. Don't chew the coca leaves if there is a chance of having to take a drug test back home.

The CDC recommends using acetazolamide (Diamox) prophylactically if you ascend very rapidly or have a history of altitude sickness. Dosage is 125 mg twice per day or 250 mg twice per day if your body weight is greater than 100 kilograms (220 pounds). Avoid taking acetazolamide if you are allergic to sulfa-containing drugs.

More severe cases of altitude illness (called Acute Mountain Sickness or AMS in the medical literature) can develop into high altitude cerebral edema (brain swelling) or high altitude pulmonary edema (swelling and liquid in the lungs). Both of these conditions can be fatal. If you have uncontrolled coughing at altitude or if you start losing coordination and cognitive function, you must descend. If descent isn't an option, the CDC recommends taking dexamethasone (Decadron) as a treatment. Dosage is four (4) mg every six (6) hours. I carry both acetazolamide and dexamethasone in my medical kit when I'm traveling in higher altitudes.

If you want more information about treatment and prevention of altitude illness, please visit the CDC's Altitude

Illness page at http://wwwnc.cdc.gov/travel/yellowbook/
2014/chapter-2-the-pre-travel-consultation/altitude-
illness

Miserable and suffering from horrible AMS at the
top of Mt. Kilimanjaro

Animal Bites

Be exceptionally cautious around any wild animals or
strays. The feral dog and cat populations in some third
world countries are astoundingly high. Very few of these
animals have been vaccinated and some carry transmissible
diseases. The stray dog visiting your restaurant table or the
stray cat on the roadside may look cute, but it's not worth
the risk to pet it.

If you are bitten by an animal in a third world country,
clean the wound copiously with soap and water, disinfect

it with whatever is available (alcohol, hydrogen peroxide, betadine) and seek medical attention immediately.

If you are more than a day's travel away from a hospital or doctor, consider starting a course of antibiotics. Speak with your health care advisor before you leave and get his/her recommendation, but a common medical recommendation would be to use Augmentin (amoxicillin/ clavulanic acid). It is a first line treatment for most animal bites. Anyone with a penicillin allergy should choose another antibiotic as there is common cross sensitivity between penicillin and Augmentin.

If you are far away from medical attention, do not close the bite wound, even if you are carrying sutures or staples. Even if you've thoroughly flushed the wound and cleaned out any debris, there is a high chance that the animal's teeth have pushed some bacteria deep inside the wound. It may not be possible to remove these bacteria even after thorough cleaning and disinfection. If you close the wound with sutures (or even steri-strips) you will be allowing the bacteria to grow and create a pocket of infection, called an abscess, further increasing your risk of a serious systemic infection. Cover the wound to keep it clean, but don't bring the skin edges together.

Bed Bugs

Bed bugs are a huge problem in third world countries. I've been lucky and only experienced them once (in a hostel in Bogota, Colombia). They are very hard to see. Usually your first indication that they are sharing your habitation is when you feel their itchy, annoying bites as you sleep.

As soon as you get into your hotel room, you should check for bed bugs. Resist the urge to place your luggage on the hotel room bed. If the bed is infested, the bugs may crawl into your baggage and reappear once you get back home. Place your luggage on another piece of elevated furniture instead of the bed or the floor. Turn on all the lights in the room and grab your flashlight.

Lift the sheets off of all beds and check the mattress. If it is infested with bedbugs it may have small blood stains near the mattress seams where the bedbugs live. You may also see pinprick blood stains on the sheets. In addition to seeing evidence of blood, there are a few other signs of bed bug infestation. Check the mattress, screw holes in the bed, under the mattress, and under the bed itself for:

- The reddish brown skin that the bed bugs shed during their growth stages
- Bed bug eggs.
- Wet, sticky, sweet-smelling, dark-colored residue that may be bed bug droppings

If you find evidence of bed bugs, change rooms quickly and wash all of your clothing and backpack in very hot water. Some insect repellents can keep them away and a tightly woven sleep sheet placed over the top of the hotel/hostel bedding may help prevent their bites, but these are temporary solutions at best.

An unconventional, but occasionally effective, emergency solution exists for a bed bug or flea exposure. If you believe you have small biting insects in your clothes and don't have access to laundry facilities or insecticide, you can hold the clothing item in the exhaust of a running car or bus for a few minutes. The carbon monoxide in the vehicle exhaust will kill the bugs. You'll smell like diesel fumes all day, but it's better than being bitten by fleas and bed bugs.

Be especially cautious to keep your dirty laundry bundled up tightly. Recent research indicates that bedbugs are attracted to dirty clothes. Keep your soiled laundry in a tightly closed dry bag in order to avoid bringing bed bugs home with you.

Even with the best precautions, it's possible to bring a few unnoticed, hitchhiking bed bugs back home in your luggage. You plop your suitcase down on your bed and begin to unpack. The bedbugs make their way into your bed and either lay eggs or breed. Now you have a serious problem.

To combat stowaway bedbugs, I've recently been throwing a couple Raid brand bed bug detector/traps into my luggage. These are small plastic traps filled with bed bug bait. When the bedbugs crawl into the trap to eat the bait, they are locked inside. There is a clear window so you can easily see if any bedbugs have been caught.

You can place these traps under your bed anywhere and know if your room has bed bugs. Checking the trap as soon as you get home lets you know if your luggage has been infested. If so, you can avoid bringing your bags into the house until they have been fumigated. It's cheap insurance to avoid a costly fumigation treatment of your entire house if you allow the bed bugs to reproduce. The only downside is that the traps will make your clothing smell like insecticide.

While bed bug infestation can be a serious problem in developing countries, occasionally, the solution is worse than the problem. In some countries, toxic chemicals are used to kill bed bugs and other annoying insects. Without regulation, sometimes these chemicals kill more than just bugs. More than 20 Western tourists in Asian countries were killed by hazardous insecticides sprayed in their hotel rooms in 2009. If you find yourself having difficulty breathing, vomiting, becoming dizzy, or notice a blue colored tinge to your fingernails shortly after entering your hotel room, seek fresh air and get out of the room quickly. You may be experiencing a life threatening insecticide poisoning.

Bleeding

Direct pressure is the standby solution for severe bleeding. It works well and will stop bleeding about 95% of the time. For it to work, direct pressure must be hard and sustained. That limits the rescuer to treating only one casualty at a time. It also may be difficult to perform on oneself, while exhausted, or while you are carrying your casualty to safety.

The solution to that problem is to use a pressure dressing. These dressings are merely a way to hold pressure on a wound with a bandage rather than directly from the rescuer. There are lots of good pressure bandages on the market. I carry the Thin Cinch or the Mini Compression Dressing by H&H Associates when traveling because they take up less space than most others. Any commercial pressure (Israeli, H-Bandage, Cinch Tight, or Oleas) bandage will work fine, however. Pick one and buy a few extra to practice with before throwing it in your kit.

Thin Cinch Pressure Dressing

You should also practice improvising pressure dressings by using gauze pads combined with roller gauze, duct tape, or ace bandages in case you are in a mass casualty situation where you have more injuries than commercially manufactured pressure bandages.

For some wounds, a pressure dressing won't be enough to stop the bleeding. That's where the tourniquet comes into play. Tourniquets were once demonized and treated as a last resort. Recent military experience in Iraq and Afghanistan has changed medical thinking on this previously controversial practice. The military is now teaching aggressive tourniquet use and cites it as the single most successful battlefield medical intervention to prevent death from extremity bleeding. Not a single soldier in our war on terror has lost a limb from a properly placed commercial tourniquet.

Use a tourniquet in these three instances:

– When bleeding can't be stopped with direct pressure or a pressure dressing

  – As a first line whenever you see spurting arterial blood from an extremity

  – On any traumatic amputation

Place the tourniquet as high on the limb as possible and crank it down until both the bleeding stops and there is no pulse distal (downstream of) the tourniquet. In approximately 20% of cases, a second tourniquet may be needed to stop bleeding. Place it directly adjacent to the first tourniquet and crank it down. Do not loosen or remove either tourniquet for any reason. There are protocols for removing tourniquets or converting them to other dressings, but these are outside the scope of this book. If you can get to definitive medical care in less than six hours, let the doctors remove the tourniquet.

The military uses the CAT Tourniquet and SOFT-T Tourniquet. I like the CAT the best, but the TK-4 and SWAT-T elastic tourniquets may be useful for travelers as they pack down to the smallest size.

North American Rescue CAT Tourniquet

Also learn how to improvise a tourniquet using a triangular bandage (or other piece of cloth) and a windlass. Don't use a shoestring or zip ties. Make sure your improvised tourniquet is 1-2″ wide for optimal effectiveness and to reduce the chance of injury to your patient. Watch the short video by my late friend Paul Gomez at https://www.youtube.com/watch?v=47yDBpyDCyM about making a simple improvised tourniquet using a key ring and carabiner. If you don't have the key ring or carabiner, use whatever you can find as a windlass and hold or tape it in place.

What if the bleeding is from a location where a tourniquet can't be placed? If the wound is on the shoulder, the neck, or the groin, you may not be able to use a tourniquet. In that case, you will need a hemostatic agent. These are basically chemical blood stoppers. There have been several generations of them over the years, but the current crop stops bleeding well and does not produce the extreme heat that earlier varieties did.

While several options are likely to be effective, I would limit my selection to Quick Clot Combat Gauze or Celox Trauma Gauze. There is a brief training video at https://www.youtube.com/watch?v=Cj4gSDivxt0 covering how to use the hemostatic gauze. Caution for those with weak stomachs; there is a lot of blood in the video.

If you don't have hemostatic gauze, pack the wound in the same way with roller gauze (Kerlix) or gauze pads.

Blisters

During third world adventure travel, blisters regularly become a problem. Most people simply walk more on holiday than they do at home. Walking in hot weather, wearing new shoes, or getting your feet wet can all cause blisters.

It's easier to prevent a blister than it is to treat it. Make sure that all new shoes or boots are adequately broken in at home before your trip. Avoid creating blisters by eliminating any "hot spots;" areas where the shoes or the socks are applying friction to the skin on the feet. One of the easiest ways to prevent hot spots from forming is to wear two pairs of socks, with a lighter, thinner liner sock underneath your normal pair of socks. The second pair of socks changes the point of friction from one where a single sock is rubbing your skin to one where the two pairs of socks rub against each other. Another handy tip is to apply antiperspirant to your feet before donning your socks. Moisture can cause friction. Reducing the amount of sweat your feet produce will reduce the chance of getting a blister.

When you feel a hot spot forming or notice an area that is being irritated by friction, take your socks and shoes off. Dry your feet. Change socks if you have a spare pair. You may also want to apply a piece of duct tape to the skin where the hot spot is forming. The sock will then rub the tape rather than your tender skin. I will often preemptively apply duct tape to my heels and the balls of my feet underneath my socks if I know I'll be walking a lot.

Once the blister forms, it's better to keep it intact than to pop it. Popping it reduces the cushion that the blister is providing to your irritated skin. A hole in the skin also provides a mechanism to allow bacteria to enter your body and create an infection.

Cover the blister with moleskin or a Blisto-ban dressing to reduce further irritation. If using moleskin, cut out a piece of the center of the moleskin patch that corresponds to the size of your blister. Folding the moleskin patch in half will make cutting the hole easier. Place the hole in the moleskin around the blister so that it cushions the area but doesn't put any pressure on the blister itself.

If the blister is very large or painful, you may have to pop it. Disinfect the skin on the blister with an alcohol wipe. Disinfect a needle or safety pin with another wipe or by heating it in a flame. Push down on the blister until all the fluid is moved to one side. Puncture the blister on the side where the fluid is amassed at a point where the blister is just starting to rise from around the healthy skin. Express all the fluid and then apply a dab of antibacterial ointment.

Some experienced travelers will replace the antibacterial ointment with a small amount of superglue instead. The glue burns for a short time, but works well to seal up the blister, prevent infection, and prevent the blister roof from tearing off and exposing raw flesh. Cover the blister with an adhesive bandage or a non-stick gauze pad and tape after the glue dries.

Constipation

Unfamiliar foods, combined with dehydration and disgusting toilet facilities can lead a traveler to experience long-term constipation. If you find that you can't defecate, the condition is almost always caused by dehydration in travelers. Start drinking a lot more (a half ounce of water per pound of body weight per day at minimum) and the problem will likely resolve itself in a day or two.

You can also increase your fiber intake and eat more fruit (after ensuring the fruit is washed in clean water or peeled) to speed the process along. If that doesn't work, try taking an over the counter stool softener. I think the stool softener is a better option than harsher laxatives when your travel bathroom availability schedule isn't consistent.

It's also important to recognize that constipation aggravates any pre-existing rectal conditions like hemorrhoids. When constipated, the straining necessary to defecate can rupture hemorrhoids or other blood vessels in the rectum. You may see blood in the toilet or on the toilet paper after using the bathroom. Don't freak out if you see some blood in the toilet water absent any other symptoms. You probably don't have any serious tropical diseases. You just need to drink more water.

Cystitis (Bladder or Urinary Tract Infection)-

One of the more common medical complaints from third world travelers (mostly female) is a urinary tract infection.

Strange bacteria combined with poor hand washing, inadequate hydration, increased sexual activity, and "holding" urine as long as possible because of lack of availability of adequate restroom facilities are all causative factors.

Symptoms of a UTI consist of burning or painful urination, foul smelling urine, and an increased frequency and urgency of urination. The majority of women have experienced a UTI at some time in their past and can readily recognize the symptoms.

Occasionally the UTI can be eliminated by consuming copious amounts of fluid and/or an acidic beverage such as cranberry juice. Many antibiotics will quickly resolve the condition. Almost all commonly-carried travelers' antibiotics will kill the E. coli bacteria that cause most urinary tract infections.

Bactrim, ciprofloxacin, azithromycin, and nitrofurantoin are antibiotics commonly prescribed for UTIs. Over the counter phenazopyridine (Pyridium) tablets will help reduce the pain from the infection until the antibiotics kill all the bacteria causing the infection.

Seek professional medical attention when you have the symptoms of a UTI along with severe back or flank pain, a fever, or blood in the urine.

Dental Emergencies

As you will likely be eating in third world countries, there's always the possibility that you will crack a tooth or lose a filling. You may even have more traumatic dental emergencies if you smash your face while rock climbing or get in a car crash. In my experience, quality dental care is even harder to find than good medical care in rural third world countries. If you are going to be traveling for a long period of time, it would be a good idea to get your teeth checked by a dentist before you leave. Fix anything that needs to be fixed at home so that you are less likely to need a dentist on your trip.

The atmospheric pressure changes caused by air travel, scuba diving, or high altitude mountaineering can make existing dental conditions more painful. If you plan on doing any of these activities on your trip, you'll want to make doubly sure that you get a clean bill of health from your dentist before you travel.

In my medical kit, I carry a few dental supplies as well. I carry dental wax, temporary filling material, and an anesthetic like Anbesol or Orajel. These items don't take up much space but may make your life much more comfortable if you have any dental related emergencies. Most of these items are tough to find in rural pharmacies.

If you have a toothache that is caused by a cracked tooth or a filling that has fallen out, you can numb the tooth with a small piece of cotton soaked in the anesthetic solution. Place the cotton in the crack or void with a small pair of tweezers or a toothpick. If commercial anesthetic isn't available, you may be able to find oil of cloves in the supermarket. The active ingredient in oil of cloves is eugenol, which acts as a potent anesthetic in the mouth. Be cautious about using too much. Pure clove oil can burn the tongue or gums. Use it on the teeth only. Taking ibuprofen (Advil or Motrin up to 800 mg every eight hours) will help control the pain as well.

If the dental pain is caused by an abscess in the gum or under the tooth, this strategy won't be very effective. You need to find a dentist to have the abscess drained and take prescription antibiotics. In an emergency situation where you can't make it to the dentist for several days, it may be helpful to empirically treat the abscess with your own antibiotic supply. Penicillin, amoxicillin, and clindamycin are antibiotics commonly used to treat dental infections. Talk to your dentist before your trip about antibiotic options and indications.

If you have a broken tooth or lost crown, filling the void with soft dental wax or a temporary filling material like Cavit or Tempanol will help ease the pain and hold you over until you can get professional attention. Use a plastic coffee stir stick or something flat like a Popsicle stick to apply the temporary filling material. Have the patient bite down on the material to mold it to the individual bite pattern and then remove any excess material before it dries. This operation is difficult to do by oneself. Another person can do the work much easier for you.

If you are unlucky enough to have a tooth knocked out, stop the bleeding by biting down on a couple gauze pads for several minutes. A tea bag can also be used as a mild astringent to stop the bleeding. Find the tooth and rinse it off gently. Re-implant the tooth in the mouth if the tooth has been out for less than 30 minutes. There is some chance that the tooth will be functional (after a root canal) if you do this. Get to a dentist to secure the tooth as soon as possible.

If you can't place the tooth back in the mouth, store it in sterile saline solution or milk in order to transport it to the dentist.

Diarrhea

A two year survey of 784 Americans traveling overseas (published in the *Journal of Travel Medicine*) found that 64% had some type of illness on their trip. Each day of travel increased the chance of getting sick by a little over 3%. The single most common reported illness was diarrhea, affecting 46% of the travelers. When you look at the fact that somewhere around half of all travelers develop a food-borne illness abroad and compare that to the rate of food-borne illness in the United States in any given year (0.5% of the population), you'll see that there is a very significant risk of getting travelers' diarrhea from the food that you consume during your travels. The good news is that even though lots of travelers get sick, very few actually die from their illnesses. Out of all the travelers who die abroad, only 4% die from communicable diseases or infections.

Traveler's diarrhea is a common complaint in third world countries. Sometimes it is caused by a virus and sometimes by bacteria. Occasionally, it is caused by a parasite. This isn't a medical reference book and I am not a doctor, but I can pass on some of the recommendations I've learned in the numerous military and wilderness medical classes I've taken over the years. As always, do your own research and/or talk to a medical professional before taking any drug.

Before making any efforts to control the diarrhea, honestly assess whether it must truly be controlled. Is it a couple of loose stools a day or is it five trips to the bathroom every hour combined with agonizing stomach cramps? Are you sitting by your hotel pool or are you scheduled for a 20-hour bus ride? Most traveler's diarrhea will resolve itself within 72 hours given adequate hydration. If you don't really need to control your bowels, it may be safest to let nature take its course.

If you decide you want to stop the diarrhea, the first step is by using loperamide (Immodium). This is an over-the-counter medicine in almost every country. Take four milligrams (usually two pills) at the first onset of diarrhea and then two milligrams (one pill) after every subsequent loose stool for a maximum of 16 total milligrams per day.

Do not take Immodium if you have bloody stool or a fever. In that case, get to a hospital as soon as possible.

With any diarrhea, it's important to stay hydrated. Drink at least two glasses of clear fluid (not containing alcohol or caffeine) for each bowel movement. This should be a minimum guideline. If you are seriously dehydrated or have severe diarrhea, you will need to drink even more.

An even better course of action is to mix an electrolyte replacement powder into your (disinfected) water or drink a half-strength sports drink like Gatorade. The sugar and salt in these mixtures will actually enhance fluid absorption in the intestines when you have diarrhea. You can make a homemade oral rehydration salt mixture by adding two teaspoons of sugar and a quarter teaspoon of salt to an eight-ounce glass of water. The mixture may not taste great, but it will help keep you hydrated.

Avoidance of dehydration is even more important for those travelers who are taking diuretic medications (water pills) for their chronic disease conditions. The most common example is Lasix (furosemide), taken for certain heart conditions. Diuretics will exacerbate the effects of dehydration. If you are taking them and notice that you are getting dizzy when standing from a seated or lying position, seek medical attention. You may need IV re-hydration and an analysis of your electrolyte levels to ensure you don't end up with more serious health concerns.

Immodium will solve most problems. If it doesn't work, military medical protocols (when they are in the field and don't have access to lab tests) call for dosing with either a fluoroquinolone antibiotic (Cipro or Levaquin) or azithromycin (Z-Pack) for three days. If you still have diarrhea after three days of the fluoroquinolone treatment, switch to metronidazole (Flagyl) for up to 10 more days. If it is a bacterial infection, it should be gone after completion of this protocol. Remember, don't drink alcohol while taking metronidazole.

Many family physicians in the USA will write a prescription for ciprofloxacin (Cipro) for traveler's diarrhea before you leave. If your doctor won't, it is easy to get once you arrive in the country. In most third world pharmacies, prescriptions aren't necessary. Just walk up to the pharmacist and tell him or her exactly what you need.

You can purchase almost any drug you want (without a prescription) over the counter in developing countries. This is the tincture of opium I found on a drug store shelf in Thailand.

If you want more information about treatment and prevention of traveler's diarrhea, please visit the CDC's Travelers' Diarrhea advice page at http://wwwnc.cdc.gov/travel/yellowbook/2014/chapter-2-the-pre-travel-consultation/travelers-diarrhea

Fevers (Dengue and Chikungunya)

Many travelers are aware of and (rightfully) concerned with catching malaria in their travels. But few travelers know about other common diseases spread by mosquitoes in tropical countries. Dengue Fever (also known as "Bonebreak Fever") and Chikungunya are both spread by the bite from an infected mosquito. The mosquitoes that spread Dengue Fever are from a different genus than those that spread malaria.

While modern anti-malarial drugs are quite effective at preventing and treating a malarial infection, there are no such drugs or vaccines to prevent Dengue or Chikungunya. The only thing a traveler can do to avoid the infection is to avoid being bitten by the mosquitoes that carry it. In areas where Dengue is endemic, travelers should ensure that their accommodations have window screens and sleep under a mosquito net at night. During the day and evening, exposed skin should be treated with an insect repellent containing a 20%-30% solution of DEET.

Symptoms of Dengue typically start four to seven days after the mosquito bite. They present with sudden onset of a high fever, headache (most commonly behind the eyes), joint pain, vomiting, and a spotted rash on the torso (in 50%-80% of patients). As noted above, there are no drugs effective for treating the infection. Treatment should consist of maintaining adequate hydration status and treating symptoms with NSAIDs and anti-nausea medication.

Most infections will last between two and seven days. If patients have worsening abdominal pain, continual vomiting, an enlarged liver (which looks like a distended abdomen), mucosal bleeding, or severe lethargy they should be taken immediately to the hospital. If these severe symptoms are present, mortality can be as high as 26% without treatment. If the severe symptoms are not present, mortality is less than 5%.

Chikungunya has symptoms similar to Dengue, occurring three to seven days after the mosquito bite. No spotted rash will be present. Joint pains will be extensive, but often limited to the hands and feet. Treatment is the same; supportive care only.

Fractures and Dislocations

Breaking bones or dislocating joints are not common occurrences among travelers, but these injuries can happen. Their frequency increases if you undertake adventure sports like rock climbing, rappelling, horseback riding, and sky diving. Fractures are usually diagnosed by obvious deformities, pain, swelling, discoloration, and loss of use. In reality, you likely won't be able to distinguish between a fracture and a serious sprain or strain without having x-rays taken.

First aid for a fracture and a sprain is very similar. Your goal is to immobilize the joint so that it can't be moved. This will decrease pain and reduce the chance that additional damage will be done to the bone or joint. Immobilize the injured area by splinting the joints above and below the damaged site. Improvised splints can be created from sticks, lumber, back pack stays, or even folded up cardboard. If you can't create a makeshift splint, immobilize the area by using a sling or securing the injured limb to the body or another limb by "buddy taping." For arm injuries, a very simple immobilization can be obtained by using a few safety pins. Simply pin the sleeve on the affected arm to a piece of clothing covering the torso.

With any splint, you should leave fingers or toes uncovered so that you can check for adequate circulation. If the extremities turn blue in color or get cold, your splint is too tight and you will have to loosen it. Any serious joint injury or suspected fracture should be evaluated by a medical professional as soon as possible.

Heat Illness

Heat illness consists of a range of symptoms along a broad continuum from dehydration to heat exhaustion to heat stroke. It is common in tropical third world countries and usually follows strenuous exertion in hot weather. Symptoms include headache, dizziness, nausea, and a rapid heart rate. As the condition becomes more serious, body temperatures can exceed 104 degrees Fahrenheit, the patient will become confused or delirious, and may lose consciousness.

Early cooling and rehydration are the key treatments for heat illness. Getting the patient out of the hot sun and removing excessive clothing along with giving the patient fluids to drink may be all the treatment necessary for a mild heat illness. When body temperatures are high, the patient has stopped sweating, or suffers from altered mental status, more aggressive treatments are necessary.

In the event of heat exhaustion or heat stroke, rapidly cool the patient using any means available. Cold water showers or towels soaked in ice water are the best option. If those aren't available, douse the patient with water and sit him in front of a fan. If body temperatures don't drop or if the patient loses consciousness, seek professional medical attention immediately

Malaria

Malaria is a parasitic protozoan disease that is spread by mosquitoes. It is endemic in the majority of tropical third world countries. Symptoms start to appear between 10 and 14 days after being bitten by an infected mosquito. Similar to many other viral illnesses, the patient begins feeling chills, nausea, vomiting, and body aches. Symptoms in the classic malarial cycle last for six to ten hours before abating. Depending on the type of malaria the patient contracted, this cycle is repeated every three to four days. The cyclic fever and relief is one identifying characteristic of the disease. One other symptom that differentiates malaria infection from viral illnesses is the presence of extremely dark colored urine. If you get a cyclic fever with dark colored urine, you should get checked out by a doctor. A simple blood test will identify the virus.

The type of mosquitoes that carry malaria feed at lower altitudes, primarily between dusk and dawn. Interestingly enough, they are more likely to bite males than females because they are attracted mostly by sensing body heat. Since men give off more heat than women, men get bitten more frequently. The easiest way to avoid contracting the illness is to avoid being bitten by infected mosquitoes. Wear light colored clothing, use mosquito nets when you sleep, and liberally reapply an insect repellent containing 20-30% DEET. Pre-treating clothing with a Permethrin spray will also be helpful.

One other trick you may try is to cover your body in some type of oil. Baby oil or olive oil works best. The locals in Honduras and Belize swear by baby oil as a repellent for biting insects and sand flies. The oil creates a physical barrier on the skin that the small biting flies and mosquitoes have difficulty penetrating.

You can also take anti-malarial prophylactic medications. There are four primary drugs approved in the USA to prevent malaria. Each drug requires a different dosing schedule and has different side effects. Some drugs work in some countries, but not others. To find out which drug you need for your travels, check out the CDC Malaria Information Page found at http://www.cdc.gov/malaria/travelers/drugs.html

– **Chloroquine** was one of the first anti-malarial medications and is still effective in some locations, namely Central America, the Caribbean, and the Middle East. Travelers must take the drug a week before arriving in affected areas and continue for four weeks after returning home. The most common dosage is one pill (500 mg) per week. This isn't a good choice for last-minute travelers as it must be initiated at least a week before travel. Chloroquine overdose is potentially fatal.

– **Mefloquine** follows the same dosing schedule (one pill per week) for the same time period as chloroquine. The dosage is 250 mg rather than the 500 mg chloroquine pills. Mefloquine can be taken by pregnant women. Be very cautious when considering this medicine. It has been banned for use by the US Military Special Operations Command because of the potential mental health side effects. This pill is known to cause very vivid and strange dreams. It should not be taken by anyone suffering from mental illness or a seizure disorder.

– **Malarone** (atovaquone-proguanil) is a combination of two drugs. It is very effective at preventing malaria and has minimal side effects as compared to other drugs. One pill per day is taken, starting two days before travel. Prophylaxis is continued for one week after returning home. Malarone cannot be taken by pregnant or breast-feeding women.

 – **Doxycycline** is an antibiotic that is used in both prophylaxis and treatment of malaria. It is taken daily (100 mg) staring two days before traveling and continuing for up to four weeks after returning home. The primary negative side effect of doxycycline is an excessive sensitivity to sunlight. Use caution when relying on this drug in very sunny locations or at high altitude. The pill will also affect the reliability of birth control pills. Doxycycline is a good choice for hikers and those who plan to spend considerable time in wilderness areas as it also treats many tick-borne illnesses as well.

If you don't want to take antimalarial medications because of concerns about side effects or cost, I would recommend that you buy a couple cheap Malaria test kits (available in local pharmacies) so that you can rapidly diagnose and treat any potential cases of malaria that you may acquire. Absent a test kit, general medical guidelines call for presumptive treatment of malaria if you are in a malaria prone area and have a fever combined with chills and vomiting.

Treatment for malaria is taking four adult Malarone tablets one time per day for three consecutive days. An alternate treatment is taking one 100 mg doxycycline tablet twice per day for seven days. If you presumptively treat yourself with these medications, you are advised to seek medical attention as soon as possible.

Be alert for malaria symptoms even after you make it back home. Symptoms usually manifest somewhere between one week and three months after the bite, but occasionally can be delayed for up to a year. If you have visited a malaria-prone country and have uncontrolled fever and chills after returning home, seek medical treatment and let your doctor know about your possible exposure to malaria.

Marine Envenomation

Many third world vacations involve spending time in the ocean swimming, diving, boating, surfing, or snorkeling. When you are spending time in the ocean, there's a chance that you could get bitten or stung by a marine creature. Jellyfish stings are the most common marine envenomations. Fire coral exposure, stingray stings, and sea urchin spine punctures occur frequently as well.

The most important preventative measure you can take is to learn how to recognize the hazardous marine life that populates the area where you are traveling. Know what marine life can harm you and what is relatively safe. Spending a couple minutes looking at Google Images will allow you to clearly recognize what stinging coral and sea urchins look like. If there is any doubt, don't touch it.

Jellyfish stings and fire coral exposure are extremely common. I've lost track of how many times I've been stung by various types of jellyfish around the world. Depending on the species encountered, most reactions are fairly mild consisting mostly of pain and a rash at the site of the sting. In certain sensitive individuals and with some more dangerous species reactions can become more serious with anaphylaxis, vomiting, and paralysis being reported.

For any jellyfish sting, remove any attached tentacles with a gloved hand, tweezers, or even duct tape. Flush the area with vinegar or rubbing alcohol. If these liquids are not available, flush with sea water. Exposure to fresh water can cause any remaining tentacles to "fire," causing more pain. If only freshwater is available, a forceful spray from a pressurized source (like a garden hose) can remove the tentacles from the skin before they have a chance to fire.

After the area has been flushed, apply topical lidocaine and/or a corticosteroid (hydrocortisone) cream to reduce the pain and inflammation.

In serious exposures or contact with some of the box jellyfish species, a severe allergic reaction (anaphylaxis) can occur. If the patient has difficulty breathing, a feeling of narrowing in the air passages, or severe facial swelling, seek medical attention. Pre-hospital treatment consists of giving the anaphylactic patient an antihistamine (50 milligrams of diphenhydramine) and administering injectable epinephrine through the use of an Epi-Pen or similar autoinjector device. A second dose of epinephrine should be delivered if symptoms worsen or fail to resolve within five minutes. Any time epinephrine is given, medical attention is mandatory.

Fire coral exposure is treated exactly the same way as a jellyfish sting.

Sea urchin spine punctures are common when travelers wade in shallow waters on or near coral reefs. The punctures are usually on the feet and occur when a person steps on the sea urchin. Sea urchins also have venom in their spines which can cause an intense burning pain at the site of the puncture. If you are penetrated by a sea urchin spine, remove any obvious fragments of the spine. Immerse the site of penetration in very hot (45 degree C or

113 degree F) water for 30 to 90 minutes to reduce pain and deactivate the toxic venom.

Wound infection after a sea urchin puncture is very common. Be alert for any redness, swelling, or red streaks radiating from the puncture wound for a few days after the injury. If you are far from medical care and you see signs of infection, treatment with an antibiotic from the fluoroquinolone family (Cipro) would be appropriate.

Stingray spine punctures are treated in a similar manner to sea urchin spine punctures. Remove the obvious spine fragments and soak in hot water for 30-90 minutes. If the spine is left in an area of the body that has major blood vessels (like the chest), immobilize the spine and leave it in place for removal at the hospital. The spine may be physically blocking a damaged blood vessel. Severe bleeding may result if the spine is removed. Some locals will advocate using a suction device (like the Sawyer Extractor) on stingray stings. Avoid this practice. Medical studies have shown that suction is ineffective at removing venom and may cause swelling and damage at the wound site that will delay healing.

Systemic flu-like symptoms for a few days are common after a stingray sting. I once took a sea kayaking trip off the coast of Belize. My support boat captain was stung in the foot by a stingray he had stepped on when checking the boat's anchor. He was bedridden (actually hammock-ridden) for three days with severe nausea, body aches, and vomiting. Stingray stings are no joke. Be prepared to provide supportive care and pain relief if you or a companion is stung.

Motion Sickness

Motion sickness is the single most common malady I see in my travel companions. Winding mountain roads, boats, and erratic driving are the prime culprits. If you know you get motion sickness, try to sit in the front of the bus near a window to reduce the chance of experiencing it. Some people use over the counter medicines like Dramamine or Gravol to prevent or treat the illness. Once it occurs, I've had best luck with the prescription anti-emetic called ondansetron (Zofran). Take four to eight milligrams as soon as you feel nauseous and you should be fine within about 15 minutes. Another standby anti-emetic is promethazine (Phenergan). It works well but causes extreme drowsiness. Both of these medicines can be purchased without a prescription in most third world countries.

There is some newer research showing that inhaling the fumes of rubbing alcohol will also reduce symptoms of nausea. If you carry alcohol prep pads for wound cleaning, try opening one up and inhaling the fumes. This works very quickly and may be a very easy alternative to using prescription drugs.

Sexual Assaults

My female readers might consider carrying prophylactic drugs for a possible sexual assault, especially if they are traveling in the back country or far away from pharmacies and medical care.

The generally recommended medical treatment for the event of a sexual assault is taking the "morning after" pill (often available at U.S. pharmacies without a prescription) along with a three broad-spectrum antibiotics.

The latest guidelines call for an injection of ceftriaxone (can be substituted by a 400 mg Cefixime tablet) combined with 1000 mg of azithromycin and 2000 mg of metronidazole.

While I've never had to use it, I carry this pill combination in my travel medical kit in the event one of my traveling companions is raped. Carrying a few extra pills is a great insurance policy in the event that a friend or family member is sexually assaulted.

Skin Rashes

Whenever you travel, you will be encountering insects and plants that your skin has never experienced. Combine those with hot and humid weather and you will see tons of skin rashes pop up. Keep the skin clean and dry and make sure to remove whatever is irritating it. If the rash itches, apply a topical steroid like hydrocortisone cream for relief. Taking an antihistamine pill is also helpful for stopping the itch. If the hydrocortisone cream isn't stopping the itch, you could also try a topical corticosteroid called triamcinolone. It is commonly sold in foreign pharmacies and is more potent than the OTC hydrocortisone you can buy here in the States. The triamcinolone shouldn't be used on sensitive areas of the body (genitals, face, etc.) because it may cause irritation or skin thickening.

If the rash persists for more than a couple days, visit a doctor. You may also check out the local pharmacy. They sell tubes of combination steroid/anti-fungal/antibiotic creams over the counter in most countries outside the USA. That makes a precise diagnosis unnecessary if you can't make it to the doctor. No matter what the cause, these multidrug creams take care of the problem.

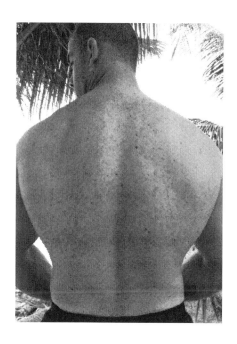

The author's heat rash (prickly heat) after a hot and dusty bus ride through Belize

If itching insect bites or rashes are driving you crazy and you have no medication, try hot water. Place the affected area under water (as hot as you can stand) for three to five minutes. The hot water will neutralize the toxins that cause the rash. The effect is only temporary, however. You may need to repeat the process every few hours. Ammonia may also work to temporarily relieve the itching.

Worms and Parasitic Infections

Many uninitiated travelers are worried about being infested with some type of worms on their trip. It's generally not worth worrying about. In all my years of travel to the most inhospitable areas on the planet, I've never gotten any worms.

Most of the patients who get worms (helminthic infections) are locals who have poor nutrition and even worse hygiene. If you can avoid constant exposure to human or animal fecal matter, you should be able to avoid getting a case of worms.

Roundworms (Ascaris) are the most common worms that infest humans worldwide. They are spread by food contaminated with the feces of another animal (including humans) that is infested by the worms or larvae. These parasites can be avoided by using proper hygiene and thoroughly cooking your food. Even if you do acquire the parasite, there are seldom serious consequences and they can be eliminated with a simple anti-helminthic drug.

Hookworms are usually acquired after they penetrate the skin. The worms can burrow through the skin and cause an intense itching. They can also travel to the eye, organs, or the intestines. Most commonly, the skin penetrated is the sole of the foot after exposure to the worm by walking barefoot on the beach. The parasite is acquired in beach areas that are contaminated with fecal matter, usually from wild or infected animals. Wearing shoes will usually prevent the acquisition of this parasite. Systemic symptoms are generally not present until the person has acquired enough of the worms to form a colony. The migration of the worm through the skin however, will cause an itchy, moving, red line as the worm burrows. Most travelers who are exposed get only one or two worms. The worms die on their own without their human host ever even knowing he was infected.

Threadworms or pinworms are transmitted through fecal contact with an infected person or animal. They are usually noticed when the traveler feels excruciating itching coming from his or her anal area. The itching is worse at night. If you notice such itching, get to a doctor for a stool test. The worms are easy to treat, but you'll want to make sure your fingernails are trimmed short and that you wash your hands thoroughly after using the toilet so that you avoid passing the worms on to someone else while the drug takes effect.

Depending on the type of worm you've contracted, one of two drugs is commonly prescribed. For most worm infestations (roundworms, pinworms, and hookworms) the drug of choice is albendazole dosed at one 400 milligram tablet per day for three days. Ivermectin (dosed at 200 micrograms per kilogram of bodyweight) tablets are prescribed for one to two days for other helminthic infections. Ivermectin cannot be given to children and should only be taken under medical supervision as high doses can be toxic.

Wound Care

By far, the most common injuries you will have to treat in the backcountry are simple cuts, lacerations, and abrasions. It's important in a third world environment to prevent infection. We get lazy with wound care when we are at home because we know we can go to the doctor or hospital if we have any complications. If you are in a remote or rural area in a third world country, that option may not be as readily available.

If you are cut, the first thing to do is to stop the bleeding. Holding direct pressure on the wound using a gauze pad for about 10 minutes will suffice for most cuts. If not, see the "Bleeding" section above.

After the bleeding is stopped, you need to clean the cut using soap and lots of water under pressure. The water to clean your cuts doesn't have to be sterile, but it should be clean enough to drink. That rules out most third world tap water.

If you can't use water from the sink or shower to wash the cut, how do you get pressure? The easiest way is to poke a small hole in a plastic water bottle and use squeeze pressure to generate a stream. You can also do the same thing with purified drinking water poured into a plastic bag. The hole should be very small. The appropriate size is approximately the size of an 18 gauge needle. In fact, they make irrigation syringes with special 18 gauge catheter tips made just for cleaning out wounds. If you don't have one of these, just use a clean needle or safety pin to poke a small hole in a bottle and do the best you can.

You must flush the wound with a significant amount of water. Most wilderness medicine professionals recommend one quart of water per inch of cut length (approximately one liter for every three centimeters for our friends who use the metric system). Ensure that there is no debris left in the wound after washing.

A thorough cleaning with soap and water should be enough to flush the bacteria from the wound. If the wound is exceptionally dirty or deep, you may want to chemically disinfect it as well. Apply rubbing alcohol, hydrogen peroxide, or diluted betadine one time before bandaging. Many people want to apply alcohol or another disinfectant several times a day for a few days. That will actually slow wound healing. If you clean the wound correctly, you will heal more quickly than by using a disinfectant numerous times.

You may apply a topical antibiotic at this point if you think there is a risk of infection. The most commonly used topical antibiotic in the USA is called "triple antibiotic ointment" or by the brand name "Neosporin." Few people recognize that one of the antibiotics in this three drug mixture (neomycin) has a very high allergy rate. The allergy expresses itself as a skin reaction. The affected area becomes red, inflamed, and hot to the touch. Those reactions mimic the early signs of infection and can be easily misread, leading to even more application of the antibiotic and a progressively worsening reaction.

To avoid this infection mimicking allergy, choose a single or double antibiotic ointment that doesn't contain neomycin. Simple bacitracin ointments or a double antibiotic ointment have proven just as effective at reducing infection as the triple antibiotic ointment.

One topical antibiotic that I carry is called by the brand name of "Bactroban" and the generic name mupirocin. It's prescription only in the USA, but sold over the counter in many other countries. It works the same way as the topical antibiotics listed above, but also has some coverage against the dreaded MRSA skin infection. It is the best topical ointment if MRSA is suspected.

Notice that I'm using the term "ointment" rather than "cream." Ointments have a Vaseline type base and last longer on the skin than creams. Apply the ointment twice a day for no more than three days. Longer application will slow wound healing times.

If the wound is not contaminated, a bite wound, or a puncture. you will reduce healing time and the chance of infection if you close the wound (bring the edges of the wound together). If the wound is the result of an animal bite, see the separate "animal bite" section above.

It's out of the scope of the book to talk about suturing, skin glues, and staples, but one very easy method of skin closure is by using Steri-strips. These are essentially pieces of medical grade reinforced packing tape. You simply dry the wound, pinch the skin edges together and tape the wound closed. Steri-strips will stay on for three to five days under most conditions. If you don't have Steri-strips, you can actually use thinly cut strips of duct tape for the same purpose. Some first aid kits include "butterfly bandages" for this purpose, but they are not as strong or as durable as Steri-strips.

After closing the wound (if necessary) cover it. You can use various sizes of adhesive bandages (also called plasters or Band Aids) for this purpose. You can also use small gauze pads covered by roller gauze or co-flex bandaging material. I really like the co-flex because it stays on for a long while and sticks to itself without needing additional tape.

Keep the wound clean, dry, and covered. Evaluate it for infection at least daily and get medical attention quickly if you think it is becoming infected. Signs of infection include: redness, itching, swelling, smelly discharge, pus, or reddened streaks leading up from the wound toward the heart.

If you notice wound infection and are far away from medical care, it would be appropriate to start taking broad spectrum antibiotics until you can reach definitive care. Antibiotics like cephalexin, ciprofloxacin, Augmentin, Bactrim, or azithromycin will likely slow or stop the infection until you can get the wound treated by a doctor.

Yellow Fever

Yellow Fever is a viral hemorrhagic fever that gets its name from the fact that the illness typically causes jaundice (the yellowing of the skin) in its infected patients. Similar to malaria, the disease is spread from the bite of a mosquito. The virus appears sporadically in both Africa and South

America. If the more serious type of the disease is contracted, it has a fatality rate of approximately 50%.

Yellow fever is a disease of short duration and varying severity. The severity of the disease is often far worse in patients who are chronically malnourished or have other diseases causing immune compromise. It is characterized by fever, chills, headache, muscle aches, nausea, and vomiting. One particular identifying characteristic is called Faget's sign, a cyclic raising and lowering of resting heart rate in concert with fever. The heart rate uncharacteristically DROPS as the patient's temperature increases and then increases again when the fever breaks. This is opposite of most viral illnesses where fever and increased heart rate are commonly seen together.

Most cases of Yellow Fever resolve within a few days, but about 15% enter into a second, more toxic phase a day after the perceived recovery. This second phase is where jaundice appears. Bleeding from all bodily orifices as well as the gums begins. Fifty percent of patients who reach this stage die of liver or kidney failure.

There is no treatment for yellow fever, but there is a vaccine that is very effective in preventing it. If you live in the USA, you'll likely have to visit a travel medicine clinic to get the vaccine. Most family physicians do not administer it. You can find a local clinic at the CDC's Yellow Fever web page (http://wwwnc.cdc.gov/travel/yellow-fever-vaccination-clinics/search).

When you get the vaccine, the clinic will give you a yellow colored vaccine record. Place this record with your passport. Some countries (mostly in South America) require the proof of vaccination before they will allow you to enter if you are arriving from another country where yellow fever is endemic.

Other than getting the vaccine, the best way to prevent becoming ill with Yellow Fever is to avoid being bitten by mosquitos. Wear appropriate clothing and use an insect repellant with at least 20% DEET. Interestingly, the mosquito species that spreads Yellow Fever generally bites victims during daylight hours as opposed to the malaria-spreading mosquitoes that tend to bite around dusk or at night. If traveling to an area where Yellow Fever is present, make sure to apply insect repellant during the day as well, even if there aren't many bugs flying around.

Scam Artists, Beggars and Hustlers

"With time, one comes to realize that if you don't occasionally get scammed on your travels, you aren't pushing yourself enough. Scams happen to confused people in unfamiliar places, people who don't take preapproved tours and deviate from their guidebooks."
– Matt Kepnes

A quick way of determining if you are being approached by a scam artist or hustler is by recognizing the language that scammers use. If the first thing they say is any one of the statements below, you are probably dealing with a hustler:

"Hello friend!"
"Where are you from?"
"I just want to talk to you."
"Hello, pretty lady."

When you hear these phrases, don't engage. The phrases are the mark of either a desperate salesperson or someone who sees you as a wallet with legs. If you aren't interested in what the person is selling, keep moving. Pretend you didn't hear them. If it's obvious that you have taken notice of the speaker, either shake your head from side to side without saying anything or point to your watch and hurry off. Let them find an easier victim.

Beware of appeals for help– Indigenous people rarely (if ever) legitimately solicit help from foreigners. Think about it: If you were lost in the United States, would you ask someone who is an obvious Japanese tourist for assistance? You wouldn't.

Excepting an emergency, the locals in the countries you visit aren't going to ask you for help. Unless the local asking for assistance is spurting blood or missing a limb, walk away. The appeal for assistance is most likely serving as an excuse for an interaction you will generally want to avoid. Any appeal for assistance is likely to be a way to get you to stop to hear a sales pitch or to set you up for a pick pocketing. More serious criminals may use an appeal for help in order to provide some seemingly legitimate reason to approach you in order to commit a robbery.

The scam artists aren't the only potential problem you will encounter. If you do much traveling in developing countries, you will also encounter a significant number of beggars. While most beggars are not criminals, some are. Some beg to distract you so their buddies can pick your pocket. Some also use it as an opportunity to assess how much money you have for their mugger friends. It's not safe to give money to beggars. Just like above, keep moving and don't engage.

You will see lots of adorable children begging as well. No matter how cute and needy they appear, you still shouldn't give them money. Most are forced to beg by their poor or criminal parents who exploit the sympathy people have for dirty, hungry children. If you give these kids money, their parents will keep them on the streets. As cruel as it sounds, refusing to give begging children money will help them in the long run. If they make a lot of money, there's no way their parents will put them in school. It's just too profitable to keep them on the streets "earning" money. If you really want to help the kids, you shouldn't give them money. That way there is at least a small chance that their parents will pull them off the streets and put them in school instead.

Be especially cautious around large groups of very young (age four to eight) children. Some enterprising criminals will enlist the aid of local beggar kids (or their own relatives) to pick the pockets of tourists. No one expects a four year-old pickpocket. When 10 kids surround you, tugging on your clothing, begging, or asking you to buy something, it's hard to keep track of your wallet.

One exceedingly dangerous version of this scam is when a very young child grabs your property in an obvious manner and then runs away. When you give chase, the kid will run around the corner where he will join the rest of his gang, generally a larger group of teen age kids. The teens will then attack you and take everything in your pockets. You will be lucky if you are not hospitalized. It's tough to fight eight to ten teenage males by yourself. Be careful. This set up is especially popular in Peru and Brazil.

Identifying Common Scams

> "The bad guy can lure you to an isolated place. This is almost infinitely varied. Anything from offering a cheap, unlicensed cab to telling you that there is a beautiful shrine just down the alley that isn't on the tourist maps. It's hard to pass up. I have learned an incredible amount and had some great times because I was willing to be adopted by locals. With this one, watch for isolation. If they are taking you to the best local restaurant, you should see more people as you approach, not less."
>
> – Rory Miller

Every location you visit is likely to have a few specific scams that con artists like to pull on tourists. If you are unfamiliar with the local scams, check your guidebook or ask the staff at your hotel. You could even do an internet search on "scams in (your location)."

The majority of scams targeting foreign travelers have at least some verbal component. The con artists use words to either reassure the victim or to close distance. Shawn Smith, in his book "*Surviving Aggressive Behavior*" classifies these verbal interactions as "testing rituals." The testing rituals all have the following similar characteristics:

- Persistence
  - Talking too much
  - Contradictions between words and actions or behaviors
  - Triggering your intuition

As a reliable general guideline, any time you are engaged in conversation with someone and you notice one or more of those characteristics in the conversation, you should expect that you are being scammed.

Another quick identifier of scams is when the scam artist hands you something. This is always bad. Don't ever accept anything that a stranger hands you on the street. At best, it will be a "gift" to guilt-trip you into donating money for the scam artists' "charity." At worst, it could be a set up for a robbery.

I've seen that happen in tourist areas of Thailand where scam artists will dress up like fake Buddhist monks and hand travelers cheap "prayer beads" with a request for a donation, usually to support an orphanage. Besides prayer beads, this scam often targets women with small bracelets, flowers, or even herbs. The con artist will give the traveler a single flower or a sprig of rosemary and then demand an exorbitant price. He will make a scene if you don't pay for it.

This scam could end up costing you serious cash if the scammer hands you something valuable and claims that you broke it and demands payment. Some of the scammers will even have corrupt cops working nearby to pressure you into paying for the "broken" valuable.

The best non-specific scam avoidance advice is to avoid accepting any item given to you by a stranger in public. If approached by a scam artist who uses any of the "testing rituals" identified above, you should walk away. Be rude if necessary. Keep your hands in your pockets.

You should also avoid giving any information about where you are from, where you are staying, or what your occupation is. All of this information can be used later to construct more elaborate cons. If the con man isn't working on a long-term scheme, these simple questions become introductions to the testing rituals I mentioned above. Most people will answer questions from a stranger on the street. You shouldn't. Just stay quiet and keep walking. Avoid verbally engaging with people you don't know or with anyone who initiates conversations with you in public.

Those three pieces of advice will keep you safe from most scams. If you want some more information about common ruses, keep reading. I could never list all the possible scams you may experience, but I'll attempt to explain the more common hustles that have been attempted on either me or my travel companions. Most of the scams you are likely to see will be variations on the following themes:

The "spill" scam– You should be careful if someone "accidentally" spills something on you and then offers to clean it off. There's a good chance that the "spiller" has an accomplice waiting to pick your pocket. Criminals will also covertly squirt something white and gooey onto your shoe and point out this "bird dropping." Some may even offer to clean it for you. This is another way to distract you for a pickpocketing accomplice.

The worst version of this scam is when criminals dump buckets full of urine or human excrement from the roof of a building onto unsuspecting travelers walking below. As the tourist stops to clean up the mess, the dumper's accomplice picks the traveler's pocket under the guise of helping to wipe up whatever was "spilled."

In general, any invitation to invade your personal space with some sort of distracting contact is the potential source a robbery or theft attempt. If someone legitimately points out a potentially embarrassing blemish or flaw, they will usually identify it by pointing to themselves and miming or gesturing that you should remove it. Act appropriately embarrassed and clean it yourself, thanking them for their consideration.

The non-pickpocket version of this scam is often perpetrated by shoe shine men. The shoe shiner (or his friend) squirts some nasty liquid onto your shoes in order to drum up business for himself. When he points out the goo, he cleans and polishes your shoes and makes a couple dollars. Sometimes this scam is run by three people, one of whom is an attractive woman. The accomplice with the "goo" walks near you in a public park and waits for you to look at the hot girl bending over. The accomplice then squirts the stuff (or flings it with a small slingshot) on your shoe. The hot chick is a paid distraction. She, the goo squirter, and the shoe shine man all split the profits from the shoe shine. This regularly happens in Latin American (or Brazilian) public parks. If you see an incredibly attractive woman acting more seductively than is "normal" recognize that you may be getting set up.

Another, more malicious version of the shoe shine scam is when a shoe shine man suddenly drops down right in front of you to shine your shoes. Before you can even tell him "no," you look down and there is a big glob of "bird poop" on your shoe (covertly squirted there by an accomplice). Since he's there, you allow him to clean it off, expecting to pay him a dollar or two for his services. When he's finished, he asks for an exorbitant fee. When you protest, he turns around his wooden shoe shine box and there is a very clear sign saying something like "Shoe Shine $25." You've been had.

Most tourists will end up paying the money because they are scared or intimidated. They just don't want the hassle of dealing with the guy. Don't be like most tourists. Don't ever stop for a mobile shoe shiner unless you want your shoes shined. Just keep walking no matter what the man says or does. If you do find yourself scammed like this, pay the man a couple of dollars and walk. No matter how much he protests, he won't call the police. They know he's a scam artist and likely will make him leave the area. He doesn't want that. Don't fight or argue, just leave. He'll be forced to work his scam on someone else.

The "baby throwing" scam- This one is most often perpetrated by large numbers of "gypsy" child beggars and is most often seen in Eastern Europe. You will be approached by a large crowd of dirty and disheveled children begging for money. As you attempt to get away, they surround you, but not in an aggressive manner. One older child will be holding a "baby" wrapped in blankets. When she gets close enough, she will throw the "baby" at your head. You will naturally either try to catch it or make sure it is OK if it hits the ground. The gypsy kids will use that opportunity to pick your pockets or steal your camera. The "baby" is usually a piece of firewood or a large water bottle covered with dirty blankets.

The "drunk" pickpocket scam– You are walking down the street when you see a staggering, boisterous drunk approaching you. He stinks and has remnants of his vomited-up dinner smeared on his clothes. As you try to avoid him, he falls onto you, mumbling his apologies as you push him away. He staggers off and you later realize that your wallet or passport is missing. You've just been pickpocketed.

The repulsive "drunk" is the ultimate distraction. You would do anything to avoid his stream of vomit. He's counting on that fact to ensure you will be too distracted to notice his hand in your pocket.

Anytime you see an obvious staggering drunk, be on your guard. Cross the street or walk into a store to avoid him if possible. If avoidance isn't possible, place your hand on your wallet or valuables as you actively disengage. The same defense can also be used against the other types of distracting pickpockets (extremely hot girls, hookers, or large groups of kids) as well.

The bag slash scam– This one is very common on busy public transportation in Europe and South America. If you are wearing a backpack, day bag, or purse, the thief casually approaches you. Because of the crowded conditions, you don't even notice as he slices your bag open with a razor blade and takes whatever he exposes. I say 'he' but this scam is also perpetrated by women as well. The best defense is to keep conscious control of all your bags, even going so far as wearing your backpack on the front of your body so that you can see if anyone tries to slash it.

Street criminals will also use razor blades to slash purse straps to facilitate grabbing the purse and quickly running away. In any crowd, ladies should carry their purse like a football (under the arm) rather than relying on a strap thrown over the shoulder

The "date" scam. If you are a man looking for a romantic relationship in another country, don't be surprised if your new "girlfriend" doesn't have the same idea of the meaning of the word "date" that you have. It's common for local women to view foreign men as nothing but sources of extra income.

Your new girlfriend might bring her parents, siblings, or friends on your "date." They will all expect you to pay for everyone's meals and entertainment. Be very clear with any local women you date that such conduct won't be tolerated. Avoid the standard "dinner" date until you know her better. Shorter dates that involve drinks only or a walk around a local park are less costly and send a message that you expect her to show up by herself.

There are also girls who use their looks and flirtation abilities to maliciously scam male travelers. You will meet these girls on the street, in a bar, or online. They will be happy, flirty, and will seem genuinely interested in a relationship with you. The girl will suggest going to a certain bar or restaurant that her friends own. You go. There is no menu. Her "friends" serve you dinner and drinks all night. When it's time to leave, you get an itemized bill adding up to several hundred (or thousand) American dollars. You've just been scammed.

The girl who seemed so interested in you actually works for the bar/restaurant. She gets a percentage of the money that you pay for your "bill." And don't even think about not paying. The owners of any establishment of this type likely have cops on the payroll as well. If you don't pay, the bouncers will beat you up and take the money. If that doesn't happen, you will be arrested. The only way to win this game is not to play.

If you end up as a victim of this scam, pay the bill with a credit card. Get out of the restaurant and then dispute the charge with your credit card company or report the card as stolen after you arrive in a safe location.

Another variation of this scam that regularly occurs in Asia looks similar, but the girl will try to take you to a "traditional tea house" or "tea ceremony." You will be led to a tea house with no other patrons and will be served tea. You will then get a massive bill.

To avoid being scammed, you (not your "date") should be choosing restaurants in a foreign country, at least until you've known him/her long enough to fully trust them. One enterprising way to avoid this scam is by telling any new girl you meet that your credit/debit card was stolen yesterday and that you only have a few dollars to last you the whole evening. If she's legitimately interested in you, that shouldn't matter. If she wants your money, she'll ditch you quickly for a richer mark.

You should also be exceptionally cautious when any of the women you are dating are very eager to meet you at your apartment or hotel room for your first date. Most females (anywhere on the planet) want to meet a man in a safe public location so they can make sure you are not a psychopathic killer before being alone with you. A girl who is eager to meet you at your residence may have other ideas in mind. Recently there have been reports of numerous men in South America who have been drugged by women they have met on local dating sites. The woman brings a pre-opened bottle of wine or a water bottle full of "flavored water" to the date. She pours you the wine (or secretly adds some of her "water" into your drink when you are not looking). You pass out only to wake up with all your valuables gone. The "flavored water" contained a drug (most likely GHB or a benzodiazepine) and your "date" was a thief.

Girls in third world countries don't bring gifts for men on first dates. Be cautious if she gives you any food or wine and watch closely to make sure she's actually drinking from the water bottle she carried on the date.

If you use dating apps like Tinder, be cautious of women using the app to sell package tours. This is especially common in South America. You "match" with a girl and quickly set up a date. The date turns out only to be her trying to sell you a package tour deal. If your date starts telling you about any type of package tours, she isn't interested in you for your good looks and charming personality. She's looking to get paid. Ditch her.

Tinder and other online dating apps are also widely used by prostitutes in Latin America and the Caribbean. If you don't normally "match" with hot 23-year old girls at home and suddenly your phone is blowing up with hot chicks from Tinder, they are likely all professionals.

One last (and more serious) caution for my gay male readers: please be exceptionally careful using dating apps like Tinder or Grindr in Middle Eastern countries where homosexuality is outlawed. Police regularly use such apps to set up sex stings against both gay residents and gay travelers.

Egyptian authorities are most well-known for employing this tactic. They will use a fake profile and quickly start chatting about sex. Their goal is to get you to agree to sex and meet your "mate" at his hotel room. Police will be there waiting to arrest you.

Just like I mentioned for my heterosexual friends in the advice above; if things seem to be moving more quickly than normal, take that as a warning sign that something is amiss. Slow things down. Always meet in a public location first. Never meet in a stranger's hotel room. Avoid talking about illegal sex (even if you are chatting on a hook-up app).

With all foreign romantic interactions, things may not be what they seem. Be careful.

The fake ticket scam– This is common in both Africa and South America in busy public transit areas like train or bus stations. The stations are chaotic, and sometimes it's hard to figure out exactly where to buy your ticket. A professional-appearing man or woman will approach you, ask if you are lost, and ask if they can help you. When you tell them you want to buy a ticket, they will escort you to their "friend" at a ticket window. The "friend" is actually an employee of the bus or train company and he sells you a ticket. Unfortunately, the ticket is counterfeit and the clerk pockets the money.

Usually, the ticket looks authentic enough that you will actually be allowed to board the bus or train. The problem isn't noticed until someone else possesses a legitimate ticket with the seat number of the place where you are sitting. If the bus isn't full, you may get away with just finding an empty seat, but if the bus is packed with passengers, you may be escorted off.

It's usually safer to buy your tickets in advance online. If you are buying at a station, do some research on the company you are using and find out the proper window or agent to use to get a legitimate ticket. You should also research the fares ahead of time as well. Occasionally, even real employees of transportation companies charge foreigners a "gringo tax" and pocket the extra money.

The Flat Tire Scam– If you rent a car, the scam artists will drive a nail into one of your tires. They will approach you in a public area (usually in the parking lot were they placed the nail as you were eating or shopping) and point out the nail. Miraculously, they will know a tire repair place that will remove the nail. They will offer to take you to their buddy's garage and he will remove the nail for an exorbitant fee. Avoiding scams like this is another reason why I prefer public transport.

Don't fall for this one. Keep the phone contact for your rental company handy. If you have problems, call the rental company. Don't rely on "Oscar's Garage" to make a repair.

You should also be aware of this scam's more dangerous older brother. The scam artists will flatten your tire the same way, but will follow you until you start having car problems and pull over. If the area is remote enough, they will pull weapons and steal all of your property when you stop to check out your tire.

Most of the criminals performing this trick, flatten the tire(s) of a series of rental cars from the same rental location. The thieves then stake out the closest highway to the car rental place and wait for you to pull over to check your rental's flat (or low) tire. When you get out of the car, they stick a gun in your face and steal all your money, phones, and luggage. More cautious thieves will work in pairs. They will pose as "good Samaritans" to help you change your flat tire. While one thief is distracting you as he changes your tire, the other is stealing valuables from your car. It would be prudent to take a quick look at all of your tires and your exhaust system (look for plugs) every time you leave a rental vehicle unattended.

Gas Station Scams- Foreigners who choose to rent cars are regularly targets of scams operated by gas station employees, especially in Latin America. Most gas stations in the developing world require pre-payment before pumping gas. Some stations don't accept credit cards and only take cash. Gas station attendants are notorious for providing incorrect change when tourists pre-pay for their gas. Count your change after every transaction.

Also, pay attention to the pump itself. Make sure that it is reset before you begin pumping gas. Gas station attendants have been known to fail to reset the pump when tourists arrive. That way it looks like you purchased your gas and the previous customer's purchase as well.

Know if you are purchasing your gas in liters or in gallons. Every country is different. Some enterprising attendants will tell you that the price on the sign is per liter when in reality it is per gallon. Every country will be standardized to one unit of measure or the other. If you are charged per gallon at one station and per liter at another, you are being scammed.

The "money envelope" scam- This is another pickpocket scam. It preys on a common human reaction. The thieves will toss an envelope with a widow in it (like you would get at a bank) filled with fake bank notes at your feet. When you see the envelope of "money" you will likely touch your own money supply to verify that you haven't lost it. That identifies where your money is for the pickpocket. If you bend over to pick up the envelope full of banknotes, it works even better for the pickpocket. In that moment you are distracted and ripe for the picking. If you see what appears to be a bank envelope lying in the street or on the sidewalk (especially when there are kids around), either ignore it or kick it down a gutter so that the thieves lose their "bait." A slightly different version of the scam uses a wallet on the ground instead of the envelope full of money. It accomplishes the same goals.

The "Counterfeit Money" Scam– This one is common in all parts of the developing world. You will be approached in public by one or two men. Both will claim to be police officers and flash you a fake badge. They will tell you that there has been a huge problem with criminals passing counterfeit bills in the area where you are walking. They will ask to "inspect" any currency you have in your possession. While "inspecting," they will covertly pocket a few of your larger bills. A real police officer will never ask to inspect your money. If you are approached with this scam, just pretend you don't understand and walk quickly away. Never allow anyone access to your money, or even knowledge of where you might be hiding it.

Another scam involving counterfeit currency occurs when you go to pay your bill at a bar or restaurant. The waiter will take your cash to the cash register. When he returns to your table, he will hand you back the bill you gave him and explain that he doesn't have change. He will ask you to pay with a smaller bill. Unbeknownst to you, he has stolen your money and replaced it with a counterfeit bill. If you don't know the country's currency well, you likely won't be able to tell the difference. Any time a shopkeeper, waiter, or bartender returns a bill to you or gives you change, examine the bills closely to ensure that they are not counterfeit or the wrong denomination.

The "Hotel Front Desk Scam"- This scam occurs most frequently in countries where English is widely spoken.

Soon after checking in, you will receive a phone call in your room. The caller will claim to be from the front desk and will ask for your credit card information, even though you already provided it at check in. It isn't the front desk calling. If you get a call like this, hang up immediately and go down to the front desk and speak to the clerk in person. If you need to provide your credit card again, you can do so. If it's a scam, you won't get taken.

Also be cautious of any restaurant "carryout menus" slid under your hotel door. While it's certainly possible that the restaurant has a legitimate carryout operation, it's just as often a scam. When you call to order, the person answering the phone will ask that you prepay for the order using your credit card. Don't do it. They will steal your credit card numbers and you won't get any food. Pay cash on delivery or don't order anything from a flyer slid under your hotel room door.

One additional hotel scam is when a couple of people dressed as hotel employees appear at your door telling you they are there to perform a "room inspection." They may say they are inspecting the electrical appliances, the heating or A/C units, or even the plumbing. The presence of more than one person is your clue that things aren't quite right. While one "inspector" is distracting you, the other will be stealing anything he can get his hands on. If the hotel sends someone to check something in your room, it will usually be a single employee. No matter how many people arrive, don't allow anyone into your room until you have called the front desk to determine if they are actually hotel employees performing a legitimate service.

The Tipping Scam– In some countries the "tip" or a "service charge" is automatically added to the restaurant bill. A common scam is when the waiter adds a few extra items to your order. He calculates the service charge based on the inclusion of the extra items. If you notice, he apologizes and says something like "*I must have given you another table's order*" and then removes the items you didn't order. Despite dropping the unwanted items from the bill, he doesn't take the time to adjust the service charge. He gets a bigger tip if you don't watch closely. Know what the service charge percentage is in the country you are visiting and watch your bill closely.

One thing that is not a scam is when you go someplace with live music and you get something called an "artistic cover" added to your bill. This is just a more convenient way of paying a cover charge to see a band or performer. Instead of charging you extra money at the door, bars add a small fee to your bill.

One other thing about your restaurant or bar bill: In some countries, the paper copy of the bill that your server gives you is collected at the door when you leave. You pay the bill at that time, and don't give money or a credit card to the waiter or server. Don't lose your bill. There will be a "fine" of several hundred dollars if you lose the bill or ticket. You will not be allowed to exit and some very large gentlemen will suddenly appear to "convince" you to pay. It gets ugly. I've had this happen to friends in both Brazil and in Southeast Asia. Keep those bar bills until you are sure you don't need them again.

The "Asian Gem Scam"- This is one of the oldest scams in the book. You will be approached by a gem seller who will ask you where you live. When you tell him, he will explain that he would like to export some gems to your home country, but he doesn't have an export license. He will offer a deal where he will sell you some gems for a very inexpensive price and give you the phone number of his "contact" back in your home country. When you take the gems home, he will tell you to call the contact who will then buy the gems from you for 10 times the amount that you paid.

There is no contact. You just got scammed into purchasing some worthless stones.

Currency "misunderstandings"- Hawkers of typical touristy gifts will occasionally use currency confusion to get higher prices for their items. They will intentionally misrepresent their prices in cheaper local currency, wait for you to agree to buy the item, package it up, and then charge you the price quoted in dollars rather than the local currency.

In Mexico, for example, 19 pesos equals one dollar U.S. at the time of this writing. The "salesman" holds up an item and says "10." You think he wants 10 pesos (less than $1.00) and you agree. He packages the item and then tells you it's $10. When you refuse to pay that amount he will get mad, yell at you, threaten you, or tell you that he is going to call the police. A lot of tourists fall for these antics. You shouldn't. Just walk. You won't get into any trouble for not being the victim of a scam.

Taxi Scams- A common taxi scam is when you hire a taxi to take you to the airport for your return flight home. Many countries levy additional fees if taxi drivers drop off passengers on airport property. The taxi driver has to pay a fee to exit the airport after doing so. Some taxi drivers will tell you that the parking lot is closed and drop you off outside the property on the street to save the price of the airport fee. The airport isn't closed. Insist that the driver take you to the terminal.

Another regular scam occurs after you agree on a price. As an example, let's say you agree to a price of 100 pesos for the fare. Your driver will stop along the way for gas and ask you for 60 pesos to purchase it. You tell him that you will give them the 60 pesos now and that you will only owe him 40 pesos at the end of the journey. He will agree.

When you get to your destination, he will conveniently "forget" that you paid for his gasoline and charge you the full fare. He will make a fuss, maybe even threatening to call the police because you agreed to pay him 100 pesos and he only got 40. His English speaking skills will suddenly drop to zero and he will enlist the aid of numerous other locals by telling them you are skipping out on your fare. Most tourists will relent at this point and pay the full amount just to avoid being delayed or hassled.

Never pay anything upfront. Never pay for anything on the drive. The only way you can really beat this scam is to refuse to pay your cab driver any money at all until you are safely at your destination and your luggage is in your hands.

A less common, but still widely practiced (especially in India and Egypt) taxi scam, is when the driver agrees to a fare and then adds a small amount to it at the end of the ride for "baggage handling." Some taxi drivers will even double your quoted fare, stating that your baggage is an additional "passenger." Most tourists just pay it to avoid the argument. That's what the driver is hoping for. The only way to avoid this one is to steadfastly refuse to pay. Pay him the agreed upon fare, grab your luggage and walk. He won't protest for long.

Make sure you have small bills available to pay the driver. Many taxi drivers will refuse to provide change for large bills claiming that they don't have any smaller bills. That forces you to stop someplace else to make change or just give him a very large tip. The driver is betting that your frustration and impatience will alter your judgment.

He thinks you'll just give him the large bill without expecting any change back. Don't play that game.

Also, be alert for "Bill Swapping." You give the taxi driver a 1000 rupee (or other local currency) bill. He quickly pockets it and pulls out a 100 rupee bill and tells you that you paid with the smaller bill and you need to give him more money. Don't just quickly hand a bunch of cash to your taxi driver. Count out your money slowly, taking note of each bill's value before you hand it over in order to prevent the driver from working this scam on you.

Many foreign tourists rely on taxi drivers to provide them with connections to drugs or prostitutes. Even if such activity is legal in the country you are visiting, avoid using your taxi driver as a connection. Drivers are often in collusion with either the police or criminals. They will offer to sell you drugs and then tell the cops as soon as the transaction is completed. The cops give the drugs back to the driver and you have to pay a bribe to stay out of jail.

The drivers may also use your desire for drugs and prostitutes as an excuse to take you to a more seedy part of town where they can set you up for an ambush. They call their robber friends and arrange a location, pull up on the street and get out of the car without saying a word. The next thing you know there is a gun stuck in your face and a demand for money. The driver just set you up.

It's always safer to stay away from hookers and dope in foreign countries. It's especially important to stay away from taxi drivers who offer to provide hookers and dope.

The hustles listed above are common, but some others occur with even more frequency. The most likely taxi scam you will experience is simply being overcharged for your fare. Taxi drivers charge the "gringo tax" even more than merchants. If your cab doesn't have a meter, negotiate the fare BEFORE getting inside.

A very common scam that I've experienced in Argentina, Brazil, Colombia, and Thailand goes this way: You agree on a price (let's say $5.00) and get into the cab. When you reach your destination, you hand the driver the $5.00 bill and he says "No! $5.00 PER PERSON!" Make sure you clarify in advance if the price agreed upon is per person or per trip.

Ask the front desk staff at your hotel what a cab ride to your destination should cost. If your hotel has a bellman, give him a couple dollars to negotiate the fare for you. Doing this might save you far more money in the long run, especially if you don't know the average fare or can't speak the local language.

The worst taxi scam is actually a kidnapping scam. This one usually occurs in Africa or South America and generally targets a wealthy male/female couple. The taxi driver feigns engine trouble and pulls over along the side of the road. He convinces the male half of the couple to either help him with the "engine trouble" or start walking to get help. As soon as the man gets out of the cab, the driver speeds away with the female passenger.

Sometimes the motive is rape. Sometimes it is ransom money. In either case, the outcome is undesirable. Be alert and on your guard any time a taxi has engine problems. If you are traveling with another person, stick together. If one person gets out of the car or starts walking for help, the other should accompany him/her. Don't get separated and this scam won't happen.

Rigged meters- The commonly-touted advice of ensuring that the taxi driver always uses the meter is generally good, but it isn't very helpful if the meters are rigged or inaccurate. Most tourists aren't likely to even notice that the mileage or fare has been inflated by an erroneous meter.

The best way to avoid rigged meters is to use only the most reputable taxi companies. Smaller cab companies and gypsy cabs are more likely to rig their meters, in my experience. Pick a taxi company that is large and has a good reputation. Most foreign cities have one or two highly recommended cab companies that offer good service. If you are not sure which cab companies are the best to use, ask your hotel desk staff or bellhop.

The "Milk for my Children" scam. Many scam artists are aware that tourists often avoid giving cash to needy beggars. To avoid an obvious appeal for cash, some scammers with one or more kids in tow will approach a traveler and ask for "milk for the children." The scammer will point to a local corner store and ask you to buy some milk for his/her children. When you buy the milk, the scammer will thank you and quickly walk away. She will then return the unopened milk to the store; get a refund of the money you spent and give the store owner a share. The store owner gets his milk back, and makes a little cash. The scammer just got you to give him or her the cash that you swore you would never provide a beggar.

The Egyptian Camel Scam- This one is obviously most common in Egypt, but the same scam is used around the world with different animals. The scam is simple. The scam artist will quote a price for you to get on his camel to have your photo taken. You will pay the price and get on the camel. Once the camel stands up, you are too high off the ground to get down. The scam artist will then tell you that he requires more money to get you down. He says that the money you paid him initially was just for the ride up. You have to pay again for the ride down.

Never get on a camel, elephant, or any other large mammal in an obvious tourist area.

Prostitutes

> *"There are, in my experience, three kinds of*
> *travelers. There are those who are leaving*
> *something behind and wish to forget. There are*
> *those who are facing forward and looking to learn.*
> *And there are those who wish to get laid."*
> – Becci Coombs

I already mentioned not using taxi drivers to locate drugs or prostitutes, but I think a few more words of warning are necessary regarding "ladies of the night."

I'm not one to judge what type of conduct may be moral or immoral. I will say that in all my travels, I've never paid a prostitute. Even where it is legal, I've avoided using their services. It's simply not safe.

In addition to the tremendous disease risk, many prostitutes are opportunistic thieves and drug addicts as well. I've seen and heard many stories where prostitutes have stolen wallets, watches, passports, and other valuables when their clients are enjoying a post-coital nap.

Most third world hotels will specifically prohibit local overnight guests for this exact reason. They don't care about someone staying in the room with you; they just don't want to deal with the hassle when the prostitute steals everything you own and then jumps out the window. Don't think you can skirt the hotel rules by going to her place either. The extremely enterprising girls will take you back to hotel rooms that are equipped with audio and video recording capabilities. They will record your amorous interaction and then threaten to send the tape to your family or post it to the internet if you don't pay them a large sum of money. Lots of bad things can happen when you start paying for affection.

I would imagine that most of my readers would be more interested in avoiding prostitutes than hiring them. The best way to avoid them is to recognize how they operate and avoid where they hang out in the city you are visiting. There are dozens of websites and forums on the internet that describe where the "red light districts" are in cities around the world. I use those sites to find out where I should AVOID staying or walking through. Out of all the ones I've used for research, I think the International Sex Guide Forum, (http://www.internationalsexguide.nl/forum/) is probably the most complete. It provides in-depth details about exactly how and where the prostitutes work in each city. Simply avoid booking accommodation in those areas if you don't want to deal with prostitutes.

If you don't want to research the prostitution trends of the cities you are visiting before you leave, a simple tip will help you to avoid third world prostitutes...

If you are in a bar or on the street in a third world country and a local woman approaches you and initiates conversation for any reason, you should assume she is a prostitute. Most developing countries have very traditional cultural norms. Men are the initiators in social interactions. Women simply don't approach men they don't know. Men do all of the approaching in these countries. If a woman approaches you, more often than not, she wants something. Be on your guard. Not all prostitutes are as obvious as the ones in Southeast Asia who simply say: "*You. Me. Taxi. Hotel.*"

Another tactic to be wary of is when a female you don't know starts showing excessive interest in you. She will fawn all over you, tell you how handsome you are, and touch you as much as possible. All of this is an effort to stroke your ego. You'll start feeling like a stud and take her back to your hotel. After having sex with her, she will then tell you her "fee" and threaten to call the police if you don't pay. If women aren't falling all over you in bars and clubs at home, you didn't suddenly become more attractive because you are in another country. Unless you look like a movie star (and maybe even then) you should suspect that any woman showing you excessive attention is likely to be a prostitute.

One additional red-flag prostitute identifier is an unusual and unexplained proficiency in speaking the English language. Most working class girls in developing countries don't have a great command of English. If she speaks to you in fluent English, but isn't college educated, doesn't work in the tourist industry, or doesn't have family in the States, she's probably a hooker. Prostitutes and bar girls recognize that speaking English will help them negotiate with "rich" foreign travelers and will often have a better than average ability to converse with you. Be very careful with any girl who speaks English without having an obvious reason for having learned it.

Recognize how whorehouses advertise themselves. Each country is different. In Brazil, for example, the brothels are clearly labeled and called "*Termas*" or "*Spas*." In rural Thailand brothels are denoted by the presence of Christmas lights (year round). Red lights of any type indicate the presence of prostitutes worldwide. It's a smart idea to figure out how the locals identify the whore houses so that you can stay away from them if you don't want any problems.

If you are the average straight male, you will also want to avoid the transgender or cross-dressing prostitutes that are far more common in some countries than they are in the United States. Especially if you are traveling in Brazil or Thailand, you will be approached by cross-dressing prostitutes. Most start their lives as men and are somewhere in the middle of the process of becoming women. Some of the prostitutes have their "man parts" and some do not.

If you are out on the town to pick up "girls" and don't want a surprise when you get back to your hotel room, pay attention to your "girl's" height, hand, and foot size. A tall woman with really big hands and feet may not be what you are expecting. An exceptionally deep voice and fake breasts can be additional clues. You should also look out for a strange voice, broad shoulders, and narrow hips. Most of the transsexual prostitutes make their money from tourists, not locals. Stay away from the tourist traps and expat bars and you are far less likely to encounter one.

One additional note: Oftentimes these transsexual prostitutes will also be engaging in petty crime like theft or pickpocketing. They almost always operate in gangs. Beware if you decide to fight back against a "lady-boy" criminal who tries to rip you off. You may end up fighting a whole pack of transsexual prostitutes instead of the single criminal who targeted you.

It's also important to note the difference between "*hotels*" and "*motels*." In The USA, the difference is that "motels" have doors leading directly into the parking lot, whereas "hotels" have doors entering into a shared hallway. That is not true in other countries. Words may sometimes differ depending on the language, but in developing countries "*motels*" are usually rented by the hour for sex. "*Hotels*" are where travelers sleep at night.

Prostitutes know that men traveling away from home are more likely to desire their services. Because of this knowledge, you will see more prostitutes in the tourist areas than anyplace else in town. The women will line the streets between the cheap hostels where travelers stay and all of the city's famous sites within walking distance. They know they'll have two opportunities to engage the tourists, once when the traveler is heading out to see the sights and again when he is walking home.

Sometimes it seems that you will truly be running "the gauntlet of whores." These street prostitutes are very persistent and won't let you pass by without trying to make a sale.

Most male travelers who aren't interested in the prostitute will have one of two common reactions. The majority will just ignore the women and keep walking. That's not a bad plan, but the girls are used to that response. They will grab you, touch you, or block the sidewalk to force you to talk to them. Ignoring them completely never works as well as it should.

The other reaction they get is when the man they are soliciting blushes, stammers, or attempts to run away from a situation where he is clearly uncomfortable. Your red face gets the same reaction from a hooker as a red cape gets from a bull. Charge! As soon as the girls sense weakness they will gang up on you, flash their breasts or butts at you, grab your hand and place it on their boobs, or pinch your ass. You definitely don't want to show weakness or embarrassment when running the gauntlet of whores.

The best response I've found to deal with this situation is to learn a simple phrase in the host country's language:

"*Love is free.*" When the whores start talking, I smile, shake my head and say "*Love is free.*" That generally gets a laugh from the prostitutes and they will get the message that you don't want their services and aren't intimidated. They'll usually leave you alone after that.

There is a common worldwide prostitution scam that also bears mentioning here. This one rarely affects casual travelers. The prostitutes who use it tend to target expats or long term travelers with whom they can develop relationships as a regular client. Having regular contact with the same traveler provides the prostitute with additional opportunities to extort money. Most commonly the prostitute will tell her "regular" client that she is pregnant with his baby. She will then parlay the traveler's concern into getting him to either pay for some amount of her housing/food costs to "take care of your baby" or con the traveler out of money to be used for an "abortion." The pregnancy never happened so the "abortion money" usually goes to purchase drugs or pay down the hooker's gambling debt.

The prostitute who is working for a pimp or crime syndicate can also exploit her "relationship" with a regular client. Once the pimp recognizes that you like a particular girl (and if you didn't like her, why would you be engaging her services regularly?), he will approach you directly with extortion threats. He will tell you that your "relationship" with this girl is keeping her from doing her regular work. He will then demand money as payment for the loss of her services, either actual or imagined. Another version of the scam has the pimp approaching the regular client and telling him that his favorite whore has a drug or gambling debt to be paid. If the regular client doesn't want to pay the debt, the pimp will threaten to kill the girl. It puts the prostitution customer in an awkward and dangerous position. Again, it's better to stay away from the local whores.

I won't belabor the issues involved with prostitution any longer besides stating that if you are inclined to partake, you should recognize that some developing countries have HIV rates up to or exceeding 50% in the female population. If you do engage the services of a prostitute, make sure you use a condom. No exceptions. Some girls will allow you to pay extra to avoid using the condom. Don't fall for that trick. Those girls are probably the most likely to have a sexually transmitted disease. Wear the condom. And don't trust the condoms that are supplied by the prostitute. Besides having size variations between countries, there is a higher rate of failure in third world condoms than there is from condoms made in the USA, Western Europe, or Japan. Bring your own rubber from home and use it.

"*Painful urination? You may have a sexually transmitted disease*" Sign on Brazilian restroom wall. Wear a condom.

Identifying Criminals and Pre-Assault Indications

"An experienced traveler knows how to properly disengage people – you have to be fast, decisive, confident, and completely cool. Looking the other way and ignoring someone doesn't work, showing fear is perilous, being rude is dangerous. The art of disengagement is an act that's learned, nobody knows how to do this at the start."

– Wade Shepard

It was day time on a crowded big-city street. It seems my girlfriend and I attracted the attention of a gang of bag thieves.

I noticed a guy on an opposite street corner talking on a cell phone. He caught my attention when he seemed to be pointing us out to some unseen other person. As soon as he pointed at us we picked up a tail. Two guys appeared out of nowhere and started following us very closely. The dude on the cell phone supervised from a distance.

I slowed down our walking pace. So did our followers. Not a good sign. The man on the phone paralleled us from across the street. I made a quick stop and forced our followers to walk past. They didn't like that at all and we could tell that it screwed up their plan.

It was quite the study in the criminal assault paradigm. The two men were obviously together, but walking a half step apart to seem separate. They weren't talking. One guy was pretending to look at a cell phone in a very unnatural posture (trying to look inconspicuous). The other was giving off constant "grooming cues" touching his face, neck, and hair as he nervously kept looking over his shoulder to check our position.

They were obviously up to something. I warned my girlfriend and slowed the pace even more. The two guys slowed down as well, keeping the same distance between us. In between nervous strokes of his neck, I saw one of the men dart his hand into his pocket. He pulled it out and had something gold and metallic-colored in his palm. I couldn't tell what it was, but it looked like brass knuckles of some sort. Go time.

I maneuvered aggressively between my girlfriend and the two men so that I could give her a chance to get away as I accessed my knife. She saw what I was doing (without knowing what had prompted my draw) and was astute enough to say "Hey! Let's check out this restaurant!" as she pulled me into an eatery we were passing. Smart girl. The crooks kept walking and I didn't have to stab anyone.

Pre-assault indicators are universal. It doesn't matter what country you are visiting. Be alert when you start seeing any predatory movement patterns or deliberate approaches in a crowd.

Pay attention to all of the following body language:

Hands- Hands above the waistline and or being clenched are a warning sign. Look at people who are calm and are not angry. Their hands will be relaxed and generally below waist level. When the hands come up, get ready for action. Any time a person is hiding his hands may indicate that he is in possession of a weapon.

Lower body- Standing in a bladed stance with one leg (and the same side hand) back and out of view is a sign that the person has hostile intentions or is concealing a weapon. Standing on the balls of the feet indicates that the person is getting ready for rapid movement, which may also precede an attack

Arm movements– Wide gesticulating outside the framework of the body is threat and posturing. It's the sign of a person who is trying to blow off some steam. Gestures inside the body frame and pointing are more closely associated with violent actions.

Breathing- As adrenaline spikes, the criminal's breathing rate will increase. If you notice someone who appears to be "panting," it should be a warning sign. Likewise, it should also be a warning when you see or hear someone take a big, deep, breath or audibly sigh. The criminal may be taking these actions to consciously slow his breathing rate and calm down so that he doesn't prematurely alert you to his plans.

"Thousand yard stare"- Be especially alert if you see someone with an empty stare who isn't responsive to his environment.

Other signs- If the person is mentally ill or exceptionally angry, you might see clenching or grinding the teeth. Occasionally you'll see the contemptuous snarling of lips. Their face will flush red. They will also be breathing more rapidly than normal. Angry people and the mentally ill are often unpredictable and it's best to avoid them, even if they aren't posing an obvious immediate threat to you.

Obvious Danger Signals

Beyond mere body language, there are other indicators to watch for that may give you an early warning that you are dealing with a potential criminal. Look out for these indicators as well:

Masking Behaviors, Pacifying Actions and "Grooming Cues"- One of the really obvious pre-assault indicators is the unnecessary touching of the face, neck, or upper body. Described using different terms depending on the expert cited, these actions all have the same purpose, to "hide" psychological discomfort.

As criminals are evaluating you as a victim or planning their attack, their stress levels rise. The criminals don't want to get hurt and they don't want to get caught. The idea of pain, death, or imprisonment amps up the criminal's fear and baseline level of stress. They know this is happening and subconsciously fear that you will pick up on their nervousness and do something to prevent their successful commission of the crime.

The criminal doesn't want you to see his psychological stress reactions, so he subconsciously "masks" them by covering his face, eyes, or neck. It is very common to see criminals do the following immediately before their attack:

- Touching the face or neck
  - Wiping at the nose or mouth
  - Rubbing the eyes
  - Smoothing the hair
  - Rubbing the neck
  - Scratching the head
  - Rubbing the arms or chest as if shivering
  - Or making any other gesture that partially conceals the criminal's face/neck area from view

These cues occur very late in the game. If you are seeing them, the attack will happen within the next couple seconds. Get ready to act.

"Target Glancing"- When a criminal wants to steal something from you, he has to figure out how to physically remove it from your protection. Sometimes that takes time. While the criminal is figuring out his plan of action, he will likely be staring at what he wants to take. This is called this "target glancing."

Any time someone stares intently at some item (especially a valuable item) in your possession, assume that he is planning on stealing it. Immediately implement countermeasures to ensure that he won't be able to proceed with the criminal activity he is planning. If you take immediate action, there is a good chance the criminal will become frustrated and move on to another victim.

"Looking Around"- Immediately prior to his attack, the criminal has to make sure that there is no one in the immediate area who can frustrate his plans. The criminal will take a quick look around to ensure there are no cops or security guards in the area. He may also be looking for cameras or escape routes. This indicator almost always occurs. If you are being approached by someone who displays a grooming cue and then looks left and right in a furtive manner, get ready. You are about to be attacked.

While we are discussing the direction that a criminal may look, I should also mention criminals often "check their tail." They look behind themselves to see if anyone is following or watching. If you are observing someone and you notice frequent looks to the rear, you can safely assume that the person you are watching is a criminal, a cop, or a spy. In a foreign country, you don't want to have contact with any of those people.

Predatory Movement Patterns- Criminals targeting you will regularly move in a predictable fashion. Anyone attempting to correlate their movement with yours (following, paralleling, directly approaching in crowds) should be viewed as a danger. Running directly towards you is an obvious threat cue.

People who turn or look away when you notice them are worthy of your attention. A conspicuous lack of movement should also ping your radar. People who are sitting in parked cars without getting out should be watched suspiciously.

A sudden change in status (focusing of attention) – If someone is watching you then suddenly looks away, he is probably trying to hide his attention. Likewise if someone "locks in" on you with his eyes, you should be ready for a potential attack.

The display of any one pre-assault indicator or body language cue is not enough to instantly brand the person who displays it as a serial killer. "Normal" people sometimes make these gestures as well. Look at clusters of signs. When you start seeing two, three, or four different indicators, recognize that you are likely being groomed for a criminal attack.

"I knew something was wrong."-When speaking to crime victims, they almost universally tell me about a "sixth sense" or "bad feeling" that they experienced immediately prior to the attack. I firmly believe that this intuitive sense that something isn't right is your subconscious mind alerting you that it has noticed one or more of these pre-assault indicators. Don't try to deny or rationalize the feeling. It's your own body's early warning system.

Perhaps the best use of this list of behaviors is to provide a conscious structure to what your subconscious mind already understands. When you get a "creepy" feeling combined with obvious pre-assault indicators, you must act without hesitation. Flee the scene, call for help, or access a weapon and prepare to fight. Implement whatever self-protection plan you have devised. If you don't, you too will join the ranks of the thousands of tourists who are victims of crime every year.

Other Potential Danger Signs

Tattoos- Numerous studies have shown that the presence of visible tattoos is far more prevalent in criminal populations than people who have never been arrested. This holds true across almost all cultures. It doesn't mean everyone with a tattoo is a criminal; but most criminals have tattoos. Look at tattoos as one of many possible warning signs.

"Branding" style of dress- People use clothing and accessories to communicate their association with certain gangs or cultural elements. A common type of "branding" is the wearing of "colors" by street gangs. Each gang has a particular color members wear to show alliance or solidarity.

Some Latin American countries have gang members that ascribe to the use of "colors" as well. You may not know which color signifies which gang, but you should be extra alert when you are approached by groups of people all wearing the same dominant color. There is a good chance that those people belong to a criminal gang.

Beyond colors, other "branding" efforts can include wearing the same style of clothing (like oversized T-shirts), clothing created by the same company, similar tattoos, the same style of jewelry, or the same kind of hat. When you notice "branding" be extra cautious.

Facial Expressions- A person's facial expressions are another reliable indicator of potential threats. Fortunately for us, Paul Ekman, the world's foremost authority on facial expressions, has determined that certain key expressions are universal. That means the expressions are the same no matter what geographical area of the world or culture a person comes from. In his book *Emotions Revealed*, Dr. Ekman categorizes these universal facial expressions and describes their significance.

We don't have to learn all of the expressions, just the ones we need to keep ourselves safe. People displaying facial expressions involving anger, hatred, contempt, and disgust are most likely to have bad intentions. These are the people we want to stay away from.

What does an angry facial expression look like? The easy way to find out is to look at yourself in the mirror while imagining a situation that makes you mad. Take note of what happens to your face: your eyebrows are pulled down so that their inner corners move towards your nose, your eyes widen, and your lips are pressed closed. The eyebrows are the big indicator. When they are pulled down, you should consider it a danger cue.

Other worrisome facial expressions are those of contempt or disgust. According to Ekman, these emotions can be identified when we see someone combine a wrinkled nose and a raised upper lip. People showing open contempt for you may be planning on doing you harm.

While we are discussing facial expressions, it's important to recognize what your own facial expressions may mean to an attacker. Displaying fear and surprise may embolden a criminal. Ekman states "*An attacker looking for an easy victim may interpret a fearful expression as a sign that we won't fight back and will be easily overcome.*" Even if you are scared, it's important not to allow the fear you are feeling to show on your face.

We all easily recognize the look of surprise or fear on a person's face. The scared or surprised person will have wide open eyes and may have an open mouth. Practice getting used to changing fearful expressions into angry expressions. The wide open eyes are common to both emotions. The difference is in the eyebrows. When the eyebrows are pulled down, it signifies anger rather than surprise.

Here's a drill for you to practice in the mirror. Start with a surprised expression with eyes wide open and mouth agape. Then simply pull your eyebrows down and press your lips together. You've changed a fearful look into an angry look. When a criminal predator sees that change in facial expressions, he may move on to find a victim who isn't as likely to fight back. Practice changing fear into anger at every opportunity you can. It needs to be a reflexive act if you want to be able to depend on it in a crisis.

Other odd appearance cues– Any obvious signs of drug abuse should be considered warning cues. Metallic spray paint around the mouth and nose, the presence of lots of scabs on the skin, itching motions (crank bugs), needle tracks, and small bruises on the extremities all indicate drug use. While not all drug users are predatory criminals, many predatory criminals are drug users. It pays to be alert to these indicia of drug abuse.

How to Avoid Looking Like a Victim

We've talked about criminal pre-assault indicators, now it's time to discuss "victim indicators." What makes a criminal choose a particular person as a victim? The authors of the book *Left of Bang* describe behavioral clusters that they have named "*submissive clusters*" and "*uncomfortable clusters.*" These behaviors are universal across all cultures and nations. When several of these behaviors are seen together in the same person, it signals that a person is overly submissive or extremely uncomfortable with their surroundings. Uncomfortable and submissive people are victimized more often than calm and confident people. The following behaviors form the submissive and uncomfortable clusters:

- Bouncing feet
  - Feet oriented towards a door or escape route
  - Legs crossed while seated or feet wrapped around chair legs
  - Torso leaning away from a potential threat
  - Torso rotated towards exits or escape routes
  - Arms across the chest or pulled into the chest
  - Arms or hands covering the groin
  - Shoulders raised
  - Darting eyes
  - Any body posture that makes you appear smaller
  - Wrists or palms exposed
  - Failing to make eye contact

(Van Horne and Riley. *Left of Bang.* pp 80-88)

These clusters are difficult to detect by yourself. Give the list to a friend and have the friend evaluate you one day when you are out in public. If you or your friends notice any of these behaviors, work to stop displaying them. If you seem less like a victim, you won't be victimized as often.

Besides the behavior clusters identified in *Left of Bang*, we can also look at some other victimology research to learn what we shouldn't be doing. A well-known study showed videos of people walking down the street to incarcerated prisoners. The prisoners were asked to subjectively rate each person as a "good" victim or not. There was wide agreement between all of the prisoners about who exactly they would attack and who they would avoid.

The prisoners looked primarily at the physical characteristics of the victim and the victim's relative awareness. Among the physical characteristics they evaluated, they looked primarily at gait patterns, body type, sex, and relative fitness levels. Fatter and less fit people were chosen more often than fitter-looking folks. Women were chosen more often than men. Anyone from either sex who had a gait abnormality (was walking funny) was chosen. All of these factors indicate relative weakness. In any predatory system, the weak get eaten. Don't display characteristics of weakness.

The prisoners assessed relative awareness by looking at whether the people were paying attention to their surroundings or not. They also assessed whether the person appeared "clueless" or seemed to understand what was happening around him. Unsurprisingly, criminals chose the least aware people as victims. In total, the crooks tended to pick those people who were weak, alone, and not aware of what was going on. Do your best to avoid fitting into any of those categories when out in public.

Dealing with Crime: The Fight/Flee/Comply Decision

"Fear-mongering aside, travelers are chosen as targets because they are not completely in tune to their surroundings. Maybe you are jet lagged, or you just ate a dangerous meal that has left you weak with intestinal anxiety, or you are lost in an uncomfortable part of Paris – these are all circumstances where you are in a vulnerable state and therefore a target of thieves. Like hyenas hunting for weakened game, thieves seek out confused tourists and map clenchers with wayward eyes."
– Justin Delaney

What should you do in the event of a physical attack in a foreign country? Should you flee, fight, or comply?

That's an extremely difficult decision to make. Personal factors such as your age, skills, and weapons availability come into play. On the other side of the equation, crime type, number of attackers, your attackers' level of armament, and local crime trends are also factors. Above all, your personal nature should be considered before making this complex decision.

I can't tell you exactly what you should do. Every person has differing skills, abilities, and motivations. You must decide the best course of action for yourself.

You must make this decision by analyzing all possible responses and figuring out which will work best for you. In any criminal attack, you have several options. Look through all the possibilities and see which makes the most sense to you:

1) Resist
-Verbally

- By screaming
- By calling for help
- Don't ever argue with or insult the attacker

– Physically

- Take the weapon away from him
- Deflect the weapon
- Strike him with your hands, feet, elbows, knees, or head.
- Use your own weapon
- Any combination of the above

2) Comply
  – Complying with the attacker's demands does not automatically keep you safe. Some criminals will shoot you even if you are being compliant. Sometimes what they want is your life instead of your money.

In general, compliance is usually a successful option if you want to avoid being killed or injured in the event a criminal is targeting your property. It does not work as well when the criminal's motivation isn't taking your stuff, but instead assaulting, raping, or kidnapping you. If you choose to comply with the criminal's demands, you must also have a backup plan in the event that your compliance doesn't generate the desired response from the attacker.

3) Flee

– Run away

– Run to cover

-Always run toward safety rather than away from danger. If you blindly flee, you may find yourself in a worse location.

4) Negotiate

– Try to talk your way out of it

5) Bluff or Posture

– Pretend to be sick or have a heart attack

– Say something like: "*You can't shoot me. You know my boys got my back right now.*"

– Say something like: "*Don't do it! There's a cop right behind you!*"

– Bluffing and posturing are strategies that work best when employed by good liars who feel comfortable using deception as a ruse. If that doesn't sound like you, choose another strategy.

6). Freeze

– the conscious or unconscious decision to do nothing

You will likely resonate with one or more of these tactics. Likewise, you will certainly find some ridiculous. I'm not in a place where I can tell you what's right for you or judge your actions. The only thing I can tell you is that based on my experience, freezing yields the worst outcomes. Doing ANYTHING except freezing would be a better choice.

Unfortunately, freezing will be your brain's default choice unless you find a better solution. Do your homework. What is your choice of action?

There is one other factor to consider...

Recognize that male residents of the developing world are far more willing and likely to fight than residents of more "civilized" countries. I've seen some hellacious fights in South America and Africa, all because one party insulted another. In Panama, I even watched an entire bar empty out on a Sunday afternoon to watch and participate in a kind of "fight club." Drunken bar patrons called out other drunken bar patrons who had somehow insulted them during the previous week and they fought out back behind the bar while everyone else watched and made bets. It was insane.

Sociologists postulate that the masculine culture of dueling, fighting, and protecting one's "honor" didn't disappear from Western culture due to any kind of moral enlightenment. It was instead the result of the increasing power of the police state. A reasonably efficient police force protects families and property by punishing men who stand up for themselves and fight. People in developed countries realize that fighting in defense of "honor" is likely to be extremely costly in the long run. Fearing arrests or lawsuits, successful men in Western countries (outside of urban ghettos) don't generally fight.

In the developing world, there are no "reasonably efficient" police forces or legal systems. There are virtually no consequences for fighting. Because of these factors, people will fight over seemingly insignificant insults. It's your job to be extra careful to ensure that you don't unintentionally offend a local, especially a young, local male. If you screw up, your first notice that you violated social norms may be a punch in the face.

It's much easier to be polite and apologetic than it is to fight a bar full of 20-year old local men. Mind your manners.

Discreet Travel Weapons

"To do adventure travel means accepting a certain amount of risk. If you're too scared to face a country's populace without a firearm, then join the military (no disrespect meant to the military) or stay at home, because if you don't feel capable without the security blanket of a gun, you're going to make a piss poor adventure traveler."
– Perrin and Randall in *Adventure Travel in the Third World*

Assessing the level of threat, determining what weapons you might need, figuring out how to bring them with you, and understanding how to improvise weapons are important considerations for your overall safety when traveling. In this section, I will discuss these topics and provide some recommendations. If you have no intention of carrying weapons while traveling, feel free to skip ahead to the next chapter. If you are curious about how you might arm yourself in a foreign country, read on.

Firearms– My travels regularly prompt my cop and gun-owner friends to ask me how I plan on protecting myself in a third world country where it is illegal for me to carry a firearm. I've spent an average of at least six weeks a year for the last 15 years traveling outside of the country. My usual vacation spots are the kinds of places that most experts will advise you to avoid. Despite that fact, I've managed to survive pretty successfully without a gun, spending a grand total of more than an entire year traveling through about 40 third world countries.

If you think that you absolutely need a gun to survive your travels, you are seriously misguided. Furthermore, you are missing out on some awesome life experiences by limiting yourself to traveling in only those places that allow your concealed pistol. Here's the crux of what I have learned in my travels: **If you don't act like an asshole, people generally won't try to kill you.**

Author Marc MacYoung echoes this sentiment in his book *In the Name of Self Defense* by stating:

> "It's amazing how well not breaking social rules can keep you from being involved in a violent situation (especially if you think those social conventions are stupid). The same goes for not insisting on your rights (especially rights involving breaking local rules or misbehaving). It's even more impressive how not insulting, belittling, or looking at people like they are dog turds can keep you out of conflict and violence."

Pay attention to these words of wisdom.

I've traveled through some of the most dangerous countries on the planet without a gun. I try to make friends with the locals. I don't act like the "Ugly American." I don't pick fights. I try to smile a lot. I don't display indicators of my wealth or throw large sums of money around. I buy my new friends a round of beer on occasion. I learn some of the local language. That's it. That's my grand gun-free self-defense strategy. It's kept me quite safe throughout my life. If you are honest with yourself, doing these same things and not acting like an insufferable bore will keep you fairly safe as well.

Just because I'm not carrying a gun doesn't mean that I intentionally ignore the firearms present in the places I visit. While it's never happened in my travels, it is possible to encounter a dangerous situation that can only be resolved with the use of a defensive firearm. If I absolutely need a gun, I want to be able to get one. I also will need to know how to competently use it, given the fact that it may operate differently than the guns I use at home.

A standard pre-travel ritual I engage in is to prepare myself to use any "battlefield pickup" weapons I may be able to acquire overseas in an emergency. I look at the weapons that local cops/soldiers/security guards carry and make sure I can use those particular guns proficiently. The chance of me needing some local cop's gun is extremely low, but so is being caught in a hurricane or trapped in a volcanic eruption. Even though they are rare, I've experienced both of those disasters while traveling. I want to be prepared for the rare weapons-related emergency as well.

All across the world, the most common gun that you will see in public is a double action .38 special revolver. Armed security guards are more prevalent than the police and military in many developing countries. Almost all those guards carry a .38 wheel gun in some kind of cheap nylon holster. In a crisis, if I had to arm myself, I would either offer to buy one of those guns for an exorbitant sum of money or I'd choke out an unsuspecting security guard (sorry dude) and "acquire" his weapon.

The problem doesn't end with the mere acquisition of a revolver. Some other limiting factors necessitate that you not only have the gun in your possession, but you be exceptionally skilled in its use. Because the security guards who carry these revolvers rarely carry spare ammunition, and the ammunition they do carry tends to lack stopping power, you must focus on extreme accuracy and making fast head shots. One round nose .38 bullet to the chest isn't a fast fight stopper and you won't have extra cartridges to spare. Every shot must be an effective one.

Plan on using head shots more often than you might normally consider. The combination of faster stops and fewer cartridges expended is exactly the solution you will need to prevail in a third world gunfight.

Would you know how to operate this gun in an emergency? Carried by a security guard in Quito, Ecuador.

You will find a variety of weapons carried throughout different countries. In Latin America and the Caribbean, the .38 revolver that I described above is exceedingly popular. You will also see a lot of pump action shotguns, many of which will be equipped with pistol grips. The ubiquitous nature of those two types of weapons dictates that the knowledge of their use is critical before traveling.

In all my other travels in third world countries, I see the following other guns most commonly carried on a regular basis by the local cops/soldiers/security guards:

- Glock Pistol
- Beretta 92 (or Taurus Copy) 9mm Pistol
- M-16/AR-15 semi-automatic or automatic rifle variant
- Ruger Mini-14 semi-automatic rifle
- FN/FAL Battle Rifle
- AK-47 and AK-74 fully automatic rifle. As a pro-tip for you American gun owners, recognize that the manual safety positions on a fully automatic AK rifle are different from the semi-automatic AK rifles you see in the USA. Up is safe for both. Once click down on American semi auto rifles is "fire." One click down on real AK rifles is "full auto." Semi-automatic on a foreign made automatic AK is the farthest position down.

To be a well-rounded and better prepared traveler, you should understand basic operating functions of all of those weapons. They are the ones you will most likely see. If the topic interests you, talk to your gun owning friends and ask them to take you to a shooting range and show you how guns like this work. You may also be able to talk a friendly gun store clerk into giving you an impromptu lesson. If you have time, use Google Images and search "xxxx country police weapons." Look at the guns you see the cops carrying and make sure you are at least proficient on those weapon systems.

Knowing what types of guns the police and military carry in your destination country may have additional benefits as well. If you are stopped by a group of criminals who are posing as police officers or soldiers, you may be able to recognize that they don't have legitimate authority because they aren't carrying the kind of guns that cops/soldiers carry in that area. That bit of knowledge saved the life of a friend of mine when he was stopped at a roadblock by a gang of criminals posing as soldiers on the border of Guatemala.

As he was driving up to the roadblock, he recognized that the weapons the "soldiers" were carrying didn't fit those carried by other soldiers he had previously seen. He sped through the roadblock and escaped. When he reported the incident at a military base down the road, the real soldiers returned to the area of the roadblock and found six people stripped naked and bound in the jungle. The thieves had tied them up and were planning to execute all of them at the end of the day after victimizing as many other travelers as they could. It pays to know your local weapons.

Recognize that as a foreigner, you stand a high likelihood of spending the rest of your life in jail if you get caught with an unlicensed firearm in a third world country. In most cases the additional security a gun provides it isn't worth the risk of acquiring it and carrying it in a third world country. Save the gun stuff for only the direst of emergencies.

If you can't get a gun from a security guard like I mentioned above, you might be able to get one from a cop. Most police officers in third world countries drive some type of pickup truck as a police cruiser. They generally do not have locking gun racks like the police cars in the USA. Cops in third world countries often keep extra guns (both rifles and pistols) as well as body armor behind the seats of their trucks. Breaking into a police car might be a good place to get what you need.

As a final option for getting your hands on a firearm, you could consider contacting a local pimp. In educated circles, those guys are now called "human traffickers." They are adept at smuggling girls across borders for prostitution. If they smuggle people, they can probably also get you a gun. It's a very risky operation and you are far more likely to get ripped off or killed than to acquire a weapon, but in an absolute emergency, it may be something to consider.

If you do choose to acquire a firearm in country, be very careful in selecting your gun. If the police catch you armed, you will most certainly be jailed. That may not even be the worst case scenario. Some types of guns may get you shot right on the spot instead of being arrested.

Let's say you acquire a Glock 9mm or .40 S&W pistol and the cops find your gun when you are stopped at a random roadblock. What do you suppose the local police are going to think about you? As an American, most will assume that you are an undercover DEA or FBI agent trying to stop "corrupt" local cops and host country drug trafficking. They may also think you are CIA. Both of these assumptions will ensure an unpleasant experience and may get you shot on sight, depending on the country. Don't carry "cop guns."

Instead of selecting the state of the art semi-automatic pistol of your choice, consider acquiring a gun that doesn't make the local cops think you are there to shut down their bribery/extortion/drug smuggling activity. Think about picking up something like a short barreled .38 revolver or small .22 automatic pistol. These guns say "prudent traveler" or "business owner" rather than "undercover

American cop." You'll still likely go to jail if the cop finds your gun, but you aren't nearly as likely to be shot in the back of the head and left in the jungle to rot.

Airplane Weapons

Considering long flight times and strict "security" policies about bringing weapons on board, many people ask me about improvised weapons that they can use on an airplane. While the chance of experiencing a hijacking or violent passenger is exceedingly rare, it does make sense to take some precautions when you fly.

Without bringing anything extra onto the plane, first take a look at the improvised weapons that are already available. Ask your flight attendant for a seat belt extension and extend it all the way. By itself, it works as a great impact weapon.

If you don't want to do this, lift up your seat cushion and take a look at how the seat belts are attached. Most just use a simple clevis pin to attach to the seat base. If you remove the pin and disconnect the buckle end, you have a nice flexible impact weapon as well. The seat cushion could be pressed into service as an emergency shield that may defeat a small edged weapon.

In airports, look for any place where you might be able to acquire weapons for a hostage situation or terrorist bombing. Food preparation areas will generally have knives. Maintenance areas will generally have tools. Look for cleaning carts to find irritant chemicals. You might need items like that if things go really badly.

There are many other weapons that can be both taken onto a plane and carried innocuously once you land. Consider one of the following:

– **Canes**: Canes are legal on an airplane. You don't even have to feign a limp. As long as the cane doesn't have a sword inside, it's pretty much allowed to go through, even nasty fighting canes. While I don't think canes are the best weapons to use ON a plane because they require space to wield, they work well in the airport and in the terminal.

   – **Flashlights**: You should definitely have a flashlight in your carry-on. I always carry at least two. One of them is a headlamp that allows me to see and operate without tying up my hands. It also works great when you are trying to read and you happen to be in the seat with the malfunctioning overhead reading light.

   In addition to the headlamp, I also carry a flashlight that I can hit someone with. I generally carry flashlights from either SureFire or Fenix in my travels.

   – **Tactical pens**: Some pens are made stoutly enough to serve as impact weapons. I would avoid the ones that are spiky or look like a weapon. Those may be confiscated by TSA. I prefer the lower profile tactical pens. I carry one made by my friend Rick Hinderer all over the world and have never had an issue.

   It's probably a good idea to pack a pre-stamped, self-addressed envelope in your carry-on bag. If for some reason the TSA doesn't like your pen or flashlight, you can mail it home to yourself.

   -Improvised impact weapons. Think along the idea of "a rock in a sock." A couple of D-cell batteries inside a long tube sock (put together after you clear security) make a very nasty impact weapon. I generally use an old biker weapon instead, a bandanna threaded through the hasp of a padlock. You are limited only by your imagination.

Neither bandannas nor padlocks are prohibited by
the TSA....

Pepper Spray

Pepper spray is commonly carried in the USA and is a
useful tool for deterring a criminal attack. It is seen less
often in other countries. Some countries ban its
possession, but in the third world it won't attract much
attention if you are discreet about carrying and using it.
Pepper spray is hard to source locally in some locations.
If you plan on carrying it, it's probably best to bring it
from the USA. Once you are in-country, check for it at
hardware stores (South America) and police supply stores
(everywhere else).

There are essentially three different types of chemicals that are marketed to the public for self-defense purposes. They each have long chemical names, but they are abbreviated with the initials CN, CS, and OC. CN (the original formula in Mace) and CS (military tear gas) are irritants. They were developed for military use. They work by irritating the mucous membranes causing tearing, coughing, and pain. OC (pepper spray) is a hot pepper extract that is an inflammatory agent. Rather than just irritating the mucous membranes, it causes them to become inflamed. This inflammation makes it difficult to open the eyes or to breathe normally.

Of the three chemicals, OC is the most effective for self-defense use. Because the irritant formulas (CS and CN) depend on the attacker's reaction to the pain they cause, sometimes they prove to be ineffective. Many attackers you may face are under the influence of alcohol and/or drugs or are mentally ill. These people are likely to have a diminished pain response as compared to a "normal" human being. OC causes inflammation, which is not dependent on the body's pain response. OC also takes effect much faster than the other chemicals.

If you purchase your defensive spray here in the USA, choose an OC formulation. In other countries, you may be forced to carry CS as OC is occasionally illegal or unavailable. While CS isn't as good, it is definitely better than nothing.

If the chemical irritant you are considering for purchase does not list either the chemical composition you should avoid purchasing it if you are in the USA. In another country, there may not be any other options. The product may be very good, but unless you plan on spraying yourself before carrying it, you will never be sure how effective it is.

If you have any doubt about your spray's strength, spray a small amount onto a cloth and wipe it on your skin. You should feel a burning sensation within about 10 seconds. I personally recommend Fox, Aerko, Bodyguard, Sabre Red, and Counter Assault brand OC sprays. I've been exposed to each of these brands and can attest to their effectiveness.

Chemical deterrent sprays range in size from the ubiquitous 1/2 oz. keychain units to fire extinguisher sized models designed to help police quell riots. Each size has its own unique attributes. The small keychain-type units are convenient and easy to carry. Their downside, however, is that they contain only a small quantity of chemical (usually about five seconds worth) and they only spray a distance of two to five feet.

If you choose a keychain model, I would recommend that you carry one that is fully encased in plastic and has a simple-to-operate sliding safety. This type is much easier to use in a stressful situation than the traditional snap leather holster seen on so many key rings. In addition to the poorly-designed holster, older models require a difficult twisting action to disengage the safety before spraying. Both of these factors increase the amount of time it takes to bring the spray into action.

One step up in size from the keychain models is the one to two ounce spray containers. These have much more chemical (up to 30 seconds spray time) and, depending on spray type can reach out to about 15 feet. This is the size I recommend for most people at home, but they may be hard for the traveler to conceal. When traveling, I carry a small Sabre Red keychain unit. I would prefer something a little larger, but discretion is the better part of valor when in another country where you don't understand the law and the culture. A bigger container is much harder to hide and more likely to attract unwanted police attention. I'd rather sacrifice a little range and capacity to avoid having to pay off a local cop for possessing an "illegal weapon."

Another idea for travelers is to carry one of the pepper spray canisters that is designed to look like a large pen. Putting the "pen" into a rubber-banded bundle of Sharpie markers and a small notebook in your daypack will ensure that nosy police officers will overlook your spray if you encounter a roadblock or get searched.

Cold Steel Inferno pepper spray pen. Very inconspicuous, but be careful of the nozzle. It can fall off if the cap is removed in a hurried manner.

Even more important than all the other factors previously discussed is the proper use of the chemical you are carrying. The best chemical and spray pattern in the world will not help you if your attacker takes it away or even worse, uses it against you. Be able to get to your spray quickly! Too many people keep their sprays in their purse or on their key rings where they are virtually inaccessible. Try a little test right now. Grab your spray, disengage the safety if it has one, and prepare it for use. How long did it take you to perform those operations? If it took longer than two seconds, your spray is likely to be of little use to you in an actual attack.

If you are able to get to your spray in an attack situation, do not announce to the attacker that you are going to spray him. He should not know you have the spray until his eyes slam shut and he can no longer breathe. Any warning you might give only allows your attacker the time he needs to come up with a plan to avoid your spray or take it away from you.

Use your thumb to depress the button on your canister. This will make your spraying more accurate than using your index finger. It will also give you a stronger grip on your canister to make it more difficult for your attacker to wrest it away from you. Target your attacker's face with short bursts of spray lasting one to two seconds. Once your attacker's face is covered, stop spraying. More spray is not more effective. In fact, more spray only washes away the active ingredients from the face, increasing the amount of time it takes for the spray to take effect.

After spraying don't stand around and admire your handiwork. Use the spray as a distraction in order to make your escape. Get away as soon as it is safe to do so.

Have a backup plan. While chemical sprays are effective most of the time, sometimes they just don't work. Occasionally they take a considerable time to put your attacker down. Be prepared for the spray to be ineffective.

Consider other weapons options or be ready to fight with your hands and feet. If the spray is not working after a reasonable time period (five seconds or so) throw the can far away so that the attacker cannot gain control of it and use it against you.

Don't take the spray on board an aircraft in your carry-on luggage. That is illegal everywhere. Pack it in your checked bag instead. Pack it in two Ziploc bags just in case the pressure changes cause the canister to leak. I generally pack mine in some type of opaque plastic bag and throw it into a larger plastic bag with other types of liquids in my checked luggage. When being carried next to similar size containers of Lysol spray, bug spray, and sunscreen, most customs agents won't pay any attention to it.

If confronted by the police or customs agents, plead ignorance of the law. Tell them that the spray is legal where you live and you assumed it would be legal there as well. I've never heard of a tourist arrested for having a defensive spray in a third world country unless he gave the police officer a hassle when confronted. Simply apologize, plead ignorance, and give up your spray to the police officer.

Chemical spray deterrents add a potent weapon to anyone's arsenal. If you follow the simple steps outlined above, you will dramatically increase your ability to utilize a chemical spray deterrent in the most effective manner possible. Good chemical spray selection, combined with viable tactics and excellent situational awareness will make you into a formidable opponent for any potential attackers.

Knives

When I'm at home, I carry a gun for protection because it is both legal for me to do so and it is the most effective weapon in my arsenal. Overseas, with very few exceptions, the average traveler will not be able to legally acquire or carry a firearm. Although widely available on the black market in almost every country, the penalties for getting caught with a firearm are so severe that it is in most travelers' best interests to avoid acquiring one. The increased protection one may receive isn't worth the cost of doing time in a third world prison in the event you are discovered carrying an illegal pistol by police.

Since guns are not recommended, the most effective lethal weapon for most travelers is a knife. Knives can be legally brought into almost every third world country in checked luggage. Unless the knife is massive in size or the traveler has dozens of them in his luggage, customs officials rarely look twice if they see a knife when searching your checked bags.

Even though it's rare that carrying a knife into a country would be questioned, the traveler should still have a believable "justification" for the presence of the knife in the event that customs or law enforcement officers ask you why you are carrying a blade. "Self-defense" is never a good justification to use with corrupt third world officials. Remember, most people in foreign countries don't have the same "right" to self-protection as they do here in the USA. It's best to have a more innocuous reason for carrying the knife.

I generally carry a Spyderco Salt folding knife when I travel. The knife is made of a special type of stainless steel that does a phenomenal job resisting salt water. Thus, I have a handy justification for my blade; it's my "diving knife." That excuse has worked for me no matter where I have traveled. "Dive knives" are commonplace and cause no additional scrutiny. You could even get by with a larger fixed blade knife so long as it looked like it had marine applications. Other "justifications" could be that you are going "camping in the jungle" or that the knife is your "cooking knife." No matter what justification you choose, have a ready answer for when the cops ask you about the blade. "Cutting throats" is not generally a recommended response.

If you want to avoid the hassle completely, you can purchase a knife when you arrive in country. Hardware stores or large outdoor stores will have the largest selection. You may also be able to acquire a knife at a local market as well. If you buy a knife locally, keep the receipt. If you do get caught carrying it, you can tell the officer that you just bought it as a souvenir to take home with you. Playing the role of the clueless tourist with this excuse might keep you out of jail.

I purchased all of these knives at third world markets as "souvenirs."

If you can't find a hardware or outdoor store, don't forget that you can buy cooking knives at almost any grocery store. A small paring knife won't cost more than a couple of dollars. Use a folded piece of cardboard or aluminum can secured with duct tape to create a makeshift sheath for safe carry.

If all else fails, stealing a steak knife from a restaurant table is a valid option as well. That may be the best option for cruise ship passengers who have to go through a metal detector every time they get back on the ship. Take a sharp knife from the dinner table and carry it around with you on your land excursion. Make a sheath with the inner cardboard tube from the roll of toilet paper in your cabin and a little duct tape. Dispose of the blade on land before your re-board the ship. Grab another knife at dinner to repeat this process for the following day.

In addition to carrying my Spyderco Salt folder, I also carry a small ceramic fixed blade knife. I carry this one because it contains absolutely no metal. While not quite as sharp or durable as a metal blade, the ceramic knife isn't detected by metal detectors. That being said, DON'T CARRY IT ONTO AN AIRPLANE!

Even though it makes it through metal detectors, an X-ray or a pat down physical search will find the blade. If you try to smuggle it into the passenger cabin of a commercial airplane, there is a very good chance you will get caught and go to jail. Spending time in a Federal Penitentiary will ruin your vacation.

I honestly don't know the laws regarding knife carry for most of the countries I visit and I really don't care. I recognize that I may be breaking local laws by carrying a blade, but my personal protection is very important to me. I'll risk being arrested or forced to pay a bribe in exchange for being able to save my own life if I am attacked. You'll have to make a decision for yourself with regard to what you are willing to risk. It's "Big Boy Rules." If you can't do the time, don't commit the crime.

With that said, the chance of getting caught and/or arrested when carrying a knife in a third world country is next to zero. If you are smart about carrying the blade, you won't get caught. If you do get caught, you'll usually be able to pay off the cop who catches you to avoid going to jail. I've only been caught with a knife one time in all of my travels when I had to go through a metal detector unexpectedly. I gave the knife to the cop. He pocketed it and that was the end of the issue.

To avoid being caught, you have to be smart. Don't carry your blade clipped to your pocket like you may in the USA. No one carries knives like this in other countries. It's a huge red flag that cops and security guards will notice very quickly. If you have a folding knife with a clip, carry it down in your pocket or clip it inside your waistband with an untucked shirt. It will be harder to access this way, but you won't get shaken down by the cops.

Be careful of metal detectors. In third world countries, you will encounter metal detectors in places where you might not expect them to be. Depending on the country and the area, you are likely to find metal detectors in hotel lobbies, train stations, bus stations, government buildings, banks, and museums. If you are sightseeing in those locations, carry the ceramic blade.

If you forget your ceramic blade and are carrying a weapon that will set off a metal detector, you won't want to be hassled with dealing with the security guard. I often will just walk right around the metal detectors without even acknowledging the guard. Adopt the air of the "clueless tourist" and just ignore the guard's protests. Often he won't even notice or care. In the worst case scenario, you will have to go through the screening- which was going to happen anyway.

If you are a regular at a certain location, you might be able to bribe the guards to avoid security. I was once staying in a reasonably high dollar hotel in Egypt that had a metal detector at the door. Not wanting to constantly be shaken down for my knives, I bought the guard a soft drink one day and thanked him for "keeping us safe." Whenever I returned to the hotel, I brought the man another cold beverage. I very quickly was determined to be "safe" and no longer required to go through the metal detectors.

Metal detector in a Bangkok subway station. I walked through with two knives and a SureFire light and didn't set it off.

I carry my ceramic blade in what's called a "slip sheath." I attach the cord on the sheath to my belt or belt loop and then position the blade in my waistband. When I draw the knife, the sheath falls off as soon as it reaches the end of the cord. If I need to have a lower profile, I will shove the knife completely down the front of my pants. The only thing visible is the cord attached to the belt. If you use paracord that is the same color as your belt or your pants, the cord will be barely noticeable. Even if you do get searched by the police, there's a good chance that they will miss the knife. Male cops don't tend to check other men's genital regions in a thorough manner.

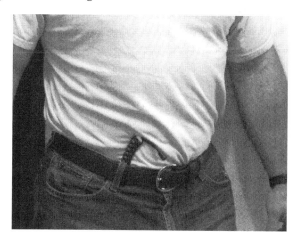

Talonz Ceramic Knife in "slip sheath" stuck in
waistband

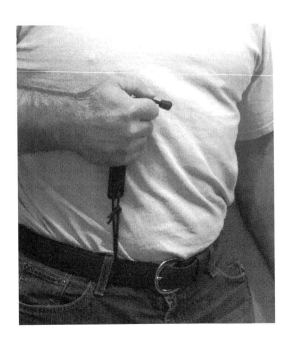

When I pull up on the knife, the cord attached to the belt reaches the end of its range of motion and the knife clears the sheath.

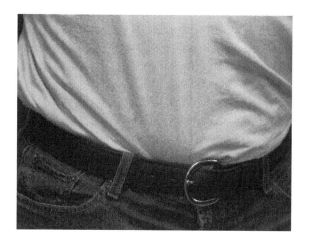

But when the cops are around, you can push the entire blade down into your pants and only the cord shows.

If you are carrying a metal blade and stumble into a location with searches or metal detectors, you may still be able to get through the security checkpoint without being arrested. Often, police and security guards use metal detecting wands instead of using walk-through metal detectors. The cops get lazy and grow tired of bending over. They regularly won't sweep body parts that are low to the ground with their metal detector wands. Sticking a knife in your sock or shoe will often allow it to make it through security undetected.

If the shoe isn't an option, clip the knife to the front of your underwear right behind your pants zipper. That area won't likely be searched well. If the metal detector does go off, you can blame it on your metal zipper or metal belt buckle.

One other technique that is regularly used by criminals here at home is to allow their female companions to carry the weapons. Women aren't viewed as being "suspicious" enough to warrant a search in lots of situations. If they are searched, male security guards and cops will usually avoid searching the breast area or genitals of females. These practices are even more evident in foreign countries than they are here. Clip your knife to the front of your wife or girlfriend's panties or to her bra strap and she will probably get the blade past security.

Women carrying knives in this manner under their clothes will often go right through security without incident.

In addition to the two blades I mentioned above, I also carry the knife that I designed, the KaBar TDI Last Ditch blade. I designed it specifically to be a last ditch weapon or escape tool that could be hidden anywhere on your body and would likely be missed by a cursory pat down search. I made the blade smaller than a credit card so that it can be hidden in a wallet. The sheath has multiple attachment points so that it can be taped or safety pinned anywhere inside your clothing. You can even lace the knife up in your shoelaces.

My LDK knife design

When I travel to countries where kidnapping is a probability, I use a safety pin to attach the knife inside my pants. I position it just below the belt line in the small of my back. I've also used a wire keychain to attach the blade to my rear belt loop so that it hangs down inside my pants. In that position, it isn't likely to be found on a search. Again, most men don't want to spend time feeling another dude's ass. That position also makes the knife easily accessible if my hands are tied or taped behind my back.

The knife is just the right size to cut my way out of a lot of problems. I've seen some folks tape it to the inside of their belts, carry it on a cord around their necks, or pin it under a lapel. It's truly a versatile knife that you can carry anywhere.

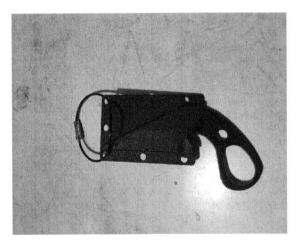

The LDK on a key chain looped over a rear belt
loop and hung inside the pants

Those three blades have traveled around the world with me for many years. No one ever gives them a second glance, but in a pinch, they'll work very well as defensive weapons.

Lower profile blades- Some of these recommendations may be too "aggressive" appearing for some of you. If you are worried about getting arrested while carrying a knife, there are a couple of other options to consider. The options below look less weapon-like than some of the ones I mentioned earlier. With that said, recognize that in general, having a lower profile blade also means that it will be slower to get into action and potentially less useful in combat.

> – **A slip-joint folder**. Some folding knives don't have locks to keep the blades from closing on your hand. Knives without locks, while a poor choice for combat, look less aggressive to authorities. In some countries (especially in Europe) it is illegal to carry a folding blade with a lock.

> My favorite slip joint folder is the Spyderco UK pen knife. It is a knife designed to be legally carried even under the strict anti-knife laws prevalent in the United Kingdom. It has a small two inch blade and no lock. While not the best choice for fighting, it can certainly do the job in the right hands. Slashing with these blades is a safer strategy than stabbing. If you hit bone on a stab, the knife will likely close on your fingers.

> – **A Multi-Tool**. Lots of travelers carry multi-tools like the ones made by Leatherman. They contain

pliers, screw drivers, blades, cap lifters and other handy tools. They really are nothing but an updated Swiss Army knife. No one will give a traveler with one of these things a second glance as long as he is not trying to take it into a secure facility.

There's no way you'll get this blade out and open in the heat of combat. Leatherman –style tools work best for defending a fixed position (like your hotel room) when you have some type of forewarning that an attack is coming. If I had to use a multi-tool defensively, I would open the blade and then fold up the handles so that the blade can't close on my fist. Most knife blades on these tools don't have any additional locks to keep them from folding if you stab something hard.

– **A Swiss Army knife.** This type of knife says "backpacker" not "knife fighter." It has many of the same weaknesses as the multi-tool mentioned above, but it won't attract any attention at all if you carry it.

Of all the Swiss Army knives available, I like the model named "The Trekker" best. It has a lockable blade with a large thumb hole for fast opening, yet still remains innocuous looking.

– **The DPx Heat.** Famed adventurer Robert Young Pelton designed this indestructible little folding blade. It has a two-inch blade that meets even the most stringent blade length laws anywhere in the world. It's made from extremely hard steel so that it stays sharp much longer than most other knives. Since you probably aren't traveling with a knife sharpener, having a knife can cut a lot of things before getting dull is an important feature.

The handle allows for a slip-free grip and there is a bottle opener (which also serves as an additional opening method) on the back side of the blade. The knife also has an automobile glass breaker on the end. The entire package makes a nice fist load for punching as well. This is a real tank of a knife, but it looks far more utilitarian than the average "combat-style" folding knife.

– **Fruit knife.** A small paring knife is easier to explain to the cops than just about any other type of blade. Pick up one that has a two to three inch blade length. Use an apple as your "sheath" and no one will think anything of it.

DPx HEAT (on top), the Trekker Swiss Army knife, and a small ceramic paring knife (won't set off metal detectors) that I picked up at a grocery store in Mexico.

The Grocery Bag Trick– People everywhere are used to seeing someone walking around with plastic grocery bags in their hands. The same ubiquitous bag can be found in

confrontation immensely because you no longer have to worry about drawing or opening your weapon. It is already in your hand and ready for action.

That bag in his hand might contain more than just groceries

I've used the technique dozens of times in dodgy third world countries. If I get caught in a dangerous part of town, I'll just stop into the corner store and buy a couple bottles of water. They'll put them in a plastic sack and I take it into a restroom. I remove the water, place my knife (opened and ready for action) in the bag and walk out. No one notices and I feel a whole lot better prepared to handle a violent attacker.

Here are some additional tips...

1) It works best if you have a darker colored opaque bag. Clear or grey colored bags often don't conceal the weapon enough

2) If you need to use it, don't remove the knife. Just stab right through the bag. It is faster than removing the knife. After the initial stab, you will be able to use the edge of the knife to slash or pressure cut, as most of the blade will be sticking through the bag

Don't remove the knife, it takes too long. Just stab through the bag.

3) Reserve this technique for only the most dangerous of situations where you need a weapon in your hand. In less-dangerous spots, it may limit

your options as it is difficult to respond physically (to an attack that doesn't require lethal force) if one of your hands is tied up holding a weapon. It will also certainly cause a prompt reaction from the local police if one of them takes notice. It's better to err on the side of caution and save this one for when you really need it.

4) Be careful of thieves and purse snatchers. Sometimes criminals will target the bag in your hand, thinking it contains something valuable. I once had this happen to me in Egypt. I was walking through a *souk* (outdoor market) in Luxor very late at night. I probably shouldn't have been there as it was a "local" place far off the tourist routes. I had a knife in a bag and was quickly walking through the crowd trying to leave the area when I was accosted by a teenage boy. He grabbed toward my bag and screamed "GIVE IT TO ME NOW!" in perfect English. He thought I was carrying something expensive I had purchased in the market and decided to rob the "clueless" tourist.

Fortunately, his robbery attempt was unsuccessful and I got out of the situation unscathed. It helped that I outweighed the boy by 150 pounds. Sometimes I wish I hadn't been so quick to pull the bag out of his reach. He would have received quite a shock if he was able to forcibly grab my knife blade.

Be careful with this technique. Carrying a weapon in your hand while walking through a crowd isn't the safest option, but there will likely be times in your life when it is necessary. Be alert to this technique being used against you by a criminal as well.

You may never look at a plastic bag in the same way again.

Improvised Weapons

"The first rule of unarmed combat is to always pick up a weapon!
– Orlando Wilson

Most third world countries don't have laws prohibiting public alcohol consumption on the street. That handy fact makes it easy to be armed at all time with the ubiquitous beer bottle. If you are leaving a bar or restaurant late at night and don't have any other weapons, order a beer to go and drink it on the way home.

I've found that criminals tend to avoid people walking around with a beer in hand so long as the drinker doesn't appear too intoxicated to take care of himself. Casually sipping a beer while walking down the street displays a level of confidence and security that most predators won't want to confront. They'll wait for the next non-drinking "goody-goody" tourist who will likely be a safer mark.

Besides the psychological benefit of appearing calm and cool, the beer can also be a great social lubricant. There have been a few times where I've been approached in the street by younger males just trying to size me up. Rather than fleeing or fighting, I find it easier to make friends in these kinds of tense situations. Offer to share your beer. You'll be amazed at the results this simple gesture will get for you. You might make a friend for life. If it doesn't work, you just hit the guy in the face with your beer bottle. Problem solved.

I was once out for a walk with a traveling companion in Cusco, Peru. We were tired of doing all of the "tourist" things and decided to stroll around some of the neighborhoods where the locals lived. It was one of my first international trips and I was pretty nervous about leaving the tourist zone. We walked for a few miles and didn't have any problems.

After rounding a corner, we saw three young local men blocking the sidewalk. They all appeared drunk and had large bottles of beer in their hands. The men started pointing at us and walking our way. I wasn't sure what they wanted, but those big beer bottles had me worried. I told my friend "*get ready to run*" as they came within striking distance.

One of the men said "*Where are you from?*" in halting English. I was certain that when I answered "*United States,*" the beatdown would commence. We were outnumbered, on their turf, they were drunk, and they had improvised weapons. This wasn't going to end well.

After my answer, the man replied: "*We don't see any American tourists around here. If you let us practice speaking English with you, we'll share our beer.*" We all sat down in the street and had a great time talking and drinking the local beer.

It was a pleasant surprise in comparison with the negative outcome I had anticipated. I learned that good beer is appreciated the world over and that most people aren't out to get you. It also got me thinking about how I immediately assumed that men carrying beer bottles would be a problem. I think most people would feel the same way. We can use that to our advantage as well. As long as you don't appear too drunk, carrying a beer bottle may make the criminal pass you by in search of an easier victim. The beer bottle has value as both a social lubricant and an impact weapon.

DeSantis coin purse sap– While not exactly "improvised," a leather coin purse filled with local pocket change looks harmless but could create quite a bit of damage when laid across a miscreant's skull. The one I use is made by a holster company called DeSantis. They call it the "City Slicker." It's a very low profile, but intensely effective impact weapon similar to old- school police blackjack or sap.

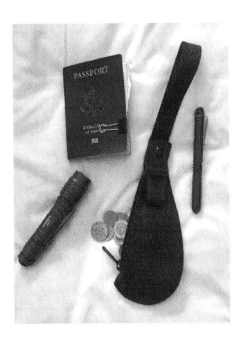

Low-profile impact weapons. Surefire flashlight,
Hinderer tactical pen, and City Slicker coin purse.

Screwdrivers- A screwdriver can be an effective
improvised weapon. I've done some pretty extensive
research testing of various screwdriver types by stabbing
them into donated animal carcasses in my edged weapons
classes. You might be surprised that the Phillips head
screwdriver will penetrate deeper than a flat head
screwdriver, even if the flat head is sharpened. Shorter
screwdrivers work better than those with longer shafts.

A screwdriver with a three to four inch shaft can be
easily buried up to the handle in a person's neck. I've found
that repeated downward reverse grip stabs to the attacker's

face/neck area (think about the *Psycho* movie shower scene) to be the most effective way to use a screwdriver as a self-defense weapon. They are legal to carry and cheap to buy all over the world. If you get caught without a weapon and need something fast, this might be a good option.

Fracture Pen- This is a slightly less effective tool, but it is extremely low profile. Take a common plastic barrel Bic pen. Remove the ink cartridge. Make a diagonal cut in the pen barrel near the tip. Cut with a hacksaw or Dremel tool and make an incision that almost completely severs the tip. Replace the ink and put on the cap.

In an emergency, you can remove the ink cartridge, break off the rest of the pen and have a sharp stabbing weapon. I would use it to target your adversary's face, eyes, or neck.

Other weapons found in the hardware store- If you are in need of a weapon quickly, duck into a hardware store. Even in a relatively poorly stocked third world hardware store, you'll likely find countless items that you can use as improvised weapons.

Hand tools work great. In addition to the screwdrivers I mentioned above, consider arming yourself with a hammer, razor knife, axe, or machete. If you want something even less conspicuous, consider a short piece of metal pipe or a length of heavy duty chain for defensive purposes. You are limited only by the selection at the store you visit and your own imagination. Be creative.

Look for weapons of opportunity. These would make fine tools for an emergency.

Adaptibility- The Final Weapon

"*Guns, clubs, and knives may well be material weapons, but abstract weapons like wits, demeanor, and attitude are just as important, if not more so.*" – Louis Awerbuck

I enjoy third world travel because it provides challenges that I don't normally get to experience. Solving the problems you encounter in a third world country will quickly make you a very adaptable person, more so than any other educational opportunity I've encountered. One of the more difficult problems to solve is deciding what weapons you should carry and what your self-protection plans might entail. You obviously think the same way if you have made it this far in the "weapons" chapter. Let me give you some other things to think about:

I once spent some time on a small island off the coast of Nicaragua. It was a peaceful place, but I still wanted to have adequate self-protection measures. Thinking through potential defensive scenarios on the island, I recognized that I was in a truly unique environment that required some adaptation from my normal plans.

As discussed above, while traveling in most third world countries, I rely on a knife (or knives) for self-protection. Depending on where I'm traveling, if I needed to use one, I wouldn't likely report the use to the local police. There just isn't much of a chance of a fair trial or judicial proceeding as an American who stabs or kills a local in a developing nation. You'll spend a long time in prison or get killed "resisting arrest" if you go to the police. It's better to quickly get the hell out of the area if you have to use lethal force.

That posed quite a problem on my little island trip. There were literally only about 20 gringos on the whole island. There were two local flights off the island and two ferry departures every day. Everyone knows everyone else and most folks are related. Escape options are few. If I stab a local in self-defense, how quickly do you think the word would spread around the island that the cutting was done by "*the big gringo dude*?" How do you think the locals would respond? Besides dealing with the initial problem that caused me to use my blade, I would have the additional unpleasant difficulty escaping the rope of the lynch mob that would be waiting for me at my hotel.

Have you ever considered something like that?

I still carried my blade, but I was also diligent in carrying my flashlight (as an impact weapon) and my pepper spray. Even though less effective in individual combat than using a knife, smashing a dude in the teeth with my flashlight or spraying him with some O.C. would probably be far better for my long-term health. The locals will be a whole lot more forgiving of some burning eyes than they will when they see a knife buried in one of their relative's throats.

Just like I teach my students here, one has to solve not only the problem of surviving the initial violent encounter, but the secondary problem with the police and the criminal justice system as well. In other countries, the "secondary problem" won't likely be a fair trial by a jury of your peers; it might be an angry lynch mob. You aren't prepared to defend yourself unless you can handle that issue as well. Walter Mitty-like fantasies of cutting throats and throwing knives in the gutter to make a stealthy escape aren't very productive. Don't delude yourself. You aren't Jason Bourne and you won't get away with it. Make a realistic assessment of your environment and your abilities and plan accordingly.

The weapon of deception: your personality

When in a foreign country, it's important to be perceived as likable even if that isn't your natural personality.

Charismatic people exude confidence and are less likely to be victimized by either the scam artist or the predatory criminal. Making people like you is a very important skill set to have and will smooth out all your traveling experiences.

The first key to molding yourself into a likable person is to smile. Not the grin of someone in an asylum, but a genuine warm smile that shows your aren't angry or a threat. That alone will take you far. Smiling and being able to laugh at yourself when you make mistakes, will endear you to many people.

If you aren't normally a charismatic person, there is another trick you can use to make friends quickly. I first heard of it from author and public speaker Arel Moodie. He instructs his clients to imagine everyone they meet has a sign hanging around his/her neck. That sign says "*Make Me Feel Special.*"

Imagine the sign and then do just that. Make every person you meet feel special or valued. True charisma is developed when people feel good when they are around you. If you take just a couple of seconds to figure out how to make the person with whom you are interacting feel special, they can't help but have good feelings about the interaction. Give it a try. You will become adored by the people you meet and will be far less likely to have to need a weapon or tool for your protection. If you are friendly enough, you can even get "cool guy" protection from the locals when things heat up.

Think about how your actions and mannerisms might appear to a local. You want to look friendly, but not gullible. Don't be afraid to alter your response quickly if you notice that your default mannerisms are placing you in greater danger.

Police and Government Interactions

"If you commit a serious offense or even look like you have done something wrong while overseas, such lofty concepts as "your rights" and being "presumed innocent until proven guilty" simply do not apply. You may have only been a bystander at the wrong place and time, but you could still be arrested on suspicion of involvement. If you are not careful, this paradise-vacation-turned nightmare scenario can happen anywhere, anytime."
– Perrin and Randall in *Adventure Travel in Third World Countries*

Outside of the USA, Canada, Australia, and Western Europe, the police will act very differently than they do at home. While you may occasionally find corruption in individual officers here in the States, it is exceedingly rare. Corruption is endemic in many other places. Expect it. Many police officers in third world countries are nothing but thugs with a gun and a badge. Your best bet is generally to ignore them.

How much training do you think he's had with that AK? It's probably best to stay away from this local cop in Cambodia.

Watch how the locals treat the police. They won't smile and wave like residents do here when a police cruiser passes their house. Locals will avert their eyes, walk away, and conspicuously ignore the police. They know that nothing positive will come from a police interaction and do their best to avoid having any contact with the cops.

If you are a police officer here in the USA, don't try to talk to the cops in third world countries. It just isn't the same. If a cop from South America walked into my police department and introduced himself, every officer there would do their best to provide him a great tourist experience. Not so in other countries. Most foreign cops will think you are an American DEA agent trying to move in on their drug/bribery/smuggling/corruption operation and will not be kind. Do what the locals do; stay away from the cops.

Even if the police officers you deal with are not corrupt, you should not expect the same level of service from the police that you would expect in Western countries. Part of the difference is a lack of resources and training. Even more prevalent (especially in Asian countries) is a different cultural view of death and serious injury. In many Buddhist countries, death isn't viewed the same way as it is in the West. In Asia, death is seen as an inevitable ending to life. It is often welcomed rather than avoided. For this reason, cops don't tend to investigate deaths/serious injuries with the same sense of urgency that you might see in North American police officers.

Police officer in Hanoi, Vietnam monitoring traffic

In most larger cities, police departments have "Tourist Police" who are often bilingual and are there to assist tourists. They are usually helpful and friendly, but may not be the best crime fighters. I wouldn't trust them if my life was in danger.

Two of my colleagues...Tourist Police in La Paz,
Bolivia

Don't take photographs of police officers, police stations,
border crossings, or military bases without asking
permission. The police in third world countries take their
personal security quite seriously and will confiscate your
camera on the spot if you are caught taking "unauthorized"
photographs.

Police border checkpoints like this one in Brazil are very common in third world countries. Notice the motorcyclists waiting on the right. They have paid off the police and will smuggle drugs past the checkpoint for the right amount of money.

Police in Latin American countries will often drive around with red and blue lights flashing to display their presence and reassure tourists. If a police vehicle comes up behind you with lights flashing, he isn't usually trying to pull you over. He will hit the siren or yell at you over the loudspeaker if he wants you to stop. If a foreign police officers is trying to stop you, slow down and turn on your flashers. If you can get to a well-lit, public location quickly, pull over there. Corrupt cops are less likely to hassle you (or worse) if you are in a location where others can see what they are doing.

Although I've seen quite a few examples of third world cops hassling folks unnecessarily and/or "requesting" bribes, overall, you are fairly unlikely to have to deal with this behavior. I've spent a lot of time in developing countries. The few times that I've dealt with corrupt cops has been spread over many, many years. In a shorter trip, you probably don't have to worry too much about corrupt cops or politicians. If you are approached by foreign police officers, be polite, smile, and play dumb.

Tell them in English that you don't understand what they are saying. If they speak English, answer their questions truthfully, but don't volunteer any extra information. Don't make a big scene when they search you or your bags. The constitutional rights you have in your home country don't apply in a foreign nation. It's their country. You have to play by their rules. In most developing countries, that means tolerating a search of your person or bags at any police officer's whim.

When it becomes obvious that a police officer wants to search you, act preemptively. Immediately empty all of your pockets and then turn them inside out. You want to do this before the officer has a chance to reach into your pockets or clothing. Turning your pockets inside out will limit the chance that the police officer doing the search will palm a small amount of drugs and then suddenly "find" them when he reaches into your pocket. If he doesn't have an excuse to reach into your pocket, it is far more difficult to plant any contraband with the goal of "requesting" a bribe.

Be extra cautious in any interaction with a police officer or soldier who appears drunk or on drugs. If they smell of alcohol, have bloodshot eyes or pinpoint pupils, get away quickly. These are either criminals masquerading as cops or are cops who are so corrupt that they don't even care about maintaining a token "good" public perception. Either of these groups is especially dangerous. The best case scenario is that you will be solicited for a bribe. Even worse, these corrupt cops might be targeting you for a kidnapping or sexual assault.

With all this said, you still shouldn't get too worked up about dealing with corrupt cops. It isn't as big of a problem as most Americans make it out to be. There are far more important things to worry about. Be aware of the typical scams, follow my basic instructions, conspicuously avoid anyone in uniform and you will likely enjoy your trip without ever having a negative interaction with the local authorities.

All bets are off, however, if you are doing something illegal. If you are drunk and stupid or mess around in the drug trade, you WILL eventually have an interaction with the cops. The easiest way to avoid being a story on "*Locked Up Abroad*" is to avoid breaking the host country's laws.

Bribery and Corruption

"The decision is between bad and worse. There is no good solution."
– J.D. Potynsky

As the taxi driver saw the roadblock and screeched to a halt, a man wearing a tattered uniform leaped out of the bushes and stuck his AK-47 through my open car window. I remember noticing that the safety was off as he jabbed my cheek with the muzzle and said *"Don't move"* in halting English.

What would you do if you were placed in that situation? I'll tell you what I did. I complied with the disheveled African cop who was jamming the AK in my face. I quickly ran through the options in my head. I was in Tanzania and didn't have a gun. Do I draw my hidden knife? Do I attempt to disarm him? Do I feign compliance and flee on foot? All of those were the wrong answer. I paid the cop some bribe money and I'm still around to tell the story.

Quite a few "experts" criticize crime victims for complying in the face of an armed threat. The writers talk about how compliance is cowardly and how resistance (preferably armed resistance) is the only "proper" course of action when one is attacked or threatened with a deadly weapon. Making statements like that is both short-sighted and wrong. While there are many situations that are best solved by armed resistance, there are some where compliance is a better option.

We start having problems when we listen to "experts" who have never truly faced violence and have never had to make the comply/resist decision when their lives are at stake. It's easy to talk about resisting a corrupt cop or refusing to pay a bribe from the safety of the computer keyboard in the writer's cozy home. It's a bit different when there is a gun wielded by a crazy man stuck in your face late at night.

Let me tell you the rest of the story I started above. It's a story where I'm not the hero. It's a story about a time in my life where I chose to comply in the face of an armed threat rather than resist. And it's ultimately a story that has a positive ending.

In 2008, I decided to climb the highest mountain in Africa. Mount Kilimanjaro is in Tanzania and stands 19,341 feet (5895 meters) above sea level. For perspective, that's more than a mile HIGHER than those big mountain peaks in Colorado. The trek up the mountain takes between five and eight days (depending on route) and starts from the desert plain at roughly sea level. It makes for a steep and difficult hike without much time to acclimate. I booked a trek with a licensed guide and made my travel plans.

While looking for airfare, I found that I could save over $2000 if I flew into Nairobi, Kenya rather than the closest airport to Kilimanjaro. Nairobi is about an eight hour public bus trip away from the town in Tanzania where I was going to start my climb. I elected to fly into Nairobi and take the public bus across the border rather than paying the extra money.

I scheduled a couple extra days in Nairobi and did some sightseeing at several nearby game parks. On the morning I was scheduled to depart from Tanzania, I caught a cab to the bus station and hopped on my bus. It left on time and we headed off across the African plains. It was a "luxury bus" and a fairly comfortable ride. After a few hours of watching the scenery, I put my headphones on and leaned up against the window to take a nap. Shortly thereafter, I was awakened by a deafening crash and a huge jolt. A dump truck hauling gravel for a road construction project had backed into our bus as it was traveling about 60 mph down a remote highway. The bus shuddered to a stop and the driver exited without ever even checking to see if any of his passengers were injured.

I looked around and saw that most of the passengers were stunned, but none had any obvious injuries. Everyone was frantically speaking in Swahili. I was the only foreigner on the bus and couldn't understand what was going on. A young college girl next to me spoke English and said to me *"Get off the bus. There's going to be a fight."*

Just before the fight began....

All of the passengers disembarked and watched as the driver of our bus and the dump truck operator screamed at each other. They yelled, began pushing each other, and eventually a full-on fight broke out. All of us watched as the two drivers struggled and punched each other in Africa's indescribable heat..

The English-speaking college girl translated the fighters' words for me. She explained that neither driver had money to pay off the police if they were called. Instead of paying bribes to the corrupt cops, the drivers were going to fight. The loser would accept fault for the accident when they turned the damage in to their respective insurance companies.

The two men fought for about 20 minutes along the side of the road. Neither landed a single good punch. It was mostly just pushing and stand-up wrestling. They suddenly stopped, shook hands and then separated. The driver of our bus dug a crowbar out of the luggage compartment and pried the damaged quarter panel away from the rear bus tire. We were on our way again. It was mind boggling, but you quickly learn to accept such events as commonplace when traveling through remote Africa.

Damage to the bus after the driver pried the sheet
metal away from the tire

The fight had some lasting consequences, however. Because of the delay, I missed my connecting bus in a little border town in Tanzania. It was 11pm and I was stuck in a dodgy African border town with no accommodations. No more buses were running. I was about 100 miles from my hotel. My choices were to either spend the night in the border town and wait for a bus in the morning or hire a taxi to get me to my destination. I chose to go with the taxi.

I found a taxi driver who spoke relatively good English. He quoted me a $30 fare for the 100-mile drive. I readily accepted. As I got in the unmarked cab, the driver suggested that I ride in the front seat with him. He said that if people saw I was riding in back they would assume that I had money and would target us for a robbery. By sitting up front, it just looked like I was the driver's friend and it would attract less negative attention. I took the driver's advice and hopped in the front seat for the two hour journey.

It was after midnight and I was both tired and hot as we drove to my destination. I had my window down because the cab didn't have any air conditioning. There were few cars on the road and we were making good time when we rounded a curve and saw something in the middle of the road. The driver skidded to a stop when he noticed a kerosene lantern in the road sitting on top of several pieces of lumber with huge metal spikes driven through them. The spikes were pointed up to flatten car tires.

As soon as we stopped, a Tanzanian cop jumped out of the bushes and struck me in the face with the muzzle of his AK-47. A thousand thoughts crossed my mind. What should I do? Even though I wanted to fight, my gut told me to comply until I had a better opportunity. I didn't know if the armed man was alone or if he had additional backup hiding in the bushes. Even if I killed him or took his gun, I still might have to fight several of his buddies. It didn't seem like fighting would have a high likelihood of success.

He kept the AK-47 pointed at my head as he explained in poor English that I didn't have a permit to be on the road we were traveling. I knew that no such permit was necessary. I also knew that the Tanzanian National Police make the equivalent of approximately $7 US dollars a day. Any foreigner with enough money to hire a driver would likely have more money in his wallet than the cop makes in a month.

I evaluated my options and decided to play it cool. I knew the cop could shoot both of us on this rural highway and have us buried before sun up. I kept my hands in sight and told the corrupt policeman that I was sorry. I asked him if I could pay the "fine" on the spot. He lowered the gun and told me that the fine for my "offense" was 300 Tanzanian Shillings. It was the US equivalent of 25 cents. For a quarter, the dude was ready to shoot me in the head.

I paid my "fine", the cop moved the roadblock and we were again on our way. For the rest of the trip, I just kept replaying the incident over and over in my mind, wondering if I should have handled it differently. I analyzed what prompted me to pay the bribe rather than do something else in that situation.

While I admit the thought of him having possible friends hiding in the bushes was a big consideration, the main factor that kept me from fighting was simply a gut feeling. The guy was dangerous, but seemed rational. I had to think of his motivation. If he wanted to kill me, he could have done so without uttering a word. No, he wanted something else. I was willing to give up what he wanted in exchange for not having to fight a rifle-wielding cop using my Spyderco folding knife.

I can say without hesitation that I made the right decision. Paying the bribe wasn't heroic. It wasn't badass. It was just using my brain and my instincts to keep myself safe. Some internet experts may try to convince you that paying a bribe isn't an option. Those guys probably haven't been hit in the face with the barrel of an AK-47.

This event was a fairly extreme example of the bribery, extortion, and corruption that you may encounter in a third world country. Most of my readers will never suffer anything so dramatic or dangerous in their travels. But if you spend enough time in developing countries, it is almost certain that you will experience some level of bribery or extortion.

North American and Western European tourists experience severe indignation at the very thought of having to pay a bribe to a police officer or government bureaucrat. That's simply not how it's done at home.

I'm not the kind of person who is going to try to change your mind about the ethical implications of paying a bribe. You have to make that decision on your own. But you must understand that bribery and corruption IS the way business is handled in most third world countries. If you don't understand the system, you will be victimized regardless of your ethical ideals.

I look at paying bribes as just another cost associated with travel. In my mind, it isn't productive to get all worked up about a small amount of money. One simply can't deny reality just because one doesn't like how the system works.

My best advice to you is to treat government corruption the same way the locals do; try to avoid it at all costs. Be prepared, be aware, but don't get too upset if you have to pay a little bit. Like I said, it's the cost of doing business. Travel requires some expenditure. You don't think twice about paying money for your airfare, food, and hotel bills. Consider small bribes to be in the same category. It's just money paid in order to fully experience a new and different culture. My friends in a large American federal law enforcement agency operating in South America call bribes "*culturally appropriate gratuities.*" I suggest that you consider them in the same light hearted way if you really want to enjoy your trip.

With all that said, there are a few strategies you can use to reduce the impact that bribery and corruption will have on your bank account or physical well-being. In some countries, bribery is the best way to deal with the police. Paying a small amount of cash often ensures a hassle-free encounter. While this idea is repulsive to many Western tourists, it is a way of life for the locals. They have figured out how best to handle the cops. Sometimes it's best to follow their lead.

A good phrase to use if the cop who stops you speaks English is "*I'm sorry. I didn't understand the law. Can I pay the fine right now?*" That is a face-saving way for the officer to extort some money from you without getting violent or making excessive demands.

As I mentioned above, it's important to carry your money in different places on your body. When the cop demands too much money for the "fine," you can pull out the smallest stash of cash (maybe $20-$50) and tell him "*this is all I have.*" I've used this tactic a few times and it has worked well. In some countries, the "fine" will be even less. The bribe I chose to pay in Tanzania was the US equivalent of 25 cents. It was a lot easier to part with the quarter than it was to argue with the Tanzanian National Police officer who had an AK-47 pointed at my head.

If you don't want to pay a bribe, your best strategy is usually to smile and pretend you don't know what is going on. Don't let the cop know you speak any of the language. Be friendly and polite, but seem confused. You want him to believe that dealing with you will be more of a time consuming hassle than what his small bribe is worth.

In each country, the locals have different terms for police bribery and the police use different slang phrases when "requesting" some cash. In Latin American countries, police bribes are often called "*morditas*", meaning "*little bites*." Locals will use the phrase regularly, but the cops will get very offended if you describe their income generating activities that way. In some African countries, officials will ask for "*Coca Cola*" or "*Coca Cola money*." They don't want a soft drink. They are asking for a bribe. It's prudent to read up (in guidebooks or online) on the local slang terminology so you know exactly what's going on when you are solicited for a bribe or payoff.

Bribes are most commonly "requested" at police/military roadblocks or when the cops stop you for some type of traffic infraction. Try to avoid any place where you see cops or soldiers operating in pairs or larger groups. In my experience, it's rare to be solicited for a bribe by a lone police officer. They feel much better about their chance for success when they have the "backup" of another officer available if things don't go the way they want. Staying away from third world cops is generally a wise idea. Take special care to avoid cops working in pairs or larger groups.

The amount of money you will be expected to pay for bribes is dependent on whether you are a local or a foreigner. Locals pay far less, if at all. If you are a foreigner, the amount you pay will be inversely proportional to the amount of other cars on the road. If there are 10 cars lined up at a checkpoint, the cop is likely extorting a little bit of money from each car. If you are the only car on a long, lonely highway, you will pay more.

Sometimes you can subvert bribery attempts by offering the officers a small gift before they ask you for money or tell you that you've broken a law and need to pay a "fine." It isn't a bad idea to have a cooler full of cold sodas and beer in the back seat of the car. As soon as you are stopped at a checkpoint, smile warmly and thank the officer for doing such a good job "keeping us safe." Offer him a cold drink or a beer. He might be so appreciative that he won't shake you down for cash. This technique also works with other small items like T-shirts, cigarettes, or CDs. It's worth a shot and it won't cost you any real money to try. It also won't get you shot and buried in the desert like some of the more aggressive ways of dealing with corrupt cops.

However you plan to deal with corrupt bribery attempts, don't get out of your car. Your car is your only escape route. If things start getting dangerous, you always have the option of driving away. Sure, you might get shot. But if you think you are going to be shot anyway, what do you have to lose? Playing the "clueless tourist" card and simply smiling, waving, and driving away often has an astounding success rate. The cops know that it will bring trouble if they shoot too many tourists. They are just as likely to let you drive away as shoot you or chase after your vehicle.

The local police want you to believe that they
aren't corrupt. Don't bet on it.

If you need to file a police report, you may be asked to pay
a fee for the police services. You may even be asked to pay
for gasoline for the police to come to your location. This
isn't unusual in very poor countries but it's still essentially
a bribe. There isn't much you can do about it however. If
you want the report, you pay the fee. Otherwise the cops
won't even respond.

Expect to spend an inordinate amount of time at the
police station should you have to file a report. The laziness
and inefficiency of some "public servants" in developing
countries is truly astonishing. A traveling companion on a
trip to Africa had a large amount of cash stolen out of the
locked safe in her room. She needed a police report to turn
the claim in to her travel insurance company.

She ended up spending several hours at the rural police
station closest to the area where we stayed. She told me

that the police department had no air conditioning and she didn't see a single computer anywhere in the building. The officer asked some questions about the theft and then painstakingly hand wrote my companion's narrative on a piece of notebook paper.

They had no actual police report forms. The cops there just threw a hand-written "report" into some file cabinet and did absolutely zero follow-up investigation. The cops stated they were not allowed to give her a copy of the report. She took a picture of the report with her phone as it was the only tangible piece of evidence that she made a good faith effort to report the crime. Don't expect a warm welcome when your report request costs several hours of the police officer's time.

Some very experienced travelers and ex-pats recommend an alternate method of avoiding the payment of bribes at police checkpoints. When asked for documents, these travelers will provide passports along with a "Press" identification card. Bribe seeking cops are afraid that their activities will be exposed by newspaper or magazine reporters and tend not to push the issue if they think you are a reporter.

This takes a certain personality to pull off. Some of you can do it, some of you can't. If you are good at improvisation and you don't get rattled under stress, it might be a viable strategy. You probably shouldn't do this on some lonely road, far away from any other people. Don't give the cop a reason to fear you. When that happens and you are all alone with him, there's a good chance you'll end up in an unmarked grave where your relatives will never find you. Play it smart if you plan on utilizing this gambit.

If you want fast and easy press credentials, I recommend printing them out from The Constitutional First Amendment Press Association website (http://cfapa.org/).

Language Issues

*"At the most remote temples and villages I visited,
everybody knew the English for 'One dollar' and 'I
love you' and "Fuck you.""*
– English Teacher X

Learning the Language- Without a doubt, the best way to learn a new language is by daily speaking practice with another person. That speaking practice can happen in a formal classroom setting or could just be a chat with a friend. It doesn't matter how you do it, just get talking. All other methods pale by comparison.

Several of my friends get daily speaking practice using the Wespeke website. Wespeke is a free global website that allows you to find a language speaking partner from another country and use the site's text and video chat software to facilitate your language practice speaking to that person.

There are a couple of smart phone apps that I have successfully used to help me learn some of the language spoken in the countries I've visited, Duolingo is one of my favorites. It's free and covers nine of the most common languages spoken around the world. The app teaches new words and phrases in a step-by-step progression that is both fun and engaging.

If you are pressed for time, you may also try the Dropps App. Dropps makes a game out of teaching English, Spanish, French, German, and Italian vocabulary. The game is limited to five minutes per day so that language students can do it almost anytime. By the time you finish each module, you will have learned the most commonly-used 4600 words in the language. The app creator states that with knowledge of these words, anyone can understand approximately 60% of all conversations in the language studied.

An additional time-tested way of learning words in another language is by utilizing flashcards. You can make them up yourself or you can use the free Anki app. Anki not only creates the flashcards for you, it orders them strategically so that you don't grow used to seeing the same words in the same order every time you practice.

Another useful thing to do when learning a new language is to hear it as often as possible. That can be difficult if you don't live in a country where the language is spoken. Some language learners like to watch television or movies filmed in the language they are learning. YouTube can be a useful reference when you use it to search for popular trending videos in the language of your choice. You can also use apps to stream music and news from any country in the world. The more you hear your new language, the easier it will be to learn.

Another excellent reference for language learning is Benny the Irish Polyglot's website. Benny is fluent in seven languages and conversational in four more. His website offers regular updates on his proven language learning techniques and shows you how you can learn a foreign language with minimal effort.

Finally, check out commercial courses by Pimsleur and FSI. I've done both and found them exceptionally helpful.

Translation-The Languages app is a very simple language dictionary and translation app that you can download for your phone. It covers most European languages and unlike Google Translate, it can be used offline.

Speaking of Google Translate, you can also use it to decipher written words on street signs or restaurant menus. When you open this app and point your phone at any sign printed in German, French, Spanish, Portuguese, Russian, or Italian, the app instantly translates the sign into English. It's amazing to see it work. I've found the app very helpful for street signs and signs outside of restaurants or businesses.

The Waygo app does the same thing for both Chinese and Japanese language characters. Downloading this simple app to your phone will save you a lot of time trying to decipher signs in a language with an entirely different alphabet.

Speaking Tips- When you are speaking to locals with limited English proficiency, speaking louder will not help them understand. Speak slowly and clearly. Ask questions that can be answered with a "yes" or "no."

Try to avoid using slang words or contractions to be better understood. I once heard an American guy trying to pick up a Brazilian girl at a bar. The Brazilian girl barely spoke any English and the guy didn't speak any Portuguese. They guy gave the girl his phone number and then said: "*Hit me up, babe. You know I'm down.*" I've never seen a more confused look on the girl's face. You can imagine someone with limited English being completely baffled by such an utterance.

Slang is guaranteed to confuse someone who isn't a native speaker. Avoid idioms and sarcasm. Locals simply won't understand what you are trying to communicate. Most will nod their heads and pretend to understand, but they will truly have no idea what you are saying.

Likewise, if you only speak a small amount of the language, you may be tempted to pretend that you understand what the speaker is saying in order not to offend him or to appear like you know more than you do. This is universally a bad idea. If you don't understand what the speaker is saying, stop him or ask him to clarify. You will avoid tragic misunderstandings if you can just suspend your ego enough to admit that you don't understand.

Be careful of hand gestures if you don't know what they signify in the country you are visiting. People who "talk with their hands" take the risk of seriously offending locals with what may seem like an innocuous gesture. If you don't know how hand gestures work, keep your hands in your pockets.

Learning even just a few words of your host country's language will pay huge dividends. Almost every local is appreciative of the fact that (unlike most travelers) you have made an attempt to learn a little bit of his/her language. Often, just speaking a couple words will embolden locals who "*don't speak English*" to be more helpful and try to communicate with you.

If you don't have time to learn much of the language in the country you are visiting, these phrases are probably the most used. Almost every guidebook will include them as a supplement. Taking an hour to learn all of these will be worth the effort:

> "*Speak more slowly*"
>> "*Yes*" and "*No*"
>> "*Please*" and "*Thank you*"
>
> The common greetings: "*Hello*", "*Goodbye*" "*Good Morning*" etc.
>> "*How much*"
>> "*How do you say xxxx*"
>
> Numbers from 1-10. If the number is larger, just say it one digit at a time.
>> "*Bathroom*"
>> "*Water*"
>> "*Where is it?*"
>> "*Hotel*"
>> "*Airport*" and/or "*Bus station*"
>> "*Restaurant*"

Besides knowing the aforementioned words in your host country's language, I also like to learn a phrase that I call "the conversation starter." If you want to get to know someone or start a conversation, you need to have a default question to ask someone after you say "hello."

In America, this question is commonly something like "*What do you do for a living?*" or "*Where do you work?*" In developing countries, this phrase doesn't work as well. Higher unemployment rates may mean that the person to whom you are speaking may not even have a job. He or she may feel self-conscious comparing his job to that of a "rich" American. Even more importantly, work just isn't valued as much in many developing countries. People work to live rather than live to work.

Instead of asking about work, I like to ask people about their home. I generally ask: "*Were you born here?*" Depending on their answer, I will usually compliment their home town telling my new friend that I enjoy his city/country or that I have heard great things about it. This almost always gets a genuine smile and prolongs our interaction.

That question immediately breaks the local's stereotype that all Americans are self-absorbed idiots. It shows that you recognize there are other great places (besides the USA) to live in this wonderful world. It also gives you lots of other threads to follow if you want to continue the conversation.

I find the question works well with most people, but it works even better when you ask it in the local's native language. Add "*Where were you born?*" to your list of "must learn" foreign language phrases.

Surviving Earthquakes, Tsunamis, and Other Natural Disasters

"Adventure is just a romantic name for trouble. It's swell reading about in the comfort of your recliner, but it's pure hell when it's coming at you in a dark and lonely place."
– Louis L'Amour

In 2006, I was traveling through Ecuador and had just arrived in the small mountain town of Baños. The town sits on the side of the active Tungurahua volcano. Although the volcano is active, it hadn't erupted since the early 1990s. There was no indication that it would do so on the cloudy July day when I visited.

I was unpacking in a small hotel when I heard what I thought was a bomb going off outside. The windows shook and there were ear-splitting blasts. Everyone ran outside to see what was happening.

My first view of the erupting volcano from the
street outside my hotel

When we looked up at the volcano, we could see the large
cloud of erupting ash. We saw the lava rolling down the
hill towards us less than two miles away. The town was
panicking. People were in the streets wailing and
screaming. Some other folks stood around paralyzed with
fear and unable to move. My traveling companions and
I organized the rental of a small mini bus to evacuate
ourselves to a government volcano shelter.

Before we arrived at the shelter, soldiers informed us that
the majority of the lava was flowing down the mountain on
the side opposite the town and that the town was not in any
danger. We returned to our hotel.

The eruption continued for hours, with window-shaking
explosions happening every 15-20 minutes. No one could
sleep, so we all pulled chairs out into the street and

watched the volcano from the front of our hotel for the rest of the night. We evacuated town the following day after fears that the eruption would cause landslides that would block the road.

Fortunately for me and my travel companions, our volcano experience ended up being little more than an exciting night and a little inconvenience. Others haven't been so lucky.

Emergency evacuations due to hurricanes, fires, earthquakes and volcanoes are far more common in lesser-developed countries. You should be prepared to leave your room in a moment's notice at all times. Keep a small bag packed with all the items you need for survival should you have to leave the room quickly without the majority of your luggage.

Have your clothes, shoes, passport and money laid out by your bed at night when you sleep. If something bad happens, you want to be able to get dressed and leave in the shortest amount of time possible. Remember, you are for more likely to experience a fire, natural disaster, or evacuation in a third world country than you are at home. Don't place yourself in danger by wasting time trying to find your clothes in the dark or when the electricity stops working.

My Cartagena, Colombia hotel room. Everything is
next to the bed in case I have to get out quickly.

As soon as you unpack your bags, place your flashlight
or headlamp on the night table or some other location
where it can be easily located. If the power goes out in
an emergency, you'll want some light immediately available
to figure out your plans, gather your gear, or make your
evacuation. Another trick is to tie a small LED keychain
flashlight into your shoelaces. If the only thing you have
time to grab is your shoes, at least you will have a small light
in order to find your way to safety.

After pre-placing emergency supplies, the next thing you
should do is fill up the hotel room ice bucket if you have
one. When the water stops flowing after a natural disaster,
the melting ice bucket may provide just enough drinking
water to keep you from getting desperate. If you have
alternate sources of potable water, you can always use the

melted ice bucket water to flush the toilet (by either filling the tank or pouring it directly into the bowl when holding the flush handle down). Having been caught in a few situations where the water stopped running, I will tell you that having the ability to flush a non-functioning toilet will make your life much more pleasant.

Don't always trust that the safety equipment in your hotel is operable. I'd hate to even guess the last time these Vietnamese fire extinguishers were inspected.

In the event that you are required to evacuate to some type of government shelter for any emergency, recognize that they may not let you in if you have too much luggage. Pack a duffel bag or day pack that contains all the critical items you might need. Bring a change of clothing, toiletry items, food and water, a sleeping bag or bedding (if you have it), and any necessary prescription medicines.

You will also want to bring some entertainment items to while away the boring hours. A deck of cards, a book, a tablet computer, or any other entertaining diversions will be valuable. Recognize that the shelter will likely search your bags for contraband. Alcohol, drugs, and weapons are rarely allowed inside. If you want to carry these items inside with you, stash them on your person, preferably down your pants. Intake officials will search your bags, but are less likely to physically pat you down.

Hurricanes and Tsunamis- Hurricanes are probably the most commonly encountered severe weather event. Every year they strike between 75 and 110 times across the globe. The best strategy to employ if you are in the path of a hurricane or tsunami is to make a hasty evacuation. If you don't have time to evacuate or can't get out of the path of the storm, you'll have to hunker down and ride out the storm. Do that by taking shelter inside and away from any windows that the storm may break. Stay on the ground floor in a closet or small room that is protected from both structural collapse and flying debris. If you are in the path of a tsunami, move to the highest floor of the building or the building's roof.

Try to stockpile as much food and water as possible in advance of the hurricane. These resources will be scarce if the storm does extensive damage. Don't go to the large supermarkets if you are in a hurry. They will likely be filled with locals who are also stocking up. Instead, hit the small corner stores and buy as much preserved food (don't forget a can opener) and bottled water as possible. If you are staying in a hotel, fill the tub and sinks with water as well. That's another reason why I advise adding a flat rubber drain plug to your luggage. Some hotel drains can't be stoppered without using your own plug.

After the storm, even if your water works, you should assume it has been contaminated until you hear otherwise from authorities. Having a supply of uncontaminated water in advance or having filtering/purifying capabilities will make your life much easier.

Things you don't think about at home...

If you are staying in an apartment or a private home, anticipate power outages and turn the thermostat in your refrigerator and freezer to the lowest possible setting to keep things cold for a longer time once the power goes out. You may also temporarily increase the heat (in winter) or the air conditioning (in summer) so that you can keep your habitation as comfortable as possible during the outage.

You will also want to withdraw the maximum amount of cash possible from the ATM prior to the storm. If there is an extended power outage, credit card machines won't be working. If you want to pay for anything, it will have to be in cash.

Unplug any electronic items and move them to a high place to protect them from flood waters. Lock doors, close windows, drapes and curtains to reduce the chance of being injured by flying debris.

Some damage caused by the hurricane may not be readily apparent. Be careful when you go outside after the storm. Downed live electrical lines, broken glass or other sharp objects in flooded areas, looters, and falling tree limbs are all serious dangers. You aren't likely to know the area well so avoid the urge to "check out the damage." It's too dangerous. Stay in a safe location or evacuate the area.

The absolute worst place to be during a tsunami (or tidal wave) is in the water. Get out of the water and off the beach if you have even the slightest indication that a tsunami is heading your direction. It's best to go is the highest place you can find. Look for Tsunami evacuation route signs. Get atop high ground or on the roof of a building as quickly as possible. Having a sturdy handhold is important as well so that you aren't swept away by the wall of water heading in your direction.

You may be separated from family or friends in the event of a flood, hurricane, or tidal wave. Pre-arrange a meeting spot that is inland and on high ground where you can reunite with any lost family members in the event of separation. Telephones, the internet, and texting may not be functioning properly, so your pre-arranged meeting place may be the only way to contact lost family members.

Floods- Flood prone areas are relatively easy to avoid. Historical records clearly identify which areas are prone to flooding and which are not. Sometimes you will even be able to see evidence of previous flood damage on buildings or roads. Floods don't normally cause too many problems for travelers. Just remember that water flows downhill. It is fairly easy to anticipate where water will move and to avoid it. Be especially cautious if you are staying near a large dam or levee system. One other thing to note is that larger floods will often cause mudslides. The mudslides can take out roads and bridges and may leave you stranded. Make sure you are on the side of the bridge where you are most comfortable staying, before said bridge is blocked by debris or the road becomes impassable.

If you plan on staying in the area without evacuating, ensure that your vehicle is parked on high ground. Many people forget about their cars when they are worried about their personal safety. You may need to change your plans and evacuate. Having a car that isn't underwater will help you accomplish that goal.

When moving through flooded areas, don't wade into any body of water that is higher than mid-calf in height. In higher water, you risk being swept away or getting your foot caught underneath submerged debris. Six inches of rapidly moving water can knock a person down. Eighteen inches can wash a car away. Use a tall walking stick whenever you are walking through water. As soon as you can, wash yourself with antibacterial soap. Flood waters often carry bacteria, viruses and chemicals that can make you ill if they remain on your skin.

If any of your gear comes in contact with flood waters, disinfect it with a solution made of chlorine bleach and clean water. Add 1.5 cups of liquid bleach to a gallon of water to create a 1:10 dilution for disinfecting any material that has been exposed to nasty flood waters.

Downed power lines are also a big danger in flooded areas. Stay far away from any down power lines, poles, or transformers if you want to avoid being electrocuted. Remember, water conducts electricity.

When you return to your lodging location after a hurricane, flood, or tsunami, realize that all sorts of critters may have sought refuge in your living space. Do a search for any bugs, snakes, or spiders that may be hiding in your room.

Earthquakes-You should know in advance if you are traveling in an earthquake-prone country. If you are, it is prudent to identify nearby earthquake emergency shelters in advance. These shelters are often pre-identified in tourist areas and hotels. Pay attention to the signs so that you know where to go should the ground start moving.

The international symbol for a safe area in the event of an earthquake is a sign with a green cross-hatched design.

If you are caught outside a shelter area, cover your head/neck with your arms to protect yourself from falling objects. It goes without saying that you should avoid areas that have heavy objects overhead. Remove anything hanging on the wall near your bed so that you aren't crushed in your sleep. If you are inside a building, take cover under a very heavy table against an inside wall or in a sturdy (load bearing) doorway. Move away from windows. If you are in a mall or larger department store, stay away from the tall display cases and larger panes of glass. Crowded venues like sporting arenas should be avoided. The panicked crowd will likely cause more injuries than the earthquake itself.

As soon as you recognize that an earthquake may be happening or is immanent, find adequate shelter and gather both your first aid kit and a bright flashlight/headlamp. Those items will likely be the first things that you need should your sheltering structure be damaged by the quake.

If the electricity goes out, don't use open flames for cooking or for light. There is a good chance that natural gas lines have ruptured in the quake. You really don't want to blow yourself up.

Expect aftershocks. Some of these will be as bad as the initial earthquake. Be alert for the possibility of flooding or tsunamis after an earthquake. If you are in a low-laying area or coastal region, move to higher ground.

Volcanoes- If you are caught up in a volcanic eruption, pay attention to the government's warnings. They generally know what is going on and can give the best advice concerning evacuation. I mentioned the problem I had with the roads and bridges being blocked by landslides in the volcanic eruption I lived through. That is a major consideration. If you are on a tight travel schedule and can't afford to be stranded in a city for a few days while they clean up the roads, make a move before the mudslides arrive.

If you are near enough to experience the toxic gasses or ash in the air, you should probably stay inside. The gasses and ash are likely to be harmful to your lungs and should be avoided. If you have to venture outside, cover your mouth and nose with a bandanna or an N-95 dust mask. I carry a couple of dust masks in my large medical kit for this very purpose.

If you are actually on the mountain during an eruption, take care to protect yourself from flying pyroclastic debris. Head protection and eye protection (even if it is only basic sunglasses and a baseball cap) is of critical importance.

In the event you should choose not to evacuate after a volcanic eruption, make sure that there is no significant quantity of ashes accumulating on the roof of your hotel, hostel, or apartment. Ash is heavy and regularly contributes to post-volcano structural collapses. It would really suck to survive a volcano and be killed when your roof collapses while you sleep.

Surviving Third World Riots and Political Demonstrations

"For people who study the universe of disorder, automatic Kalashnikovs serve as reliable units of measure...Anywhere large numbers of young men in civilian clothes or mismatched uniforms are carrying Kalashnikovs is a very good place not to go; when Kalashnikovs turn up in the hands of mobs, it is time to leave."
– CJ Chivers

Riot police in Santa Cruz, Bolivia just waiting for
trouble to break out.

In addition to having dealt with some pretty unruly crowds in my work as a cop, I've been caught up in a few riots during my third world travels. In Brazil, I was tear gassed by the police because I was in the middle of a riot that broke out during a 600,000-person free concert on the beach. In Peru, I was even stuck in a riot where one of the rioters (a striking ransportation worker) was shot by the military. There were others as well. I've seen some insane crowds.

In each of the bad spots I encountered, it was relatively easy to get out without having to resort to violence. If someone uses common sense and keeps up good situational awareness, he or she can usually get away before things get too bad.

If the country you are visiting begins experiencing some political instability, protests, or violence, it would be prudent to get out of the region. Often these events are localized and simply getting out of the involved city will reduce your danger.

If you can't get out, do as much as possible to blend in with the locals. You don't want to stand out in a situation like this. Call your embassy for advice. If you are an American, be cautious about physically going to your embassy during political unrest. US Embassies are often targeted for protests, vandalism, and violence. The American embassy may not be the safest place to go. If you are in serious danger, consider going to the Canadian, British, or Australian embassy instead. No guarantees, but those friendly embassies may be able to help.

If you are holed up in your hotel room and can't escape, call the US Office of Overseas Citizens Services in Washington D.C. They will be able to place you in contact with local embassy or consular officials. The phone number is +1 888 407 4747 (during business hours) or +1 202 647 5225 (after hours).

I prefer to be as far away from any civil insurrection as possible, but I realize that some circumstances make that impossible. The riot may be completely surrounding you or exits may be blocked. If you find yourself in a situation like this, get inside a building. A lockable location would be best, but just getting inside is better than nothing. Most riots occur outdoors and on the street. Getting inside will often keep you away from the majority of the violence.

The more dangerous situations are the riots or mob violence situations that seem to pop up without warning. The best advice I can give you is to pay attention to your surroundings and have an escape plan for every location you visit. When you see things starting to go bad (massing police, masked looters, people setting fires), GET OUT! Implement your escape plan. Don't stick around and become a target for police batons, gangs of teen looters, or panicked crowds. Usually the people who get hurt or killed in these events are the people who aren't paying attention or who want to stand around and be a spectator.

If you accidentally happen upon looters, rioters, or large political demonstrations, walk away by the most direct route possible that allows you to avoid the unpredictable crowd. Don't run; that only draws unwanted attention from the rioting crowd. Just walk quickly, avoiding eye contact or any interaction with the rioters. As you walk, keep an eye out for places of sanctuary you may be able to use to escape the violence for a short period of time until the crowd passes. Fighting against the crowd will be difficult. Think of crossing a river, it's easier if you don't fight the current. It's the same way with crowds. If you get surrounded by a group, move with the group as you work your way to the edge of the crowd or to your pre-planned escape route or sanctuary location.

If, despite your best efforts to avoid problem areas, you find yourself surrounded by a mob or overtaken by a riot, quickly get your back to a wall. That way you won't be surrounded and will only have to deal with a few people at a time. I've found this tactic works very well. If you fade back to a wall and stop moving, often the crowd will ignore you and pass right by.

Once you get your back to a wall, organize yourself and plan your escape. If you are wearing a backpack, bag, or purse, swing it around to the front side of your body where it can serve as a shield (a panel from an old ballistic vest carried in the back pocket of your backpack will give you even more comfort). This also prevents thieves and looters from trying to take it from you. Take a look at the crowd. Look for gaps. Your goal is to look far enough ahead to move from gap to gap, exploiting the openings in the crowd. Holding both arms in front of you with your hands together in a wedge shape will help get you through the crowd. Move along walls if you can with your "wedge" out in front of you, deflecting people off to the side. Turning your shoulders to make your body narrower as you squeeze through the crowd will also help.

Having some sort of less lethal weaponry is useful. Many of the criminals who are caught up in the spirit of the riot are not very dedicated or motivated. A quick blast of pepper spray will usually make them look for easier targets.

If you are attacked and you don't have any spray (or the spray doesn't work), you must act decisively. Don't get caught in the middle of two or more attackers. If possible, keep moving to the outside of the group of attackers to "stack" them, or line them up so you only have to fight one at a time. If you do get surrounded, violently attack one of the gang members and either use him as a temporary shield or blast through him to make your escape. Don't just blindly run away; you may be running into an area where there are more problems. Instead of running AWAY from the criminals, run TOWARDS safety. And remember that "safety" in this case may not be the band of police in their riot gear with batons out and ready.

In addition to your everyday carry items, there are a few other easily-carried items that may help you if you find yourself in a riot or mob:

- A bandanna or triangular bandage- Besides its obvious use as a piece of multipurpose medical equipment, a wet bandanna can be tied or held over your nose or mouth to temporarily protect you from tear gas. I prefer holding the bandanna rather than tying it over my mouth and nose. A bandanna tied over one's face screams "criminal" to the police. I would rather not be a target for baton blows or rubber bullets if I am mistaken for a criminal

- Spare contact lenses if you wear them- Tear gas will destroy your soft contacts. You will never want to put them back in again if they get exposed. If you need your lenses to see, carry a spare pair.

- Protective glasses or sunglasses- When the police start firing beanbag rounds, Stingball grenades, and rubber bullets, you will want your eyes protected. Those rounds hurt if they hit skin. If they hit your eyes, you can be seriously injured.

– Sturdy running shoes or boots- People who walk around in large crowds while wearing flip flops amaze me. If bad stuff happens they aren't able to run and their feet will likely be trampled by those who were smart enough to wear real shoes. Be smart. Save the flip flops for the beach.

– A flashlight- if you are out at night in a crowd, you should have a light. Besides its regular uses, a stout flashlight can be an improvised impact weapon. If the riot occurs at night, you will want the light to check out any unlit alleys or other areas you might be considering for escape or refuge.

Pepper Spray/Tear Gas exposure– If you get exposed to tear gas or pepper spray, don't panic. All the effects will diminish on their own without treatment in less than an hour. The definitive treatment for the spray exposure is fresh air and cold running water. Find a garden hose, shower, or sink. Flush your eyes and skin for 5-10 minutes. After that, most of the effects will be gone.

If you don't have access to running water, take a plastic water bottle and poke a small hole in the lid by using something like a safety pin. Squeeze the sides of the bottle to create a stream of water coming out the hole. Direct the stream into the affected eye or eyes. If there is an open store, purchase a cheap bottle of contact lens saline solution to do the same thing. If no water is available, open and close your eyes as hard and fast as possible to get the tears flowing. This will hurt initially, but will speed up the decontamination process.

You will need to take a few more precautions if significant quantities of tear gas are in the air. First, remove your contact lenses. The gas will get trapped under your lenses and you won't be able to open your eyes because of the intense pain. It's better to have some vision (even if uncorrected) than to be blinded when your contacts soak up a dose of pepper spray. Then wash off any sunscreen, oil-based makeup, or skin lotions you've applied. These will also bond with the tear gas and make it difficult to wash away from your skin.

Additional Riot Self-Protection Advice– If you are able to find shelter inside a building as you make your escape, lock the door you used to enter and move to the rear of the building away from the direction of the crowd. Try to find a rear-facing exit. If the building is large enough, going out the back door might put you far enough away from the hostile crowd that you can walk or catch a taxi to get out of the area. If escape is not an option, lock all the doors and stay away from the windows nearest the crowd. You'll have to wait out the rioters until it is safe to leave. It could be minutes or days. That's why I advocate always carrying some emergency supplies on your person when you travel through developing countries.

In the event that your sanctuary location becomes untenable or you have to leave it for any reason, it's a good idea to wear as much protective clothing as possible. You want protection from impacts (rocks, bottles, etc.), fire, and police chemical weapons. You should wear long sleeves, long pants, and closed toe, sturdy footwear. Attempting to make your escape in shorts and flip flops may get you seriously injured or killed.

Think about wearing natural fiber clothes like wool or cotton. Those are least likely to stick to your skin or melt when exposed to flame. The only downsides of these materials is the fact that they wick tear gas and pepper spray, soaking up the chemicals and keeping them next to your skin. To avoid problems with tear gas, carry a raincoat and put it on over your natural fiber clothing if you are in an area where chemical weapons are present. The raincoat (ideally with hood) will keep most of the chemicals off your skin.

More Mob Violence Recommendations– While there isn't much research on human mob behavior and killing, there is quite a bit of research on our primate cousins (chimps and bonobos) who also kill and maim in large groups. One of the larger primate studies of group violence was conducted by Michael Lawrence Wilson. The key learning point derived from the study was that *"They mainly killed when it was easy to kill victims, either because of a strong numerical advantage, or because the victim was weak..."*

That same study showed the following:

– Groups that contained more males and lived in greater population density killed more.

– Attackers did not kill randomly. They most often chose victims who came from different groups than themselves.

– Attackers most commonly killed when they clearly outnumbered their victims. The average disparity in the killings was 8:1.

– Ninety-two percent of attackers were male. Seventy-three percent of those killed were males. Males commit almost all of the group violence and tend to pick other males as targets.

While similar research has not (yet) been done in human group killings, 25 years of studying violent attacks has led me to similar conclusions. When people are killed in mob violence, they tend to be males who are of a different racial or cultural background than their attackers. Those killed were outnumbered by a large margin and gave their attackers the idea that they are somehow "weak."

As a traveler, it is important to pay attention to this research. YOU are the outsider. YOU don't fit in with the dominant "group." YOU are alone and outnumbered. It's YOU who will be targeted by rampaging chaotic mobs if the authorities lose control of the protest or mass gathering.

It's highly prudent to avoid any location where large numbers of angry local men are gathering. It's especially important to avoid such groups when they are drunk, on drugs, or armed. I know you want some great pictures to take home to your friends, but it just isn't worth it. Play it safe. Stay far away from any strikes, violent sporting events, protests, roadblocks, or large groups of angry people.

If you know your travel destination far enough in advance, you should sign up for a google alert searching for the phrase "(visiting city) + strike". Many strikes and protests are planned in advance. The more violent ones will certainly make the local news. An emailed news alert can help you avoid the hazardous areas where protestors might be demonstrating.

If you can't avoid the protests, you might have to just try to ride them out. As soon as you can foresee that there may be longer-lasting riots or political demonstrations, pull a bunch of cash out of the ATM. You may need to hire a local with a car to drive you away from the chaos when the taxis and public transportation stop running. You may also have to pay off corrupt cops or people manning roadblocks to ensure your safe passage. Emergency credit cards are nice, but they aren't widely accepted by terrorists or corrupt cops.

Dealing with rioters while driving-When driving your own vehicle, you may encounter mobs, rioters, or protesters who spill out onto the street and block the roadway. This type of situation is extremely dangerous. Here are a few tips to avoid/survive a mob attack on your vehicle:

1) Avoidance is key. Many protests and riots are either predictable or planned in advance. Stay away from the riots if you want to avoid being victimized. When you see masses of people blocking the roadways, STOP. Don't go any farther. Do whatever necessary to change directions and get out of the area. If you are alert, you should be able to see these masses of people far enough in advance that you can act before being surrounded. It goes without saying that if you are texting, talking on the phone, or watching a DVD while driving, you may not be paying enough attention to save yourself. Don't get distracted by electronic devices when driving.

2) You can't just run people over if they are in the road. The safest thing to do in a situation like this is to keep moving, bumping people out of the way with your car. Unfortunately, that isn't legal in any country you may be visiting. Even if people are illegally blocking the road, you will likely go to jail if you run them down absent a legitimate threat to your life.

3) The situation changes, however, once the rioters attack you or your vehicle. With your vehicle surrounded in a manner that you can't escape and your attackers being trying to burn your car, flip it over, or drag you out, it is reasonable to assume that you will suffer serious injury or death. Even if self-defense is not a right given to the people in the country where you are traveling, I think it is better to fight than die. I'd also rather go to prison for acting too aggressively than be beheaded on national television.

When people start attacking the car, it's likely best to begin driving through the crowd, hitting people with the car if necessary. Accelerate steadily and forcefully, driving away from the surrounding rioters. Steady movement is the key. Hitting folks too hard can disable your vehicle. Use your vehicle to push people out of the way rather than striking them.

4) Doors locked and seat belt OFF. Your doors should be locked when driving in a foreign country. If your doors don't automatically lock, get in the habit of locking them manually as soon as you get inside. You don't want the crowd to be able to easily open your door and drag you out.

You may not have enough time to do it, but cracking your windows and turning off your ventilation system would also be a good idea when driving in areas where crowds may gather. Windows that are down approximately 1/2" are actually harder to break than windows that are tightly closed. You want to turn off the ventilation system so you don't get overcome by any smoke or tear gas that is in the air where you are driving.

Your seat belt should be off. Seat belts will reduce your ability to access any weapons you may be carrying. They will also prohibit you from making a speedy escape should your vehicle be set on fire or overturned. In general, it's safer to stay inside the car in a crowd. If Molotov cocktails hit your car, drive quickly away. The wind will likely extinguish the burning liquid before you are hurt. If the car is disabled and under attack from firebombs, get out. It's better to take your chances on foot than be trapped inside and burned alive.

5) Beware of other forms of roadblocks. The roadblocks designed to make you stop may not take the form of people. The rioters will steal cars and then purposely abandon them in the middle of roadways. Abandoned vehicles cause you to stop and also prevent police/fire vehicles from getting to the scene. It's a common occurrence all around the world.

Get in the habit of knowing more than one route in to or out of a place to which you commonly drive. Flexibility in these situations is paramount. Keep your situational awareness up and be prepared to alter your route if you encounter throngs of people or roadblocks.

If you cannot escape a roadblock, you may have to drive through it. Don't do it like you see in the movies by ramming the blocking cars as hard and fast as you can. Doing this will likely disable your car and cause serious injuries. If you must ram a vehicle blocking a road, it's best to do it in reverse. Impact on the rear of your car is less likely to disable it than impact to the engine compartment.

Whether you strike the blocking vehicle with either the front or rear of your car, try to strike the blocking vehicles trunk area rather than its engine compartment. Hitting the car in the trunk will move it much easier than striking the heavy engine. Instead of blasting the car at full speed, hit it at 10 mph or less. As soon as you make contact, accelerate through in order to move the vehicle out of the way. You want to think of the ramming motion as a push rather than a crash. That's the most effective way to break through the barricade and will cause the least damage to your escape vehicle.

Taking care of family members in a riot-Traveling with other people adds an additional layer of complexity when it comes to surviving a riot. Not only do you have to protect yourself, you may feel responsible for protecting others in your group as well.

When attending any large public event in a third world country, you and all of your family members/traveling companions should establish at least two emergency meeting locations, one within the event perimeter and one outside the event. If you and your companions are separated and foreign cell phone service is unavailable, you should know how to reunite.

If you are together with traveling companions when you encounter a violent mob, don't assume that your companions are seeing the same things that you are. You may have to tell them what is going on as you implement your escape plan. Instantly hold hands or interlace elbows with everyone in your party. It will be safer for you if you are in a larger group.

You may not have the time or desire to explain your perceptions of danger to very young children. I would recommend that you implement a code word procedure with your young children and work it into regular emergency drills. Choose a word that you don't commonly use. A word like *"emergency"* works well. Train and drill your children to instantly and unquestioningly obey your commands after the code word is given. Saying something like: *"Emergency! Run to the car!"* and having your children immediately obey your commands without question is a useful goal when dealing with a rioting mob.

There aren't many situations more dangerous to the foreign traveler than driving in to a mass of people who are violently protesting anything. It's critically important that you take whatever measures necessary to avoid such an action. If your avoidance efforts are unsuccessful, remember the tips I've given you. They may save your life.

Surviving Bombings and Terrorist Attacks

"I had learned another vital lesson for survival in the Third World: Be especially nice to the ones with machine guns."
– Christopher Blin

The chance of getting caught up in a third world terrorist bombing is far less likely than your worried family members may believe. Despite nearly constant news coverage about worldwide terrorism, very few travelers are killed in terrorist attacks. The odds that you will be killed in a terrorist attack worldwide are around one in 25 million. The odds of your dying in a plane crash are one in 5,862.

In fact, if you look at the statistics in the 20-year time period from 1995 to 2016, you'll find that a total of 3658 American citizens were killed by terrorists in another country. A similar number (3277) were killed by terrorists in the USA. We generally don't think it is dangerous to live in the USA. Most of us don't fear becoming victimized by a terrorist in our home country; yet we are scared of terrorism abroad. It's an unfounded fear. You are only slightly more likely to be killed by a terrorist while traveling than you are being killed by a terrorist here in the USA.

Avoiding just a few countries will go a long way in ensuring your safety. In the year 2015, 69% of worldwide terrorist fatalities occurred in just five countries. These countries: Iraq, Afghanistan, Yemen, Nigeria, and Syria, aren't at the top of most travelers' "must see" lists.

Terrorism elsewhere is relatively limited. To get actual statistics about the country you plan to visit, check out the Global Terrorism Index (http://www.visionofhumanity.org/#/page/indexes/terrorism-index).

Even if terrorist attacks are relatively infrequent experiences for Americans, terrorists worldwide use bombs as their weapons of choice. Occasionally, these bombs will be supplemented by sniper fire, grenades, or active shooters but it's the bombs that get the most media attention. Fortunately, the countries that have the most terrorist bombings are those that most travelers don't plan on visiting. Nevertheless, there are some popular third world travel destinations that terrorists have targeted.

In recent years terrorists have bombed a night club in Bali, Indonesia, two tourist towns in Egypt, a tourist café in Morocco, and a bus stop outside a tourist hotel in Mombasa, Kenya. The terrorists who held the city of Mumbai, India hostage for several days intentionally targeted sites where there would be lots of Western tourists. While this book chapter isn't a substitute for formal bomb training, it will give you some tips that may prevent you from being blown up should you happen to be caught in the middle of a suicide or homicide bombing while traveling in a developing country.

First, get it out of your head that a bomb looks like a bunch of taped up road flares with an alarm clock attached. Bombs can look like or be concealed in ANYTHING. In one bomb class I took, we made a bomb and concealed it in a flowerpot with a live plant covering it. We had it triggered with a motion detector that detonated the bomb when someone came within two feet of the flowerpot. If the terrorist wants to blow you up badly enough, he'll probably succeed and you'll never know what hit you.

Despite this fact, some terrorists and bombers are not all that smart. Sometimes you might be able to identify a suicide bomber before he detonates. Here's what to look for:

- Clothing that is bulky or excessive for the weather (to hide the bomb)
- Hands hidden (possibly holding the switch to detonate the bomb)
- A strange chemical odor or excessive cologne to cover up that smell
- The bomber focused, but unresponsive. Suicide bombers often have the "thousand yard stare" and are usually unresponsive to questions or commands
- Heavy luggage or backpacks that don't fit the situation. The average weight of a bomb used by a suicide bomber is around 20 lbs. The Madrid train bombers all had very heavy backpacks. The Moscow airport bomber placed his bomb in a rolling suitcase. Not all the bombers wear their bombs.
- Nervousness, excessive sweating, or repeated mumbling of a prayer or mantra
- Exposed wires anywhere on a person's body
- Repeated attempts to avoid security checkpoints and/or police officers

Beware of any suspicious packages. The bomber might not be a suicide bomber. He or she might just plant the bomb and walk or drive away. Although it didn't get nearly the media attention garnered by the 2011 Russian airport bomb, a bomber blew up a bus in the Philippines on the same day. Two people were killed and over a dozen injured when two bombers placed a package under the seat of a bus. The package contained a modified 81mm mortar shell and a cell phone. The bombers left the package, got off the bus and called the cell phone, thus triggering the bomb. If the bomb is not worn by a terrorist, it is most likely to be hidden in a car, in a discarded backpack or duffel bag, or placed in a trash can.

What should you do if you notice a person with one or more of these descriptors or even a suspicious package? GET AWAY! Time, distance, and shielding are your only defense. Realize that a 20 lb. suicide bomb vest loaded with shrapnel is dangerous within 400 meters. That's a long distance.

Recent research has determined that 15 meters (about 50 feet) is the distance that means the difference between life and death in most suicide bombing incidents. If you are within 15 meters of the bomber when he detonates, you will likely die. If you are beyond 15 meters, you will likely live, but may be seriously injured. Ultimately, whether you live or die depends on the terrain, the type of bomb and shrapnel and how far away from the bomb you are. The farther away you can get, the better off you will be. Ideally, distance combined with some type of cover that will stop shrapnel and projectiles is best. For a 500 lb. car bomb, people were likely hit by shrapnel up to 1/2 mile away.

Personally, if I noticed a suspicious package or thought someone might be wearing a suicide bomb vest, I would make it my primary objective to get myself and loved ones as far away from the bomb/bomber as possible. Once I've made it to safety, I will report the person to police. I'm not going to hang around in the kill zone looking for a policeman.

After the Engagement or Detonation- If you do survive the detonation of a third world terrorist bomb, here are a few things you should be thinking about:

Often terrorist bomber have "handlers," "tail-gunners," "lookouts," or security people assigned to them. The role of these people is to protect the bomber in case anyone intervenes or to detonate the bomb if the terrorist gets cold feet. Watch out for these people. Scan for anyone who appears to be paying undue attention to the situation, especially if that person is behind some type of cover or at a discreet distance away. They are every bit as dangerous as the bomber himself.

Look for people watching who are not scared or stunned. Being on a cell phone may be another tip off. Many modern terrorist bombs use cell phones as triggers (switches). The handlers may be on the phone reporting to their superiors or they may be planning to set off another bomb.

Also be cautious of people in uniforms. One important tactic to recognize is that many third world terrorist bombers will disguise themselves as police officers to gain easier access to target rich environments. Remember in the "Police" section how I advised that you try your best to stay away from third world police officers? This is another reason why you might want to continue the practice.

Bombings by people dressed as cops are exceptionally hard to prevent, but there are a couple of tips that will help keep you safe. First, it's important just to recognize that the possibility of a terrorist attack by criminals dressed as cops exists. If you see a police officer or officers doing something obviously "un-policelike," be on your guard. Follow my advice. Get away from the cops.

Second, recognize that even police departments in third world countries have some grooming standards. You don't generally see cops in uniform with long beards or long hair. Cops will also be wearing a complete uniform in most jurisdictions. If a person is wearing a police uniform shirt, blue jeans, and tennis shoes, he's probably not a cop.

The last thing to remember is that if a bomb has already gone off, the people coming to "help" you might not actually be the police that you think they are. They may be additional bombers looking to plant a secondary device where it will cause the most damage. In the event of an explosion, my advice doesn't change. Don't go running towards uniformed officers for assistance unless no other option is available.

Do not approach the bomb or the body of the bomber. You don't know if there is another bomb planted on him, if the primary bomb is on a time delay, or if it is command detonated by another person. Keep far away. Try to get everyone else away too. Move quickly to cover after the bomb blows.

Some bombs have been triggered when innocent bystanders have opened abandoned luggage. Resist the temptation to open any suspicious package to see what it is inside. If you think it's a bomb, then treat it like a bomb. Get away and get to cover.

Beware of secondary devices. Oftentimes, bombers will use more than one bomb. The original bomb is just designed to create havoc and bring in first responders. A second bomb placed in an evacuation zone, obvious command post staging area, or near the body is designed to injure more people, specifically fire fighters and police officers.

After one bomb goes off, look for items that seem out of place: discarded baggage or backpacks, strange pieces of trash, or recently disturbed ground. If you see any of these things, get away from them.

If a bomb goes off, don't evacuate into a parking lot. Cars are the easiest place to hide large amounts of explosives for a secondary device. One very common tactic is to place a small bomb in or near a building or public area. The terrorist knows that the small bomb will trigger an evacuation. He will then place a bigger bomb at the evacuation site to blow up all of the evacuees. I'm repeating myself, but this is very important: NEVER EVACUATE TO A PARKING LOT! It's too easy to hide a (big) bomb in a car. Get far away from anything that may conceal a secondary device.

Medical Car – If you or others are in the vicinity of a bomb blast you will likely see deaths and serious injuries. Expect that and don't be stunned. People will be staggering around dazed and unsure of what to do. Don't be one of those people. Expect to see serious bleeding, hearing loss, confusion, head trauma, and internal injuries. The victims may not be able to walk or to hear you.

This is one time when laying the injured person down to prevent spinal injury is counterproductive. Move the injured people AWAY from the bomber or bombing area as quickly as possible as there may be a secondary device in the area. Cervical spine stabilization won't really matter if the injured person is lying on top of another bomb. Yes, movement may further injure a casualty, but bombing victims seldom have the types of injuries that are aggravated by movement. Get the injured people to a safe place so that they aren't blown up again.

Establish a casualty collection point behind some hard cover in an area that is as far away from the original bomb as possible. Clear this area of secondary devices before unloading casualties. Emergency response in developing countries is very inconsistent. It may take a while for EMS to enter the scene. Be prepared to treat life threatening bleeding first (you should know how to make or use a pressure bandage and a tourniquet) then follow up with airway and breathing stabilization and other injuries. Re-read the previous chapter on medical care and be prepared to provide first aid. With an absence of effective professional emergency responders, your first aid efforts will likely be important life-saving interventions.

This is a 500 lb. car bomb I helped build in one of my classes. This picture was taken from 3/4 mile away. This is a fairly heavy payload of explosives,

but there have been several terrorists who have
detonated car bombs with even heavier loads.

Terrorist and Active Killer Attacks

Active shooters are certainly something you must
prepare for if you are engaging in overseas travel. Despite
popular belief, these types of attacks are not limited to the
United States. Look at the recent tragedies in France, with
the Bataclan Theater attack and the Nice vehicle assault
that killed more than 80 people to recognize that these
events happen everywhere.

Besides the garden variety active killer, you must also be
aware of the Islamist Terrorist mass hostage siege. These
have ONLY happened outside the USA at the time of the
book's printing. The largest of these events have happened
in Russia. The Beslan school massacre and the Nord Ost
theater hostage taking resulted in hundreds of fatalities.

Islamic Terrorists have also recently taken hostages in
Mumbai, India; Dhaka, Bangladesh; and Sydney, Australia.
In these mass hostage sieges, the terrorists attempt to hold
onto the hostages for as long as possible while pretending
to negotiate with police. Their motivation is maximal
media attention to their cause and they will do anything
possible to grab the headlines. Eventually, they force police
to make entry by killing hostages. During the shootout
between police and the terrorists, many more hostages
die. These aren't events you want to experience.

According to the IntelCenter Database, in the years
2014-2016, The Islamic State has conducted 73 different
major attacks in countries outside of recognized war
zones. Many of these attacks involved active shooters and/
or mass hostage sieges. They aren't common, but they
do happen and anyone who travels overseas needs to be

prepared in the unlikely event that he/she becomes trapped in such an attack.

In either an active shooter event or a mass hostage siege, your first priority should be to escape. The innocent bystanders who run away almost always fare better than the folks who try any other tactic. Get out, even if you have to risk your life to make the escape.

The general advice for dealing with active killers in the United States actually is more useful in a foreign country. The "Run, Hide, Fight" model works pretty well as long as you know your individual limitations. I've been critical of the model in the USA because statistically, the most effective way to handle an active killer event is by armed resistance. That's a possibility in America where a large part of the population is armed. It's not as likely among unarmed travelers to a foreign country.

If unarmed, escape by running will usually be your best bet. While running often yields excellent results in an active killer event and I recommend it as a general tactic, there are many times when running should not be your first choice.

One prime reason running may be a bad option is the lack of physical conditioning among the "target" population. With more than half of our citizens overweight or obese, why do we think they can run away from the average college age male (the majority of terrorists are young men)? Our McDonald's guzzling and flip-flop-wearing population stands little chance against a college aged male in a sprint.

If unarmed, you should think about running as a response if there is a good chance you can get away before the killer sees you. Here are some situations where you may NOT want to make running your top choice:

- You can't run (either from being overweight or from some physical infirmity)

-You have young children in tow who will slow you down

-The power has been cut and running in the dark may be hazardous

-You are wearing clothes or footwear that makes running impossible

-When running towards the building's exit will take you into the path of the killer

-When you are within a very close distance of the killer. You aren't going to outrun a bullet when you are five feet away from the gunman

If I were in any of the above situations, I would consider another option before I took off running.

The next best option is hiding or barricading. I have very mixed feelings about this advice. Sometimes hiding is an effective tactic. Sometimes it fails miserably. Some examples of failure were the Virginia Tech shooting and the Sandy Hook shooting. Students tried to hide under desks or in closets in both massacres. Most of the hiding students were shot down by the killer. Let's face it. There aren't very many good hiding places in the average school classroom. It really depends on where you are located and if there is an effective hiding spot nearby.

Hiding makes good sense only when you have the following conditions:

-You are in a room that can be effectively barricaded and locked. That generally means that the door does not have a window the shooter can knock out and that the door contains a quality deadbolt lock.

-Your hiding place has an alternate escape route. Locking down, barricading, or hiding in a location that doesn't have an escape route means that you will be forced to fight the shooter if he breaches your hiding spot

-It is a temporary maneuver to buy you a little time because police are on the way.

-You are unable to escape due to age, infirmity, or proximity to the shooter

-"Playing dead" by hiding among other injured and dead bodies has occasionally worked. It has also failed miserably. At Virginia Tech, the killer made a second pass and shot everyone a second time if they were laying on the ground without moving. If you are wounded, can't run, and the killer is focusing on other targets, hiding by playing dead may be an effective option

I would place hiding nearly last on the list of options for the majority of active killer events. As I stated above, there are rarely suitable hiding locations to be found in the places where these active killers operate.

That leaves the final option of fighting. Again, the circumstances dictate the tactics. Is this a lone teenage boy trying to stab people with a knife or is it a team of 50 armed terrorists trying to corral you into a mass hostage event? Your ability to succeed while fighting is determined by both your abilities and the abilities of your potential attackers.

There are many situations where fighting should be your FIRST option. Researcher and trainer Ron Borsch has been studying active killer incidents for years. In his research, he has found that in roughly 2/3 of all active killer events that are stopped on scene, an UNARMED citizen stopped the killer. That citizen stopped the killer by FIGHTING. Imagine what the fatality statistics would be if all of these fighters chose to run instead. Fighting is a viable option (and potentially a first choice of action) when:

-The killer is very close (within arms' reach). Very few other tactics will work at this range

-You are armed...even with a pocket knife or pepper spray

-You can set up an effective ambush

-Your lockdown has been breached

-You have fighting skills or are among a large group of people who are willing to act together

-You notice that the killer has a weapon malfunction or is in the act of reloading and his weapon is not immediately available

-The killer sets down or drops his weapon

Going unarmed against an active killer is a dangerous thing to do, but it may be your only option. Here's how to stack the odds in your favor:

You may have to wait for a better opportunity. Charging headlong towards a man firing an AK-47 isn't a recipe for success. If possible, get yourself to cover or concealment first. In an active shooter event the gunman will likely be shooting fast. That means that he will run out of ammo fairly quickly. If you can wait a few seconds until his gun is empty and he's in the act of reloading, it's much safer to initiate your attack then.

Another good opportunity to attack is if the killer has a weapon malfunction. A startling number of active killers end up with a malfunctioning gun at some point in the attack. On the train in France, the would-be killer had a weapon malfunction that prompted the three Americans to tackle him. Learn how to recognize weapon malfunctions and exploit them. I posted a short video on youtube covering what active killer weapon malfunctions look like. Go to https://www.youtube.com/watch?v=m8V4rnkh1lo&t=4s to watch it.

Set up an ambush. The head-on charge usually isn't the best plan. If you can hide behind cover and wait for the killer to pass you, you'll have access to his back. You don't have to fight fair. Approach him from behind and hit him in the head with something hard. Many of you travelers may be carrying pocket knives. Approach from behind and bury the blade into the side of his neck. Once it is buried to the hilt, aggressively "stir the soup" with the handle of the knife. You can also plunge the blade straight downward into his chest cavity from behind. Aim to penetrate just above the collar bone and target the knife straight downward. Just like the previous technique, aggressively rotate the handle of the knife to cause more damage.

If you have a little forewarning, you may be able to set up an ambush at a natural choke point or from a "hard corner." A choke point is any narrowing of a passageway that funnels movement. Think about a doorway. That's a natural choke point. Only one person at a time can go through the doorway and everyone who enters the room must follow the same path through the door. The close-quarters nature of the choke point (often also called a "fatal funnel") makes it difficult for multiple shooters or terrorists to target you (the defender) at the same time. It also provides a location where the movement of the shooter is extremely predictable. That makes it an ideal place for you to set up your ambushing counterattack.

A hard corner is a corner around which a person cannot see without somehow exposing his body or entering the room. Think about a doorway into a classroom or office. The doorway is usually placed in the center of a wall. Immediately inside that doorway (on either side) is a space that can't be seen from the hallway. In order to see the side of the doorway from the hall, a person would physically have to stick his head into the doorway. That makes him vulnerable to attack.

When you set up your ambush in the "hard corner" of a room, it is almost certain that you will see the attacker before he sees you. When people enter rooms, they don't do so by leading with their head. Usually a leg or arm is the first body part to round the corner. By the time his head (the part that can see your ambush) has rounded the corner, you are already initiating your attack.

Get some help. If you have time, plan an attack from one of the ambush positions I identified above with willing friends or fellow travelers. If there isn't time for a plan, you may have to start the attack yourself. As you are fighting the shooter, call out for help. Give people specific instructions what you want them to do. Sometimes people are frozen in fear. They want to help, but don't know what to do. Yelling: "*You! Grab his gun.*" or "*Somebody hit him in the head!*" may be all the instructions needed to cause bystanders to spring into action.

I've tested several ways to go unarmed against an armed shooter in various training courses I've taught. If you have a small group of people, designate the first person to go for the shooter's weapon. Ideally, that person will take the weapon away from the shooter, but even if he just deflects the muzzle so that others aren't shot, he will be accomplishing the goal. Immediately following the person charged with handling the weapon will be one or two others who hit the shooter as hard as they can with the goal of knocking him to the ground.

What I've found is that one person hitting high (chest or head level) and another person hitting low (tackling at the knee level), usually brings the attacker to the ground very quickly. Once on the ground, the weight of the multiple defenders can be used to effectively reduce or control the attacker's momentum and prevent him from accessing additional weapons.

It sounds complex, but is really quite simple. You and two friends set up in a hard corner. The instructions go something like this: *"I'll go first and try to take his gun. You follow me immediately and wrap up his arms or hit him in the head. You (to the next person) follow him and tackle the shooter at knee level."*

Having been on the receiving end of such ambushes, I can tell you that they are tough to defend against. The shooter's natural urge is to put all his attention on the guy trying to take his gun. As he is doing that, he can't effectively defend against the dudes trying to take him to the ground or bash him in the head.

Once you get the attacker on the ground, beat him in the face with any hard object you can find. Cut his throat if you have a blade. If you know how to sink a good choke, put him to sleep. Most active killers have more than one weapon. Even if you wrestle one weapon away from him, he will likely have others. You need to act quickly to kill him or make him unconscious so that he can't draw another weapon and continue his attack. If you are unable or unwilling to knock the attacker out or kill him, use the weight of multiple people to hold him down as you bind his hands and feet with shoe laces, belts, or purse straps. When he is immobilized, search him and remove any additional weapons he may be carrying.

Chokes and Improvised Weapons can be game changers. You want to stack the odds in your favor as best as you can. The goal is to end the fight as quickly as possible so that more people don't get hurt or killed. Think about possible improvised weapons that may be on hand. Grab anything heavy and hard and use it to smash the shooter's head. Fire extinguishers are common in public places and work great to crush skulls. You are limited only by your imagination.

Be cautious, however, about using the shooter's firearm(s). The police will be coming fairly quickly in an active shooter event. If the only description the cops have of the shooter is "*a white male with an* AK-47" and you are standing there beating the attacker unconscious with his own AK-47 rifle when they arrive, what do you think the cops are going to do? You could very easily be mistaken for the shooter if you are using his weapons against him.

Learn how to choke someone unconscious. It's not hard. It can be taught by a good judo or jiu-jitsu instructor in just a couple hours. Seek out a quality grappling instructor and pay him for a couple hours of private lessons on applying chokes. They are the fastest and most reliable way to make people unconscious quickly.

Proper response tactics for an active killer require an analysis of your own abilities, the environment where the violence is occurring, the presence of help, the response time of the local police, and the killer's weapons/tactics.

They can't be codified into a simple "*Run, Hide, Fight*" playbook. "*Run, Hide, Fight*" is certainly a better response option than passively freezing, but anyone who is truly interested in his own safety must ignore this simple, dumbed-down dictum and think for himself.

Special consideration for hotels

Islamic terrorists have made it part of their doctrine to attack hotels that cater to Western tourists. If you are in your hotel room and become aware of an attack, I would advise escaping as early as possible. Get out before the terrorists control all of the exits.

In addition to all the advice I provided in the hotel chapter, if you are worried about terrorist attacks, I would recommend some additional tactics: Avoid getting a room that faces the street or is near the main lobby. That's where the initial terrorist attacks will focus. Avoid hanging around the hotel lobby, restaurant, or bar. Past terrorist attackers have very quickly taken over those areas. You should also avoid having a room overlooking the parking lot on the lower levels of the hotel. If terrorists detonate a car bomb in the parking lot, the windows facing the explosion below the fourth floor are likely to be broken.

If you can't escape, shelter in place in your room. Use every lock available (and a door stop) to secure your hotel room door. Additionally you may want to further barricade the door by placing heavy furniture in front of it. Most terrorists do not bring breaching tools. If you make the room hard to enter, they may move on to easier targets.

Additionally, you should do everything possible to make the room appear vacant. Don't use the "do not disturb" sign. Keep the TV and radio off. Turn the phone ringers off. Do not take showers or run the water in the sink any longer than needed. If the room appears unoccupied, the terrorists may pass by it.

Stay sheltered in place until you are sure that the police have come to rescue you. While in the room, stay low to the ground and make every effort to hide behind whatever cover is available in the room to protect you from stray bullets. Do not open the door until you are 100% certain that the terrorists have been defeated and that it is the police who are on the other side.

Surviving Kidnapping Attempts

"The person best equipped to protect you against terrorism is you."
– Anthony J. Scotti

Did you know that the American government won't publicly reveal how many Americans are being held hostage overseas? The government won't release he numbers out of "privacy concerns" and fear that the knowledge of the true number of Americans being held hostage might increase the risk for other citizens who travel overseas. If hostage takers recognize that there are benefits, financial or otherwise, to taking hostages, more Americans will become prisoners of rebel groups and foreign regimes around the world. The government wants to keep information about covert negotiations and ransom payments quiet, to avoid encouraging more hostage taking worldwide.

With that said, most estimates place the number of American hostages being held long term in foreign countries to be somewhere between five and twenty at any given time. Some sources estimate that approximately 25 American business travelers are kidnapped worldwide every year. Neither is really a large number. Almost all long term hostages are either journalists or members of the armed forces. Most are being held in war zones where there is little tourism. The recreational traveler's risk of being held as a long-term hostage is extremely small. As is true with many subjects, what people worry about tends not to be the most likely risk. Rest assured that you are not likely become a political prisoner if you travel to South America, Africa, or Southeast Asia.

Now that we've established that you won't be spending the rest of your life in as a hostage or political prisoner in most third world countries, what do you really have to worry about? Although the risk of being held long term is minuscule, that doesn't mean that there is no chance of being kidnapped. Kidnappings occur quite frequently, especially in Latin America. Most of these kidnappings are motivated by finances rather than political ideology.

The kidnappers want money or fame. They choose victims who are likely to be able to pay a ransom or bring them publicity. Casual travelers and backpackers are rarely targets. Backpackers just don't have enough money to make the crime worthwhile. The majority of Americans kidnapped overseas are middle-class business travelers with families. The kidnappers know that a business traveler's employer is likely to pay a ransom. If the employer won't pay, the traveler's family might. That's why middle-class businessmen make the best targets.

In the book *Executive Safety and International Terrorism*, author Anthony J. Scotti lists the three profiles of people who are taken hostage. They are:

1) Apparent wealth

2) Having value to someone (either family or business)

3) Represent something important (good publicity)

Business travelers reading this book often display all three criteria. If you want to reduce your chance of being kidnapped, you must work to change the kidnappers' perspective of you. If you are traveling for business, the best way to avoid being kidnapped it to keep an extremely low profile. As I stated in the earlier clothing chapter, don't wear any clothing with your company's logo. Avoid answering any type of probing personal questions by someone you don't trust or know well. Don't do anything that will flaunt your wealth, employment or status. If the kidnappers don't think you have resources, you aren't likely to be kidnapped.

Statistically, 84% of worldwide kidnappings target locals as victims. Business travelers are most likely to be kidnapped in Asia (35%), Africa (30%) and Central or South America (21%). As a traveler, when you are visiting the same city repeatedly for business, try to vary your routine. Don't get in the habit of moving in a predictable manner. Change the hotels where you stay and the restaurants where you eat. If you are unpredictable, you will be much more difficult to kidnap.

After Beirut CIA Station Chief William Buckley was kidnapped, tortured, and killed in 1984, analysts determined that kidnappers targeted him because of his regular routines. Even though he was a counter terrorism agent, he steadfastly refused to vary the route he took to work each day. That predictability resulted in his death. Keep that case in mind when you book the same hotel over and over while traveling overseas. Reward points aren't worth your life.

Business travelers must also increase their levels of awareness. Pay special attention to any suspicious vehicles that are parked near your hotel or workplace. Look for people standing around or sitting in cars without an obvious purpose, especially people who seem to be paying undue attention to your activities. Don't ignore any marked police vehicles that seem to be following you either. Many corrupt foreign cops are on the kidnappers' payroll. Police cars make great surveillance vehicles. No one thinks twice when they see them. You should. If you seem to be targeted for surveillance by a marked police car, you should be even more concerned than if you detect someone else watching you. Don't trust the local cops under any circumstances.

Anyone following you should also be an obvious red flag. The most prevalent sites for a kidnapping attempt are a business traveler's residence, his workplace, or some predictable location between these two sites. Because the route you take to work is such a common location for an abduction attempt, you should always use a trustworthy driver and frequently vary your routes. It might also be valuable to call a colleague at work as you are leaving your hotel or residence and tell that person your route itinerary and approximately when you plan on arriving. If you are late, your colleague can notify authorities and get an earlier start on any rescue attempts.

Occasionally, alert travelers will sense the warning signs of an impending kidnapping. If you notice the suspicious indicators mentioned above, your first inclination might be to go to the police. That may not be in your best interest. In corrupt third world countries, the police are often the folks who conduct the kidnapping, people don't generally resist uniformed cops and the terrorists know that. They pay the corrupt cops a lot of money for occasional "services." Even if the cops don't perform the kidnapping themselves, they may provide information about potential targets to terrorists or criminal cartels. As I mentioned in the surveillance detection paragraph above, stay away from the cops in third world countries.

If you sense an impending kidnapping, quickly make your way to the most public place possible, instead of going to the police station. You are less likely to be abducted anywhere there are a lot of witnesses. When you get to a busy public location, call any of your local friends or your country's embassy and get some help headed your way.

If you don't catch the early warning signs, you may be the victim of an actual kidnapping attempt. If that happens, make every effort to escape as early as possible. Often, you will be able to drive away or flee on foot at the first sign of attack. Kidnappers may not give chase out of fear of being caught by authorities. Nothing draws police attention faster than the sounds of gunshots and a screaming foreign traveler. If you have the opportunity to get away, take it. Don't hesitate. People are always hesitant to recommend resistance in the face of armed kidnappers. I'm not. I think you should resist at every opportunity unless you are so overwhelmed that resistance is futile.

Let's put things in perspective:

When we look at Westerners kidnapped by Jihadi terrorists since 2001, 60% were murdered by their captors. Another 25% were killed during rescue attempts by American or British armed forces (statistics from a Rand Corp. study). If you stand an 85% chance of being killed if taken hostage, why not resist? Odds of your success have to be greater in a resistance attempt than what are likely once you have been taken hostage.

Your tactics must change however, when you are overwhelmed by armed individuals or you have no chance to escape. In that case, your safest option is likely compliance. During the initial stages of a kidnapping, your attackers will have to act violently or threaten violence to ensure your cooperation. Any resistance during this stage is going to result in extremely harsh treatment by your captors. The terrorists have to establish dominance. One of the ways they will do so is by killing anyone they think is a group leader or anyone who might cause them trouble in the future. You don't want to be identified as that person.

Once you realize an initial escape isn't likely, stop fighting. Don't anger, challenge, or insult your captors. Direct eye contact may be viewed as a challenge as well. Don't stare at your captors or look them in the eye. Keep eyes averted or downcast. Go along with the program until you have a better opportunity to escape. If you are a police officer, government employee, or member of the armed forces, hide any identification cards you may have so that the terrorists don't find them. Government employees make for good "examples" to kill in front of the other hostages to ensure compliance.

If you are taken hostage, attempt to personalize yourself by developing a rapport with the hostage takers. People don't want to kill people that they see as friends or people who they respect. Talk about your life, your kids, your job...anything that you can use to construct a bond with your captors. Family life is a topic that is common to everyone. Avoid talking politics or religion. Listen to the terrorists' propaganda, but avoid getting into debates on these topics. Remember, it's your goal to make your captives fond of you, not to alienate them. It has been shown that the longer you have been held hostage, the more likely it is that you will be released alive. Most experts agree that as hostages are held for a significant period of time, they are more likely to develop positive relations with their captors. This "humanizing" effect is what increases their survival rate.

Constantly be alert for escape opportunities. Captors usually become more and more complacent the longer you have been held. That has allowed numerous hostages worldwide to exploit their captors' inattention and successfully escape. Take any opportunity that affords itself.

As I mentioned in the "weapons" section, I carry the Ka-Bar TDI LDK knife when I'm traveling in areas where kidnapping is common. While it works as a last ditch weapon, I primarily carry it as an escape tool. I carry it in the small of my back below the belt line so that I can access it and cut myself free if my hands are tied or taped behind my back. It can be safety pinned directly to your pants or hung from a belt loop on your pants using a key chain or a small loop of paracord.

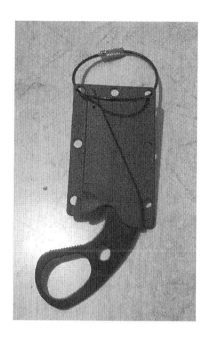

Ka-Bar LDK knife on flexible keychain. I attach the
key chain around a belt loop in the small of my
back and tuck the blade down into my pants.

While rope and tape are the most common ways that
kidnapped travelers are bound, you should also be
prepared to escape other restraints as well. If your captors
use zip ties or police flex cuffs to restrain you, you will
be unlikely to break or cut them without seriously hurting
yourself. The best option for getting yourself free from
restraints like this is to use a friction cutting method. I
replace my shoe laces with stronger paracord when I
travel. I can unlace a shoe, tie a loop on either end of the
lace and thread the paracord lace through the flexcuffs.

After doing that, I can loop an end of the lace over each of my feet. By "pedaling" my legs as if I am riding a bike, the paracord will quickly saw right through the flex cuffs or zip ties. There are several videos on the internet that show this technique

Handcuffs, although rarely used by criminals, are another method of restraint for which you will need to prepare. While it is fairly easy to pick handcuffs with a paper clip or bobby pin, it requires some practice and is very difficult to do when your hands are cuffed behind your back. It's much better to have a hidden key or keys on your person. Handcuff keys are universal no matter what country the handcuffs come from. A small handcuff key taped to the inside of your belt (best to have one both in front and behind the back) is an easy solution. Keys can also be taped under watch bands or hidden inside the waistband of the pants (after cutting a small slit in the lining). I carry a cuff key under my watch band and another one strung onto the key ring I use to hide my LDK knife in the small of my back. Smaller keys are obviously easier to hide. I prefer the plastic keys from SerePick or from TIHK. Gearward also sells what they call the "AK- Band." It is a rubber sleeve that slides over your watch band. Hidden inside the sleeve is a plastic handcuff key, a ceramic razor blade to cut restraints, and a small section of ultra-thin Kevlar cord that can be used as a friction saw in the same manner that I described above with paracord.

One last escape tool that I have found exceptionally useful is the Advanced Personal Escape Kit from OscarDelta. This piece of gear masquerades as a necklace that you can wear under your shirt. It's barely noticeable when worn. The "necklace" is really an exceptionally tough cord that can be used as a garrote or as a friction saw for cutting through flex cuffs. Attached to the cord is a handcuff key, a handcuff shim, a mini glowing light stick, and an exceptionally hard striking disc that will break window and automotive glass. Having all these items on a cord around your neck in one place is handy, but I would still suggest having a few smaller keys or shims stashed in other locations as well. You don't know how thoroughly you will be searched after you are kidnapped. Losing all of your tools at the same time when your captors find your necklace won't help your long term survival. The more items you have, the more likely one or more will be missed on a hurried search of your clothes and body. That makes your escape chances significantly greater.

Tools are important, but skills and mindset are even more valuable. Consider purchasing some of these escape tools and carrying them with you. But like most defensive tools, they require practice to master. Merely having the tool isn't enough. Practice until you can use the tool to quickly escape restraints under any and all possible conditions. Only then will you truly have options.

A last comment on kidnapping and escape: you should always be prepared for a dynamic rescue attempt. The most likely time a rescue attempt will occur is when negotiations come to a halt, when captors start executing people, or in the pre-dawn hours when the hostage takers are least alert. When military or police storm the location where hostages are being held, they usually rely on speed, surprise, and violence of action to quickly terminate any hostilities. You want to make sure that you don't appear hostile or aggressive to the rescuers. They don't have much time to process information and you may be shot by mistake. If you become aware of a raid against your captors, be ready to act and follow the orders of your rescuers. Absent any specific instruction from them, you should seek cover or drop to the ground to avoid being shot.

Express Kidnappings– Besides kidnapping for ransom, the other type of kidnapping that all travelers must be prepared for is often called "Express Kidnapping." Express kidnappers ask for money, but not in the form of a ransom paid by your employer or relative. Instead, they kidnap a traveler and then take him to a bank or ATM and force him to withdraw money. Occasionally, people are held for multiple days in these express kidnappings. The kidnappers know that most American bank accounts have a $500 a day limit of ATM withdrawals. They hold the traveler for multiple days in order to more effectively drain the bank account.

Most express kidnappers get their money by forcing the traveler to use the ATM. Actually going into the bank has a larger payoff, but a much larger risk as the traveler might inform a bank employee of the kidnapping or call the police while the kidnapper waits outside. Kidnappers don't want to enter the bank with the traveler out of fears of being photographed or arousing the suspicions of bank employees.

You may be able to avoid such kidnappings if you offer to give your ATM card and the password to the kidnapper. You may also try a ruse of incorrectly entering your password at the ATM multiple times so that the machine "eats" your card. Without a money card, the terrorists have no reason to keep you.

Virtual Kidnappings- One of the more recent trends in kidnapping (especially in Latin America) is "virtual kidnapping." In a virtual kidnapping, the perpetrators use information about you to convince your relatives or friends that you have been kidnapped. Your loved ones pay the criminal a ransom without ever realizing that you weren't truly being detained. This method is more like a telephone scam than a legitimate kidnapping and removes the element of risk for the kidnapper.

Virtual kidnappers will use a ruse, sometimes over several days, to acquire the information they need. They will need your name, where you are traveling, the name of a victim to bribe, and the victim's phone number. Occasionally they will solicit this information over the phone, claiming to be hotel staff and requesting an "emergency contact." Some other virtual kidnappers will talk to your children (either while you aren't paying attention or by telephone) to acquire the information they need.

Once they get a name and phone number, they call the victim and tell him that you are being held hostage. They will instruct the victim to either wire money or send prepaid debit cards to an address to affect your release. You'd be surprised to see how many people fall for this ruse.

In order to prevent virtual kidnapping, be cautious about revealing any personal information to strangers. No one except airline employees legitimately request emergency contact information in a foreign country. Make sure your home address and phone number are not easily visible on your luggage tag as well.

Teach your friends and family back home how virtual kidnappers work. There are a couple of easy ways to identify a virtual kidnapper. The first is that they will often try to keep the victim on the phone as long as possible. They don't want the victim to have a chance to call you to verify what's going on. Real kidnappers will never do this, preferring to keep any phone calls short and to the point to limit the chance that the call will be traced by authorities. Real kidnappers will also often use the victim's phone to call. Virtual kidnappers won't have the victim's phone and will be calling from an unfamiliar phone and/or country

Tell family members not to answer any questions from unknown callers. If they receive a call from a potential kidnapper, ask the kidnapper to describe the person allegedly "kidnapped" in great detail. Ask to speak to the kidnapped person. If the kidnappers won't allow that, ask them to verify the kidnapped person's identity by answering a question that only the victim would know.

Even more importantly, having regular contact with your family/friends while traveling can prevent being victimized. Give a "code word" to your family that indicates you are truly being held hostage. If you are really kidnapped, you can give the code word to the kidnappers and they will relay it to your family members, thus allowing them to take appropriate action. The virtual kidnappers wouldn't know the code word and would be easily identified as scam artists by your family members.

Drugs

"Everything we do is for the purpose of altering
consciousness. We form friendships so that we can
feel certain emotions, like love, and avoid others, like
loneliness. We eat specific foods to enjoy their
fleeting presence on our tongues. We read for the
pleasure of thinking another person's thoughts.
Every waking moment—and even in our dreams—we
struggle to direct the flow of sensation, emotion, and
cognition toward states of consciousness that we
value."
– Sam Harris

"Going to the middle of a war zone to buy some
three-dollar cocaine from an unstable militant, who
probably hates Americans, is an easy way to end up
dead in a ditch. Plus, there's a place back home
where the drugs flow freely and there are no
repercussions for using them. It's called college."
– Robert Koch

The issues regarding the relative merits and dangers of
drug use are contentiously debated in nearly every society
on the planet. Regardless of your personal feelings about
the use of drugs, we know that humans have been altering
consciousness by consuming certain plants and chemicals
since the time of pre-history. No one is likely to stop using
these drugs any time soon.

It's not my role to either advocate for or moralize against
drug use. Every individual has to make that decision for
himself. My job in this book is to relay information that you

can use to keep yourself safe. There are a lot of travelers who go to countries in the developing world solely to source inexpensive narcotics and hallucinogens. There are ways to reduce your personal risk of harm, even if you do choose to consume psychoactive substances.

Many drug users consume their drugs of choice at bars or nightclubs in order to enhance their social experiences. Be especially cautious if you choose to do this. In addition to the dangers inherent in altering your mental status in the presence of many people who would take advantage of you, bar staff can also exploit drug users.

Bars and night clubs often have security personnel who pat down or search everyone who enters. They will not allow you to enter while you are carrying illegal drugs. If they find your drugs, the best scenario is that they take them from you. The worst is if they have a deal going with the local police. They let you keep the drugs and then tell a corrupt cop that you have them. The cop arrests you and extorts a huge bribe that you will gladly pay in order to stay out of jail. The cop will then share a portion of the bribe (and/or the drugs) with the security guard who informed on you.

Avoid using any drugs on the street. Even in places where some drugs are legal, like the Netherlands, consumption on the street is regularly prohibited. If you are going to use drugs, don't flaunt your usage. Keep the drug use limited to your residence or a private area where you are unlikely to be viewed by the police.

Never transport drugs across international borders. That's how most drug-using tourists get arrested. Smuggling drugs across borders isn't worth the risk. Acquire all of your drugs in the country you are visiting and use them up before you come back home. Be especially alert when crossing the border into a country that has a history of fanatical enforcement of harsh drug laws against foreigners. Even though marijuana might be legal to smoke in your home state, you could get the death penalty smoking the same weed in another country.

The countries of Indonesia, China, Malaysia, and Singapore have all executed foreign travelers convicted of drug offenses. Countries in the Middle East that operate under Sharia law also have a track record for handing out excessive punishment to those who are convicted of using illegal drugs. I personally wouldn't use any drugs at all in a country where I could get a death sentence for doing so. That isn't me taking any moral high ground; it's just my best advice to keep you safe. Dead travelers won't buy any of my future books.

Sign inside a Cambodian bar where the bar girls were serving "shots" of nitrous oxide

One of the major allures of drug use in third world countries is the fact that drugs are often far cheaper and easier to obtain than they are at home. That causes some users to overdo things. Even if the drugs are cheap, don't be tempted to do too much. Start with a very low dose. Remember, you likely won't know your supplier and you may not really know the true contents or purity of the drugs you are buying. Go slow.

As a novice drug user or anytime you are experiencing a chemical for the first time, it's wise not only to start with a small dose, but to start out with a method of ingestion that creates the slowest absorption in the body. Most chemicals can be eaten, smoked, inhaled, or injected. Some can be applied topically or dosed rectally. The injection and inhalation methods get the drugs into the system very quickly. The topical or digestive method slows absorption and can be safer. If you have a bad reaction after eating a drug, your stomach can be pumped or you can be given an emetic to purge your system. That isn't as easy to do if you've inhaled or injected the drug. When starting out, consider taking the drug in a manner that allows for a potential reversal if you have a negative reaction.

If you do choose to take drugs, make sure you have a sober and trusted friend who is able to care for you if something goes wrong. Take the drugs in a calm setting with minimal distractions. Especially in the case of psychedelic drugs (like LSD or mushrooms) "set" and "setting" are crucially important aspects to control in order to avoid negative experiences. You shouldn't take psychedelics when angry or disturbed. Ensure you have a good mindset when trying the drug. Make sure that you aren't in a setting that has excessively loud noise, too much visual stimulation, or contains something that frightens you. Avoid taking more than one drug at a time; this includes alcohol. Poly-drug usage dramatically increases the risk of medical complications, especially in the novice drug user.

Despite your best intentions, "bad trips" or negative side effects can occur any time you consume recreational or pharmaceutical drugs. If you or a traveling companion begin experiencing difficulties after consuming drugs, try the following:

– Try to change the setting. Reducing the volume of loud music, getting the person away from chaotic crowds, and/or changing the temperature of the environment can make a big difference in how a person experiences a drug's effects. Try to make the person as comfortable as possible.

– If the person is feeling excessively paranoid, gently move them away from other people. Stay nearby, but don't sit close to the suffering person or stare at them.

– Provide any objects or distractions that will help the person get through his or her crisis. If you can play some relaxing music or give the person a toy or animal to distract him. Blankets also tend to help soothe a person who is experiencing a psychedelic crisis.

– Always ask the suffering person for permission before touching him. Sometimes just holding the person's hand or placing your arm around his shoulders will help reduce anxiety.

– Verbally assure them that what they are experiencing is a temporary effect of the drug they consumed. Make sure they know that their feelings are normal and aren't permanent. The effects will fade in time.

    – Get the person to focus on his or her breathing. Providing an alternate focus will help reduce the intensity of the hallucinations. Encourage the person to breathe slowly and deeply. You may even be able to get the person to match and mimic your own calming breath pattern

If you are interested in learning more about this topic, please see these tips and additional advice on Erowid's" Psychedelic Crisis" page (https://www.erowid.org/psychoactives/faqs/psychedelic_crisis_faq.shtml)

To reduce the chance of being arrested, don't carry drugs on your person. Police in third world countries will stop and search foreigners, especially those who look like "partiers" or those who appear to be under the influence of drugs or alcohol. If you are going to use drugs, purchase a single dose and consume it as soon as possible. If you are carrying drugs around in your pockets, you are dramatically increasing the chance that you will be arrested or fined.

Beware of using drugs in popular tourist nightclubs and bars. Third world sting operations are common in these locations. Cops will raid the clubs and force anyone who appears to be under the influence of drugs (usually tourists) to submit to an on-the-spot urine test. If your urine tests positive for a controlled substance, you will be immediately arrested.

It's never 100% safe to purchase psychoactive chemicals from sources you don't know and trust. Given my advice above of never smuggling drugs across international borders, how do you acquire your drugs in another country? It's generally best not to trust the locals. Too many are scam artists who prey on naive tourists. Others are in cahoots with the local corrupt police and will turn you in to the cops after they make a sale.

Other travelers tend to be the safest bets. Meet some fellow travelers and hang out with them for a couple of days. It's virtually guaranteed that you'll find a connection with someone; and hopefully someone with whom you've developed some level of trust. Other sources that tend to be slightly safer than the local dealer on the street are hostel employees, especially hostel bartenders. Every town has a "party hostel" that has a fun reputation. The bartenders there will likely be a good hookup. If your hotel is high class enough to have a concierge, he might be able to arrange whatever you might need if you give him a fat tip.

It's not advisable to experiment with any drugs that you've never heard of or haven't researched. While no drug use is completely safe, it's usually safer to make informed and well- researched decisions. Each country has a different drug culture. Even if you are a regular drug user at home, you will likely encounter drugs that you've never heard of when you travel abroad. I've been offered (but did not partake) scopolamine in South America and Yaba (methamphetamine in pill form that is smoked by the locals) in Thailand. Neither drug is widely used in the USA. Don't take chances with random chemicals you haven't thoroughly researched.

In addition to exercising caution around all the blatantly illegal and potentially harmful drugs available in many countries, you should also pay attention to what you are ordering from "normal" restaurants and bars. In Ecuadorian bar, there was a drink on the menu comically called the "*super-maldito pervertido*" (super-evil pervert) that contained hashish oil. It was labeled on the menu, but had I not spoken Spanish, I might have ordered the drink for novelty purposes and been quite surprised at its effects.

Mushroom (the hallucinogenic kind) milkshakes are sold on the beach and in bars in Thailand and Indonesia. In India, you can order *bhang lassi* which is a drink made of yogurt and hashish. It's sold everywhere during very large festivals. There are dozens of other "innocuous" foods and drinks throughout the world that contain some type of drug or adulterant. You'll also want to watch out for the "*happy pizza*" or "*herb pizza*" served in Southeast Asia (mostly in Cambodia). You can probably guess what "herbal" topping might make you happier than the pizza you order back home. Be careful. The "happiness" is dosed at an amount that will keep you completely unable to function for about 12 hours. Not a good choice if you have an early bus departure the next morning.

My point isn't to scare you. I just want you to recognize it is still dangerous to consume unknown substances even if you avoid all the back alley drug dealers. Some of the smartest drug dealers have a trustworthy appearance and a sales strategy that would seemingly fit better in a Fortune 500 company than in a third world flophouse.

Drug dealers who don't know you will generally be casual when they make their first approach to new customers. They will commonly use phrases like "*You good?*" or "*You doing OK?*" to offer their wares. Some will be a little more direct and say "*You need anything?*" All of these phrases are offers to sell you drugs. If you aren't interested in purchasing anything, keep walking and say something like "*I'm good.*" The dealers generally won't bother you anymore.

Occasionally, local terms indicating drug sales will be different. In Belize several years ago, if a stranger said "I *like your shirt*," it was an offer to sell drugs. Another strange request is asking "*Do you like snow?*" That is an obvious offer for cocaine. Anytime a stranger approaches you and says something strange in fluent English, expect that the person is a drug dealer.

While we are speaking of intoxicating substances, we cannot ignore the more mundane substances, namely alcohol. It's important to note that more people are injured or killed while drunk than when under the influence of all other intoxicating substances combined. Being drunk is very dangerous if you are in an unsafe area. Not only are you more likely to be involved in accidents, you are also more likely to be targeted for various crimes as well. Those crimes are not just petty thefts. Alcohol is the most widely-used date rape drug in the world.

You will probably have no problems acquiring alcohol in third world countries. Some countries have certain hours when alcohol cannot be sold, but these are easily circumvented by purchasing in small stores that care more about your money than the law they are breaking. Some other countries do not allow the sale of alcohol on election days. You did check to see if there were any national holidays during your trip, didn't you?

The only countries where you will have consistent problems finding alcohol are countries with Islamic laws or where Muslim residents form the majority. Alcohol may not be served in any restaurants or hotels owned by people of the Islamic faith. Work-arounds exist, however. In larger tourist areas, there will be a ready supply of young children who hang out around outdoor eating areas where alcohol isn't served. Those kids will run down to a corner store and buy beer or wine for tourists for a few cents' commission. If you choose to engage in the services of these children, get the beer FIRST, before you pay any money.

Alcohol is also served in the four and five star hotel bars in Islamic countries. In fact, that's where wealthy Muslims (who aren't very faithful to their religion) go to drink. You can generally get anything you want there. I'd buy each drink individually rather than starting a tab. I've heard of travelers who have later found large "service charges" added to their credit card bills at a later date after buying alcohol at the fancier hotels.

One other often unrecognized consequence of drug or alcohol use is the effect that intoxication has on insurance coverage. Many travel medical insurance policies specifically refuse to pay for medical care that is necessary after the traveler is "reckless" in their conduct. Drug abuse or intoxication is considered "reckless" behavior in most jurisdictions. If you get run over by a tuk-tuk after staggering drunkenly into the roadway, your medical claims may be denied. It's something most travelers should look at more carefully.

One last piece of advice I can offer is to be extremely cautious about traveling to foreign countries if you are addicted to drugs. I occasionally have come across addicts who travel to third world countries thinking that they will "escape" their problems at home and break the chains of their addictions. That strategy rarely works. When the addicts arrive in their new home country, they become lonely and find an easy escape in the ready availability of illicit drugs. Drugs in third world countries are generally both cheaper and more widely available than at home. There are also fewer support resources for addicts. Don't travel to a developing country looking to cure your addiction. It isn't a good plan. Take care of your drug problem first, and then seek further enlightenment by traveling.

Conclusion

> "Travel isn't always pretty. It isn't always
> comfortable. Sometimes it hurts; it even breaks your
> heart. But that's okay. The journey changes you; it
> should change you. It leaves marks on your memory,
> on your consciousness, on your heart, and on your
> body. You take something with you. Hopefully, you
> leave something good behind."
> – Anthony Bourdain

One of my favorite travel writers is Kira Salak. In one of her travel books she wrote:

> "The only rule I try to follow religiously in life is not
> to listen to most people."

That's good advice to follow.

You should pay heed, even if it means ignoring everything that I've written. I've shared this work sincerely. Everything I've written comes straight from my heart. Yet I still don't believe a word of it. Every strategy I've described in this book might be "wrong" tomorrow.

I urge you to filter this content through your own experiences and gut intuition as well. What works for me may not be the optimal solution for you.

Author Stephen Jenkinson described his writing as a structure to "wonder aloud with you about things that could be important." That's what I'm doing here. I'm "wondering aloud".

I think "wonder" is something that should be more widely cultivated in our culture. Jenkinson describes wonder as:

"... a willingness, decked out as skill, to be on the receiving end of how vast the world always is and how unlike your ideas of how it should be often is.

As always, I asked that people give their certainty about these things a rest for the duration and allow their wondering muscles a little exercise.

Wonder is part fascination, part ability to believe in things as they are, part willingness to be confused, even devastated at times, by the epic mysteriousness of ordinary things."

You should "wonder" about both travel itself and the nature of the guidance I've provided in these pages. Keep your mind open. Shun ignorance. Don't take yourself or anything I've written here too seriously. Smile. Cultivate a childlike curiosity.

The world needs more adventurers like you. Thank you for reading my book. I sincerely hope that the strategies you've learned will help you stay safe and avoid most of the chaos involved with traveling to unfamiliar places.

If you enjoyed the book, please give it an honest review on Amazon.com or any of the other book-related sites that you regularly frequent. That simple action will do more than anything else to help me educate and inspire more travelers.

If you would like to connect with me, please check out the book website at www.ChooseAdventureBook.com. If you are interested in taking some of my tactical, counter-kidnapping, or wilderness medicine courses, visit my company page at www.activeresponsetraining.net.

I hope to meet up with all of you in my future explorations of the developing world.

References

"If you don't feel that you haven't read enough,
you haven't read enough."
– Nassim Nicholas Taleb

Adventure Travel in the Third World- Jeff Randall and Mike Perrin

The Adventurist- Robert Young Pelton

Backpacker Points and the Quest for Aunt Sheila- Becci Coombes

Bare Naked Nomad- Liz Wright

Bug Out Gear for Travelers- Tony Nester

Come Back Alive- Robert Young Pelton

Don't Go There. It's Not Safe. You'll Die. – Jared McCaffree, Jessica Mans and Kobus Mans

Emotions Revealed- Paul Ekman

Escape Plan- Mark Manson

Escape the Wolf- Clint Emerson

Executive Safety & International Terrorism- Anthony J. Scotti

How to be the World's Smartest Traveler- Christopher Elliott

How to Shit Around the World- Jane Wilson-Howarth

How to Survive Living Abroad- English Teacher X

How to Travel the World on $50 a Day- Matt Kepnes

Kiss, Bow, Shake Hands- Terri Morrison

Left of Bang- Patrick Van Horne and Jason Riley

Looking for Lemons- Lloyd Figgins

The Lunatic Express- Carl Hoffman

Moon Volunteer Vacations in Latin America- Amy Robertson

Overlanding 101- Mark Fittall

The Places We've Been- Asha Brisbois

Pushups in the Prayer Room- Norm Schriever

The Rough Guide to First-Time Around the World- Rough Guides

Saigon Survival- Simon Miller

Sleeping with Strangers: A Vagabond's Journey Tramping the Globe- Jeremiah Allen

Swimming to Angola- Christopher Blins

Vagabonding- Rolf Potts

When Cultures Collide – Richard D. Lewis

Wilderness Medicine- Paul Auerbach

The World's Most Dangerous Places- Robert Young Pelton

101 Places to Get F*cked Up Before You Die- Matador Network

101 Travel Apps- Tristan Higbee

Resources

AirBnB

  AirHelp

  BusBud

  CDC Travelers' Health Resource

  CDC Malaria Information Page.

  CDC's Yellow Fever web page.

  CFAPA

  CIA World Factbook

  Dohop

  Global Terrorism Index

  Health Map

  Hospital Information

  IAMAT

  Momondo

  Pro Med Mail

  Seat 61

  Skyscanner.com

  The Star Alliance Visa and Health Portal

  Thorn Tree Travel Forum

  T-Mobile Simple Choice Cell Plan for Travelers

  Traffic Deaths by Country

  Tripping.com

Useful Travel Websites and Blogs

Adventurous Kate
  Art of Non-Conformity
  The Blonde Abroad
  Catch Carri
  Ed's Manifesto
  Expert Vagabond
  Girl vs. Globe
  Global Terrorism Index
  Hippie in Heels
  IntelCenter Terrorism Database
  Inside the Travel Lab
  Jessie on a Journey
  Keep Calm and Travel
  Matador Network
  Maverick Traveler
  The Nomad Capitalist
  SkyCure Threat Map
  Too Many Adapters
  Tourist Killed
  Tourist Meets Traveler
  Travelettes
  Travel Freak
  Uncornered Market
  Vagabond Journey

Pre-Travel Checklist

– Check to ensure your passport has at least six months validity before expiration. Ensure your passport isn't torn or damaged.

– Check if you need a visa for the country you are visiting

– Research general health and safety information at your planned destination

– Add your embassy's address and phone number to the contacts list on your phone

– Triple check dates for in country holidays, festivals, and elections. Use caution around dates when flying across the International Date Line.

– Compare group versus solo travel in your destination. Decide which best serves your needs

– Check all your airlines' luggage policies

– Notify bank and credit card companies about your travel

– Make backup copies of credit cards, ATM cards, and passports. Store a copy on your phone, in your email/cloud storage, and provide a copy to someone at home

– Remove extraneous cards from wallet or purse

– Ensure that both checked and carry-on luggage have no contraband and are empty before you start packing

– Download city maps to your phone for offline use

– Check currency exchange rate

Useful Travel Applications for Your Smartphone

Airports by Travel Nerd- http://www.travelnerd.com/app/

All Subway by Carmat- https://itunes.apple.com/us/app/allsubway/id299081353?mt=8

Can I Eat This from the Centers for Disease Control- http://wwwnc.cdc.gov/travel/page/apps-about

CarRental by Hotwire- https://itunes.apple.com/us/app/carrentals-carrentals.com/id506426310?mt=8

Dine Gluten Free Travel App- https://glutenfreetravelsite.com/mobileresources.php

Disaster Alert by Pacific Disaster Center- http://www.pdc.org/solutions/tools/disaster-alert-app/

Drops by PlanB Labs- https://itunes.apple.com/BB/app/id939540371?mt=8&ign-mpt=uo%3D4

Duolingo- https://www.duolingo.com/

Easy Taxi- http://www.easytaxi.com/

Food Allergy Translator by Gregg Greenberg https://itunes.apple.com/us/app/allergy-ft-allergy-food-translator/id643072499

Flush Toilet Finder by J. Ruston- https://itunes.apple.com/us/app/flush-toilet-finder-public/id955254528?mt=8

Galileo- https://galileo-app.com/

Google Maps by Google- https://itunes.apple.com/us/app/google-maps/id585027354?mt=8

Happy Cow Vegetarian Restaurant Locator-https://itunes.apple.com/us/app/veg-travel-guide-for-vegan/id435871950?mt=8

Here Maps by Here Apps-https://maps.here.com/?x=ep&map=38,-97,10,normal

Hostel Bookers by Hostelbookers.com-http://www.hostelbookers.com/mobile/

Hostelworld- http://www.hostelworld.com/mobile-app

iTranslate Voice- http://itranslatevoice.com/

JiWire Wifi Finder- https://itunes.apple.com/us/app/free-wi-fi-finder/id307217005?mt=8

Kamino by Kamino Labs- http://www.gokamino.com/

Kindle Reader App by Amazon-http://www.amazon.com/gp/feature.html?docId=1000493771

Languages App by Sonico GmbH-http://www.languagesapp.com/

MagicApp from magicJack- https://itunes.apple.com/us/app/free-calls-with-magicjack/id463926997?mt=8

MetrO by Kinevia- https://itunes.apple.com/us/app/metro/id320949132?mt=8

Packing Pro by Quinnscape-http://www.quinnscape.com/PackingPro.asp

Pocket Guide Travel App- http://pocketguideapp.com/en

Prey Project- https://preyproject.com/

Rail Planner by HaCon- https://itunes.apple.com/us/app/rail-planner-offline-timetable/id579547877?mt=8

Rome-2-Rio-https://itunes.apple.com/au/app/rome2rio-rail-air-road-sea/id569793256?mt=8

Taxi Finder by TaxiFareFind-http://www.taxifinder.com/

Tune-In Radio by TuneIn- https://itunes.apple.com/us/app/tunein-radio/id418987775?mt=8

TripAdvisor Offline City Guides-http://www.tripadvisor.com/apps-icityguides

Vaccinations App by Medicus 42 GmbH-https://itunes.apple.com/in/app/vaccinations/id383013992?mt=8

Viatour Local Tours by Viatour.com-http://m.viator.com/mobileapps/

Viber messaging app- http://www.viber.com/en/

Waygo by Translate Abroad-http://www.waygoapp.com/

Wespeke Foreign Language Practice-https://itunes.apple.com/us/app/wespeke/id825855730?mt=8

WhatsApp- http://www.whatsapp.com/

WiFi Map- http://www.wifimap.io/

WiFiMapper by Open Signal- http://wifimapper.com/

World Drugs Converter App by Ary Tebeka-https://itunes.apple.com/us/app/world-drugs-converter-find/id411442850?mt=8

About the Author

Greg Ellifritz is a seasoned traveler, spending nearly two months of every year traveling in third world countries alone or in a small group. He's traveled through more than 50 different countries and territories, visiting all seven continents in the process. When not adventuring, Greg works as a full-time police officer in central Ohio. In his 24-year career, he has served as a patrol officer, bike patrol officer, firearms instructor, tactical trainer, and sniper for his agency. He teaches firearms, self-defense, travel safety, counter-kidnapping, and wilderness medicine classes through his company Active Response Training.

Printed in Great Britain
by Amazon

every corner of the world. Carrying it draws no attention because it's a common part of the scenery. No one looks twice.

Would you pay any attention to a man walking down the street with a plastic bag in his hand?

Now, place a knife into the bag. Grip the weapon from the outside of the bag and go for a walk, letting the covered weapon hang loosely at your side as if you were carrying some groceries home from your trip to the convenience store. You have an instantly available weapon in your hands that will go undetected by almost everyone who sees it. You have improved your odds of winning a violent